# TRANSCENDENTAL WIFE

## The Life of Abigail May Alcott

Cynthia H. Barton

University Press of America, Inc.
Lanham • New York • London

Copyright © 1996 by
University Press of America,® Inc.
4720 Boston Way
Lanham, Maryland 20706

3 Henrietta Street
London, WC2E 8LU England

**Library of Congress Cataloging-in-Publication Data**

Barton, Cynthia H.
Transcendental wife : the life of Abigail May Alcott / Cynthia H.
Barton.
p.    cm.
Includes bibliographical references and index.
1.  Alcott, Abigail May, 1800-1877.  2. Alcott, Amos Bronson, 1799-
1888.  3.  Alcott, Louisa May, 1832-1888--Family.  4.
Transcendentalists (New England)--Biography.  5.  New England--
Social life and customs--19th century.  6.  New England--Biography.
I.  Title.
CT275.A46B37     1996     974'.03'092 --dc20     96-16217   CIP
(B)

ISBN 0-7618-0386-6 (cloth: alk. ppr.)
ISBN 0-7618-0387-4 (pbk: alk. ppr.)

The paper used in this publication meets the minimum requirements of
American National Standard for information Sciences—Permanence
of Paper for Printed Library Materials,
ANSI Z39.48—1984

Love though they do and try though they may, few mothers are awarded praise such as Louisa's for Marmee, "You are the best woman in the world."

# Contents

# List of Illustrations

Frontispiece

Mrs. Alcott's Intelligence Office, broadside
*by permission of the Houghton Library, Harvard University*

Bronson Alcott
*Louisa May Alcott Memorial Association*

Samuel May
*Louisa May Alcott Memorial Association*

Elizabeth (Lizzie) Alcott
*Louisa May Alcott Memorial Association*

May Alcott
*Louisa May Alcott Memorial Association*

Anna Alcott
*Louisa May Alcott Memorial Association*

Louisa May Alcott
*Louisa May Alcott Memorial Association*

Alcott family in front of Orchard House
*Louisa May Alcott Memorial Association*

Woman Suffrage Association, broadside
*by permission of the Houghton Library, Harvard University*

May Alcott
*Louisa May Alcott Memorial Association*

Mrs. Alcott
*The Fruitlands Museums*

May's frontispiece for first edition of *Little Women*
*Louisa May Alcott Memorial Association*

# Acknowledgments

To all who encouraged me in this project, thank you, with particular gratitude to the staffs at Orchard House in Concord and the Fruitlands Museums in Harvard, Massachusetts. Some of the materials are quoted with the permission of Fruitlands; publication of the bulk of the primary source material is by permission of the Houghton Library, Harvard University. Many profitable hours were spent at the Concord Free Public Library, where Marcia Moss was most helpful. I am especially indebted to those who advised me as notes became drafts: Pamela Smith, Barbara Kahn, Joanne Myers, and David Barton.

Cynthia H. Barton
Harvard, Massachusetts

# Foreword

She has lived in our hearts as the gentle "Marmee" of *Little Women*.
Abigail May Alcott was a remarkable individual, important in her own
time and ours. Her personality, convictions and actions challenged conventional norms and made her the ideal "transcendental wife." The letters and journals of Alcott family members document the vital presence
Mrs. Alcott assumed in their lives and the significant role she played in
shaping their futures. She was a guide to her four daughters, nurturing
their talents, inspiring self-confidence and preparing them to them to
take responsibility for their own lives. She was a "soul-mate" to her
husband, sharing his philosophies and complementing his idealism with
a firm practicality of her own.

In the pages that follow, Abigail May Alcott speaks to us in her
own words, a task made all the more difficult given that, at her request,
most of her personal journals were destroyed. Her story is crucial since
it connects the past with the present and remains a haunting reminder of
the feminist struggle in history. A dedicated reformer, Mrs. Alcott
worked to better the human condition, particularly that of women. She
believed in the value of individual freedom and the strength of family
bonds, and managed to incorporate both in her everyday approach to
life. Viewed from the perspective of the twentieth century, Mrs. Alcott
stands as an enduring symbol and reminder of the capacity of women to

change society and simultaneously to strengthen social bonds. She embodies the paradox confronting women: a need to foster personal independence and a strong belief in human inter-dependence.

This examination of Abigail May Alcott is both a presentation of historical fact and a celebration of contemporary womanhood.

Stephanie N. Upton
Executive Director
Orchard House/Home of the Alcotts

# Preface

It is time to consider Abigail Alcott, nee Abigail May, 1800-1877, in the context of her historical era and as a person in her own right. She was not the perfect mother, Marmee, of Louisa's *Little Women*; neither was she a long-suffering wife, hostage to her husband's transcendental philosophy. Her views and responses to circumstances reflected her unique personality and her deeply rooted commitment to reform.

> *My life is one of daily protest against the oppression and abuses of Society. I find selfishness, meanness, among people who fill high places in church and state.*
>
> Abigail May Alcott to Rev. Samuel J. May, April 28, 1851.

Abby May entered into marriage at age thirty, imbued with the ethos of what we have come to call the republican mother. Society was much changed as a result of the American Revolution. In the new egalitarian republic, officials were elected by popular vote, but corruption was creeping into the political system. Greed and self-interest were becoming rife in a changing economy, reflecting the temptations inherent in increasingly impersonal dealings. The trend away from an agrarian economy, particularly in the North, required men to spend their working hours away from the home, resulting in the identification of women as a cohesive group with a clearly defined job, domesticity.

> *She [the mother] is the most interesting as well as important member in the community.... The father, brother, husband, son all feel her importance and are rational, enlightened enough to acknowledge it.*
>
> Abigail May, Diary Fragments, 1828-1829.

Protestant ministers, concerned about declining church attendance and simultaneous social disintegration, saw women as a potent force for the return of piety and morality. In effect, by urging upon women the awesome responsibility of bringing up moral citizens for the future, the clergy both secularized the Christian ethic and elevated the status of women. Containment was implicit in the definition of the female sphere, but most women felt valued as they engaged in their important role of models and mentors for their children.

> Let [women] by their independent example adopt those measures which promote temperance in everything. Spread their tables with delicate and wholesome food, pleasant but harmless drinks. Cultivate their minds and purify their hearts that they may make intelligent and agreeable companions. If every woman would feel that this is the influence she can and ought to use in her own family, she would be promoting the great interests of society.

Abigail May, Diary Fragments, 1828-1829.

Society is moral, the church pointed out, in proportion to the morality of the individuals who compose it. The characters of its children, the citizens of the future, were formed through the guidance and example of unselfish mothers, who disciplined their passions and regulated their feelings. Self-denial was one of the most important laws in the canon of domesticity. Authors and editors, many of them female, promoted selflessness in periodicals and books of advice. Lydia Maria Child, Abigail Alcott's close friend, wrote in her *Mother's Book* that child rearing was a cause worthy of sacrifice and that family must take precedence over personal pursuits. In the mid-nineteenth century, raising the children was a sacred trust which dominated the lives of republican mothers.

> It seems to me at times as if the weight of responsibility connected with these little moral beings would prove too much for me. Am I doing what is right? Am I doing enough? Am I not doing too much, is my earnest enquiry.

Abigail May Alcott to Rev. Samuel J. May, June 22, 1833.

For women to fulfill their newly defined domestic role adequately, better education was essential, not that they might enter personally into worldly pursuits, but that they might discuss them intelligently in the home. The nineteenth century saw the foundation of female academies which downplayed "ornamental" studies such as art and music and replaced them with courses in science and mathematics, geography and history, philosophy and languages. Critics of this increased intellectual content were held at bay by the argument that it heightened the effectiveness of the republican mother.

> *Reason and religion are emancipating woman from that intellectual thraldom that has so long held her captive. She is finding her place by the side and in the heart of man, thus compelling him by the irresistible force of merit to accept her as an intellectual companion.*
>
> Abigail May, Diary Fragments, 1828-1829.

Although male prerogatives of church and state remained in place, women, for the most part, perceived their gender identification as positive. Their job was separate from that of men but equal in value, if not equal in rights under the law. They were becoming better educated and were accorded a respected social role, one with both religious and secular definitions. They were different, not inferior, and in their bosoms they bore tender hearts which made them ideally suited for motherhood.

> *But all our institutions are based on selfishness. How then can we develop love in our pupils? I know of no more effective remedy, no more powerful lever than by beginning with our own family, with our own selves. We can do little toward reforming individuals, or society, or remodeling institutions while there is any lack of this divine principle in our own lives and conversation.*
>
> Abigail May Alcott, Diary, August 22, 1842

Religious significance was often given to diet and exercise inasmuch as moral and bodily health were perceived as related. Republican mothers were called upon to evaluate and implement innovative theories about physical well being, thereby validating their study of physiology. Books and periodicals on the subject of health became commonplace. In 1835, Dr. William Andrus Alcott, cousin to Bronson, founded a periodical, *The Moral Reformer*, which featured advice linking body reform to moral reform, thus sanctifying daily life. In selecting and preparing the family's food, in sewing the clothing, in promoting cleanliness and regular physical exercise, women, Alcott said, shaped the very house of the soul. Advocates of body reforms proselytized with evangelical fervor. Sylvester Graham, who considered following in the footsteps of his father and grandfather by becoming a minister, instead chose to preach the doctrine of Grahamism, proclaiming the body sacred and extolling the virtues of vegetarianism. The mainstay of his diet was bread from unbolted (Graham) flour. Abstinence from meat and stimulating beverages would not only renew individual bodies but regenerate the body politic as well.

*I can scarcely forbear to reproach parents, Mothers in particular, for their stupid inattention to the dietetic habits of their children.... Graham is not sufficiently valued as an apostle of light on this momentous subject.*

Abigail May Alcott, Diary, March, 1842

The nineteenth century reform movement which engaged the emotions of New Englanders more than any other was abolition. Abby Alcott was an ardent advocate of the immediate emancipation of slaves. Her friends, Lydia Maria Child and Lucretia Mott, achieved notoriety in their efforts to eradicate slavery, but Abby adhered to the dictates of society and played out her part by supporting her husband's abolitionist activities and raising her girls in the conviction that slavery was a sin in God's eyes, an evil which neither repatriation to Africa nor gradual emancipation could redress.

*It [emancipation] is a cause worthy the best and most intelligent efforts of every enlightened American.... Every woman with a feeling heart and thinking head is answerable to her God if she do not plead the cause of the oppressed, however limited may be her sphere.*

Abigail May Alcott, Diary, January 2, 1836.

# Chapter One

---

# Marriage

> *I am content to see Meg begin humbly,*
> *for, if I am not mistaken, she will be*
> *rich in the possession of a good man's*
> *heart, and that is better than a fortune.*
>
> Marmee to Jo from *Little Women*
> by Louisa May Alcott

Conflict was characteristic of Abigail May Alcott's life - conflict within herself; with those close to her; with, in fact, the whole of society. She was born in Boston on October 8, 1800, and seventy-two years later, at the request of her husband, Amos Bronson Alcott, she wrote a terse autobiographical sketch which began, "I was the youngest of twelve children, born sickly, nursed by a sickly woman.... Owing to my delicate health I was much indulged - allowed to read a good deal, fed on nice food.... I was rather a good child, but willful."[1] Good, but willful, she remained. As a female brought up in the early years of the nineteenth century, she was expected to be dutiful, to be submissive, to serve society in the capacity of wife and mother. Her own parents were models for service to society, but as she grew up she realized that it was its reformation which engaged her and that she must pursue her goals in her own way, not theirs.

Abby and her father, Joseph May, had a particularly difficult relationship. Her natural inclination towards willfulness was encouraged by the family's early indulgences, but it was not long before her father began admonishing her to be dutiful. Since she was at heart a good child, she became excessively self-critical when she failed to fulfill his demanding expectations. Compromise was not in her nature; it was no more possible within herself than it was in her dealings with others. When she was not quite eleven years old, he gave her some advice, good in itself, but which admitted no latitude for personal foibles and therefore reinforced her inclination to deal in extremes. She wanted to be dutiful, but she was headstrong. If she couldn't be perfect, she believed herself not only imperfect, but worthless. Her father wrote:

> 'To be good is to be happy' is an old maxim, one to which I pay great respect and can recommend it to my young friends who are inexperienced in the ways of the world. Attention, kindness, gentleness, good nature, and a desire to please tend to procure friends and to diffuse pleasure to all around us; while industry, patience, perseverance, fidelity, and a desire to excel make a useful and valuable member of society; and moral virtue, piety, and resignation secure us peace in our own bosoms and the smiles of our heavenly father.[2]

The paternal standards to which Joseph May held his daughter paralleled those which the post-Revolutionary ethos demanded of wives and mothers. Be good. Put others first. Work hard. Serve society. Be moral. Be pious. Submit. Submission was the difficulty. Abby's willfulness was, in part, an early and healthy manifestation of self-preservation. Too many females in nineteenth century America, especially those gifted with unusual intelligence, succumbed to nervous disorders when denied an outlet for their talents. The bottling up of emotions is dangerous at any age. By the time Abby was almost eighteen, she and her father rarely communicated even though they lived in the same house. They had become, in her words, "strangers."[3] She wrote him a note to let him know that she valued his advice and guidance although, for her, his standards were unattainable. She said she hoped to live virtuously so as never to disgrace his name, but there was no warmth in her letter, only acknowledgement of the duty which he had laid so heavily upon her.

Abby's mother, Dorothy Sewall May, expected no less of her than did her father, but she tolerated human imperfections with a better grace. Abby felt for her a bond of warm companionship which was lacking in her relationship with her father. "My mother's most striking trait," she wrote, " was her affectionate disposition. She adored her husband and children. She loved the whole human family and went about doing good." Abby was expressing in personal terms that which New Englanders approved in general, maternal devotion to family and good works. Dorothy May could have played an active part in the rounds of Boston's best social circles had she so desired, for she was born both a Quincy and a Sewall; but she chose instead to do her moral duty. She devoted herself to her husband and children and quietly bestowed benevolence upon the poor and needy. After her death Abby wrote, "She loved the doing of a good action better than describing it. She never said great things, but she has done ten thousand generous ones."[4]

Joseph May's philanthropies were more in the public eye. He was a wealthy man by virtue of his successful shipping business, and he was an honorable man. When his firm was ruined due to unscrupulous dealings by his partner, he paid the creditors out of his own pocket. This accomplished, he reordered his life, devoting himself to charitable acts while working for an insurance company at a modest salary. He was for many years a warden of King's Chapel, Boston, and was instrumental in bringing about its change from an Anglican to a Unitarian church. A memorial tablet on the wall of the May pew read, in part, "Firm in the Christian Faith, sustained by an animating hope, and in charity generous, patient and judicious, he might have been traced through every quarter of the city by the footprints of his benefactions."[5] At his death in 1841, his daughter wrote of him along the same lines. "He led a useful, honorable life, holding many offices of trust and power, and was never known to do a mean or selfish act in any of them. He was truly a father of the fatherless and the widow's friend."[6] Since she admired her father if she did not love him, Abby meant no irony in the term widow's friend, but the fact is that her relationship with him became even more severely strained by his remarriage to the widow Carey in 1826, only a year after Dorothy May's death.

The May family valued education and as Abby's brother, Sam, wrote in his memoir, "spared no expense that was needful to insure us the best instruction."[7] Sam himself was Abby's mentor in an era when higher education was not yet available to females; and even when she was only four years of age and he but seven, he tolerated her trailing after him to attend Mrs. Walcutt's dame, or Ma'am, school in High Street, Boston. When Abby was an adolescent, the Mays saw to it that she became the student of a woman, Eliza Robbins, who dared to encourage girls' individual talents whatever the discipline which attracted them. Abby was interested primarily in the humanities, and her years under Miss Robbins' tutelage laid a firm foundation for further independent enquiry and aroused her curiosity about the nature of knowledge and its acquisition. When Sam was a student at Harvard and she a girl of fourteen, they carried on a correspondence debating the pros and cons of John Locke's empiricism. Having concluded that there are no innate ideas, she wrote to say, "Nothing is of unimportance in the formation of the mind."[8]

In 1815, while Abby was continuing her studies under Sam's guidance, their eldest surviving sister, Catharine Windship, died, leaving a son, Charles. Before Abby was born, her mother had lost five babies within a year or two of their births, and in 1801 Mrs. May had a stillborn boy. In 1802, Edward May died in an accident, at the age of six. The only brothers remaining to Abby were Sam, three years her senior, and Charles, who was twelve years older and had long since left home to go to sea. The oldest remaining sister, Louisa, was as interested as Sam in Abby's intellectual progress, and offered advice of her own upon receiving a letter from fifteen-year-old Abby. "With a little practice and correction of a few faults, you may write elegantly. I was happy to observe that your spelling was very correct, which is certainly of the first importance." Eliza, the middle surviving sister, studied with Abby, and Louisa wanted them to have a knowledge of chemistry, botany, and astronomy, but she admonished them to devote most of their time to history and biography. Poetry, drama, and an occasional well chosen novel were to round out the regimen. "You must forgive me for urging this so constantly upon you, but I feel anxious to have your minds well studied with everything useful and as highly cultivated as any in the country."[9] "Why?" one might ask. Women's sphere, after all, was in the home.

The Mays valued knowledge for its own sake and saw no reason to deny females mental stimulation simply because society neither provided higher education for them nor sanctioned female participation in worldly, male, affairs. Nineteenth century culture, furthermore, postulated that the better a woman's education, the better the service she could render to society as companion to her husband and mentor to her children. Motherhood was her separate and valued domain. It is telling that Louisa particularly recommended to Abby the works of the English author, Maria Edgeworth. The moral tone of her family oriented novels coincided with and reinforced the doctrine that women's sacred mandate was to make of their families moral models for a more perfect society. Both Louisa and Eliza May chose to be conventional republican mothers. Eliza married Benjamin Willis in 1817 but died in 1822, leaving two small children, Hamilton and Elizabeth. Louisa married in 1823, dying only five years later, leaving her husband, Samuel Greele, with little Samuel and Louisa. When Abby was eighteen, her parents wished her to marry a cousin, Samuel Frothingham, whom she did not love. She balked, refusing to accept her filial duty, despite protestations of valuing her father's advice and guidance. She wanted independence, or at least a companionate marriage, not the passionless subservience she saw in a marriage with Mr. Frothingham. Contemplating such a union served only to exacerbate her willfulness and compound its companion, guilt. Her spirits were at low ebb.

Abby chided herself because she had not yet brought her will under the control of her reason and had spent too much time "in trifling occupation or wanton negligence." She chafed under the impression that her studies were desultory, her talent wasted, her existence aimless. During her darkest moments, then as later, she dealt in black and white, right and wrong, good and bad. Sam May was well aware that his sister wanted no part of marriage with Samuel Frothingham and found a way to give her some breathing space. In January of 1819, on his advice, she left the home of her parents at Federal Court in order to spend the better part of the year studying in Duxbury, Massachusetts, with Miss Abby Allyn and her father, Rev. Dr. Allyn. The ten months spent there, she said, "made me a new being within myself."[10] Her brooding ceased, and she wrote Eliza, now the mother of a son, that their lives would probably be very different. "I may yet earn my bread by the knowledge this year has afforded me and spend... life in teaching a school.... Louisa's capability joined with my industry shall make us

independent of our relations and happy in ourselves."[11]    Louisa's
engagement and marriage put an end to such plans. Abby did not want
to keep a school alone. She was interested in learning but had neither a
passion for teaching nor financial need to pursue it. She was prepared
to return to Federal Court after her stay with the Allyns, though she
knew doing so would be at the cost of her independence just as surely
as would the proposed marriage to Samuel Frothingham. Her future
remained unclear and she was nowhere near the "new being" she imagined herself, but Sam had chosen well in entrusting her to the care of
the Allyns during this time of emotional turmoil.

Abby had gone to Duxbury by stage. As no public conveyance
was available for the local leg of the journey, one of the passengers, a
Mr. Soule, kindly walked the three miles to his home, procured his
chaise, and returned to drive her to Dr. Allyn's. The minister was not
at home, but his wife and daughter received her kindly with "a good
shake of the hand"[12] and a cup of tea. Abby felt comfortable there right
from the start. After two months of study she wrote home to say,

> My mind, character, and feelings are more under the control of rea-
> son than they have been. Under the constant direction of Miss Allyn my
> mind is cultivated and improved.... I have nothing here to excite bad
> feelings. Therefore by constantly entertaining good ones, I am in hopes
> they will become habitual, and strengthen with my strength. Miss Allyn
> is a model worthy of imitation. By her character I form my own, and the
> very improbability of being like her incites me to constant exertion.[13]

The young women pursued a daunting course of daily study. They
emphasized history, beginning with that of this country and reading
such works as Belknap's *Lives*, Hutchinson's *America*, Abiel Holmes'
*American Annals*. They read English histories by Hume and Gold-
smith, Gibbon's *Decline and Fall of the Roman Empire*, and a work on
the history of the Middle Ages. They pursued chemistry, botany,
astronomy, and geometry; they read and discussed moral philosophy
and natural theology. Somehow, two hours a day remained available
for the study of Latin grammar and literature, and Abby wrote home
requesting a *Caesar* as a personal gift for Miss Allyn. Every Sabbath
Abby worked at translating a chapter in John from the Latin testament,
though at first she hesitated to tell anyone about her attempts lest she
not be able to meet the challenge. "Should [I] not succeed I should be
mortified to have you know it. I wish my pride were subdued as

regards this. I am not willing to be thought incapable of anything."[14] As usual, self-criticism inhibited her from acknowledging the more positive aspects of her character. Not all pride is negative, especially when it signifies determination to meet a challenge. She did not yet have enough experience to understand that much of her fear of failure had been imposed from without by those who so relentlessly urged her to duty and perfection.

Sam was keeping in close touch with her, trying to pay attention to her personal as well as intellectual progress. He reminded her that not all knowledge is obtained from books and recommended that she indulge her curiosity in order to keep her mind constantly stimulated. Having so said he proceeded to send an alarming number of volumes on history and philosophy, easing the burden, however, with advice to progress through them slowly. "[Haste] is a great waste of mind as well as time."[15] During one of his visits Sam noticed that Miss Allyn sometimes looked anxiously at Abby, whose studies were not bringing her the peace of mind they had all expected. He warned his sister that her morose manner was increasing Miss Allyn's labors and decreasing her pleasure in their relationship. Sam wished she would try to be more cheerful. "Cheerfulness," he advised, "is a kind of oil to the springs and wheels of life."[16] He was much relieved when her spirits rose sufficiently to banish the "demons"[17] which she said she had felt hovering around her head.

Her impending engagement to Mr. Frothingham weighed on Abby's mind, and a letter from her mother chastising her for not writing to him served only to renew her despondency. She was realistic enough to admit to herself that in going to Duxbury she was merely postponing the inevitable, but fate intervened on her behalf when Samuel Frothingham died in August, 1819. Dutifully, she went home for the funeral, then returned to Duxbury, and in October was ready to live once again at Federal Court - with conditions. She wanted to be left alone in order to immerse herself in her studies, and she insisted that she be "allowed to refuse visiting." She would willingly do her share within the family, and more, but the past two years had taxed her greatly, she said, and she "*must* be permitted this winter to withdraw... If I incur the epithet pedantic or unsocial or misanthropic, I must bear it patiently." She argued that her parents could not deny her the character building program she set forth for herself so that she might "fix habits of attention and reflection." She claimed to be fond of company, though she had not given evidence of it lately; but at present she wished to chance no diversions which might distract her from her stated purpose, the formation of her character. To reinforce this reasoning she noted that since she might give offense in selecting friends, she would avoid the danger by having none. "It is better to treat everybody well and be intimate with nobody." The more she pursued this theme, the more she gave evidence of a troubled mind and spirit. She was at last living life rationally, she said, finding enjoyment in that which "philosophy activates and religion sanctifies."[18] In reality, she was denying herself emotional outlets; her life was badly out of balance.

Abby was doing her best to order her life, but upbringing and personality combined to present a daunting challenge. Frivolity had played no part in the May household. Social visits were more obligation then pleasure for them, and in the evenings, the days' duties accomplished, they held forth on reform topics of pressing interest - abolition, temperance, women's rights. Music, piano and song, gave variety to the scene but did not furnish much relief to Abby during this crisis in her life. She had a close friend, Lydia Francis, who might have been able to help but who was, unfortunately, living with a sister in Maine at the time. Like Abby, Lydia had been tutored by an older brother, a divinity student at Harvard. Unlike Abby, she taught before she was twenty and had a school of her own by the age of twenty-four. Both young women felt that education and reason would lead the way to a just and unselfish society, and the reform of early childhood education became Abby's new focus even though she chose not to be actively involved. In 1822, she found a satisfactory outlet at last, when Sam, ordained a Unitarian minister, was called to a parish in Brooklyn, Connecticut. She began to visit him with some frequency, often for extended periods, and eagerly entered into his enthusiasm for educational reform. He was committed to convincing educators that they must abandon rote learning and allow a spirit of free enquiry in the classroom. This was the year of Louisa's marriage, the event which put an end to Abby's thoughts of independence through teaching; but as her preference was for a supporting role anyway, she brightened at the prospect of doing what she could to help her brother. Sam married Lucretia Coffin in early June, 1825, and Abby more than approved of his choice. Here was no rival but a new friend, a beloved sister-in-law who shared her values and was possessed of remarkable intellectual attainments. Just after their marriage, Abby visited them in Brooklyn although reluctant to leave her mother, who had been unwell for some time. On June 13, Abby wrote her father requesting "a full statement of Mother's health. I am as happy as I ever expect to be in this life when I am in Brooklyn, but I would not stay another moment if I thought I could serve my mother successfully."[19]

Abby nursed her mother during the last weeks of her illness and was at her bedside when she died that October, on a Sunday. She was back at Sam and Lu's by Thanksgiving when, at an appointed time, Joseph May in Boston and those in Brooklyn paused to think of one another and of the departed wife and mother. The situation was not as loving a year later when Joseph May remarried. He began courting Mary Ann Carey all too soon after his wife's death. Abby was at first dismayed, then indignant. She felt he was behaving irresponsibly, neglecting his duties, and carrying on in a fashion "unbecoming the father of twelve offspring." She wrote as much to a cousin, Thomas May, "in a whisper," not really caring whether he kept her sarcasm to himself or not. "My father has been very busy in conjugating the verb to love, and I assure you he declines its moods and tenses inimitably."[20] The relationship between father and daughter deteriorated. Abby continued to respect him in principle and reconciled herself to calling the interloper Mother, but she spent as little time as possible at Federal Court.

Sam and Lu welcomed her in Brooklyn as often and as long as she could stay, and when their son, Joseph, was born in 1827 she enjoyed her visits more than ever and was useful to the household as well. Her life began to feel almost full, especially as Sam was joined by other Connecticut activists in his goal to reform education. She kept abreast of all that was going on and got at the essence of the underlying problem in a few expressive words. "Children, until within a few years, were not allowed to think and reason. They were treated like machines - machines not active in themselves, but which were to be acted upon."[21] Sam began to organize a convention of interested parties to discuss "the defects of our Common Schools, the causes of those defects, and the expedients by which they may be corrected."[22] When he sent out a call for papers, William Alcott, a Connecticut physician deeply interested in education, forwarded an account of the innovative school newly established by his cousin, Bronson Alcott. Mr. Alcott's Cheshire, Connecticut, schoolroom was decorated with flowers and pine boughs, and his materials were not standard texts but everyday objects such as blocks for mathematical calculations and pictures to facilitate reading and writing. "The Child is the book,"[23] he said. "It is not the string of names in the memory, but ideas in the understanding that constitute knowledge."[24] His method was to draw this knowledge from his pupils by means of appropriate questions.

Sam was excited by William Alcott's general description of Bronson's school and wrote to ask Bronson himself for a detailed statement of his goals and methods. The resulting paper revealed such a depth of insight that Sam "at once felt assured the man must be a genius." He sent the essay to William Russell, liberal editor of the *Journal of Education*, who accepted it for publication. He also sent an urgent message to Mr. Alcott, inviting him to visit Brooklyn as soon as possible. The invitation was accepted; Alcott passed a week with the Mays. Sam was immensely impressed. "I have never, but in one other instance, been so immediately taken possession of by any man I have ever met in life. He seemed to me like a born sage and saint. He was radical in all matters of reform; went to the root of all things, especially the subjects of education, mental and moral culture.... My sister Abigail was in my family at the time. I soon saw the indications of a mutual attraction, which afterwards became a strong attachment."[25] The attraction was physical as well as intellectual. A year her senior, Bronson was tall and fair, elegantly serene in aspect, with penetrating eyes - altogether an aristocrat in mind and bearing although the son of a poor, rural, all but illiterate farmer. Abby was his opposite by birth, appearance, and personality. She had the dark hair and olive skin of the Mays, and now, in Bronson's presence, her natural vivacity asserted itself and she became animated, even impetuous.

The visit took place in July, 1827. Sam was out when Bronson arrived, and Lu was indisposed, having recently given birth to little Joseph. It fell to Abby to welcome him, and she did so heartily, launching into a topic dear to her heart - improvement of female education. She believed that its deficiencies to date had been oppressive to women's "moral health and intellectual growth." She applauded William Russell for being a pioneer on behalf of their emancipation, for acknowledging the truth that women are "intelligent, accountable beings." Adding that "truth is no welcome guest when it comes in the garb of innovation," she further praised him for reminding the public that God created women to be used as "divine agents, not merely as objects of pleasure or sense, created only for convenience and admiration. Let us be taught to think, to act, to teach. Let us adopt and exercise the laws of our nature which nature is love."[26] In this impassioned outpouring Abby did not concern herself with equal rights for women but, rather, with the huge potential of their influence for moral good within the confines of their prescribed role.

Bronson was not put off by her tirade, for he admired a keen intellect in man or woman and agreed with the sentiments she expressed so adamantly. He stayed with the Mays for a week, long enough for Abby to be certain that here was no ordinary mortal. For the first time, she was attracted to a man personally and intellectually; and her affections were further stimulated by his uncommon zeal for reform. They both felt that society and its institutions were based on a self interest which could only be dispelled through education of the young. Although Abby was beginning to acknowledge that an emotional range was necessary for mental health, she remained a staunch advocate of the efficacy of reason. Only rational beings know right from wrong; reason, therefore, should be cultivated early. Bronson's methods were exactly to her liking. By precept and example, by engaging each student in conversations on the meaning of such values as truth and honesty, he was able to accomplish the goal which motivated his whole system - moral education.

Mr. Alcott and Mr. Russell contemplated teaching together in Boston, and Abby did not hesitate to offer her services. She quickly responded to a letter Bronson sent off soon after his visit to the Mays, telling him that she would be pleased to associate herself with the enterprise as female assistant should he and Mr. Russell decide to open a school the following spring. In the meantime, she requested that he instruct her to that end. His guidance would be helpful, even if the plan came to naught, because she had nieces and nephews whom she taught from time to time. She then made so bold as to write, "It would add much to my happiness to form an arc in your social circle, wherever you may be." Her long letter was unmistakably warm, even flirtatious. She had held herself properly in check, not writing until he began the correspondence, but with that propriety met she wrote without restraint. Her tone was light and bantering but there was no mistaking her intentions, nor did she want them mistaken. Bronson Alcott was the man for her. With mock modesty, clearly intended to show that she had spirit, she said, "I am particularly pleased that you should have retained sufficient recollection of my identity to sign a letter to me."

She admitted to regrets for not having taken the initiative in encouraging their friendship but said she dared not "ford the great gulf that heartless fashion and polar etiquette has made between us, (or rather our sex)." He had given their friendship an impulse; she would take the impetus, hoping "it will endure through time and be sublimated in eternity." She was remarkably uninhibited, marveling at her newfound sense of freedom. She closed on a sensible note, however, with a simple statement that belied the depth of her feelings. "I shall pass the winter here and hope to hear from you (if not see you) often."[27]

Abby did not see Bronson until the following April, nine months later, but both she and Sam corresponded with him and were disappointed to learn that his progressive educational practices had alarmed Connecticut parents, first in Cheshire and then in Bristol, where he made his second attempt to reform infant education. By April of 1828 he was on his way to Boston to teach, not with William Russell, but in a charitable school for children of the poor. Bronson stopped at Brooklyn for two days, en route, and inadvertently dashed Abby's hopes of furthering her suit, for it was clearly she who took the initiative throughout this unusual courtship. At their first meeting she had found in Bronson "a friend with whom I might freely communicate my opinions without embarrassing him or involving myself." Their subsequent letters through the fall and winter were not in any way intimate, professing friendship only, but Abby hoped for much more and was taken aback by the seeming coldness with which he met her at Sam's in April. "I went into Mr. May's study to see a friend. He proved merely an acquaintance, whose reserve chilled me into silence.... I formed the resolution to omit no kindness but to avoid him as much as possible." She feared that her letters "might have been more familiar than was agreeable to him and given the impression of a particular attachment."[28] This distressed her, but she determined to leave Sam's and follow Bronson to Boston where she would act in the chaste capacity of friend. There was an intensity to her need for just such a companion, and she would accept friendship if love were not forthcoming.

Since she saw only his reticence, she would have been surprised to know that at their first meeting Bronson saw in her his ideal woman. He wrote in his journal, "There was nothing of artifice, of affectation of manners; all was openness, simplicity, nature herself. There was intelligence, sympathy, piety, exemplified in the tenderness of the eye, in the beauty of moral countenance, in the joyousness of domestic performance.... Everything seemed to favor the commencement of an acquaintance of a pure and sentimental kind. The results of this interview are to be determined by time."[29] Bronson's reluctance stemmed from legitimate reservations. He was poor, with an uncertain future, a farmer from rural Wolcott, Connecticut, who brought himself to prominence in the field of education entirely through application of his innate gifts. He had only the most rudimentary of educations but read voraciously, especially in history and philosophy. Hand copying Abby's brief autobiography when in his seventies, intending to write her biography, he made an understandable correction. Choosing her words inaccurately, she had written that he was not an educated man. Bronson amended the statement to read self-educated.

Though she lacked his genius, learning was of the utmost importance to both Abby and Bronson, and they were to discover yet another important bond, one which allayed his concerns about the disparity between their social positions. He soon learned she cared no more for socializing than he. Continuing to use her studies as an excuse, she seldom mixed in society and knew herself to be an eccentric figure on the rare occasions when she was obliged to appear. "I cared for nobody and generally left a party with disgust. I saw folly worshipped, beauty adored, and worth neglected. I withdrew myself in a great measure, for which I was stigmatized as odd. Odd I shall probably be through life for I shall ever condemn those forms of society which displace the substance of life."[30] Trying to justify her attraction to a penniless idealist with few prospects, she said she was grateful to her parents for teaching her to value personal worth more than social position or financial success. She conveniently forgot that they had wanted her to marry the unremarkable but socially acceptable Samuel Frothingham. Removing her argument to a higher plane, she expressed further gratitude for the upbringing which enabled her to say, "I have been conquered by moral power, I serve moral excellence, I love moral rectitude."[31] She *would* pursue Bronson, this most moral of men, and she would do so without consulting her father. She could not chance his disapprobation, however, and was constrained to act with the utmost circumspection as she had no choice but to return to Federal Court if she wished to be near Bronson.

In April, 1828, when Bronson left Connecticut for Boston under
the patronage of the philanthropic matrons who were organizing the
Salem Street Infant School, Abby said good-bye to Sam, Lu, and little
Joseph; returned to her father's home; and offered herself as Bronson's
assistant. She felt confident there was no impropriety. Her interest in
education was well known; she was offering her services in order to be
useful, not for the remuneration; Bronson's behavior towards her was
in no way that of a suitor. He was, in fact, so indifferent that she sometimes felt her character was disagreeable to him. "Strange infatuation!
I found it made me unhappy. A man whom I much esteemed and was
so anxious to secure as a friend, should feel a contempt for me,
wounded me so much that I resolved he should know me better and
find I had some redeeming virtue." Persistence was her strong suit.

The plan came to naught for society proved no better than her esti-
mate of it, deeming her motives scandalous. In her desire to communicate Bronson's views and praise his moral character, she spoke too
warmly on his behalf when showing the matrons letters he had
exchanged with Sam. They accused her of being more interested in
Mr. Alcott himself than in his school. She feared that he might think
her a hypocrite should he hear of these accusations, and she worried
that his reputation might thus be harmed "in the estimation of those
very people I was most anxious to secure as his friends.... I said little
of him for several weeks. I kept myself secluded, lest accident might
involve me. An indescribable something made me cling to his interests. I was anxious at his absence, solicitous for his success, and
wholly incapacitated from doing anything to serve him lest I should
involve him, and corroborate the slander of fools."

She took refuge at the home of her sister, now Louisa Greele, in
nearby Brookline, Massachusetts. Bronson called upon her there and
allayed her fears. With relief, she wrote in her diary that he was "kind
in his manner" and appeared not to have heard the slander. With her
apprehensions quieted, she "resolved to be more independent of a silly
world and cherish as far as propriety would allow this good man's confidence." She was determined to further the relationship, and her
resolve was reinforced when he handed her a letter and his journal. On
reading them, she was both encouraged and dismayed. She found that
he held her character and her opinions in high regard but that he found
her deficient in expressing her real feelings. Neither one, it seemed,

had succeeded in communicating successfully with the other, and Abby complained, "He knew nothing of the trials I had been struggling with to be to him all I wished without embarrassing him or myself."

Needless to say, Abby immediately tried to set the situation to rights. "Did Mr. Alcott really love me?" she wondered. She went to Brookline for another visit with the Greeles and asked Bronson to call on her there, for such a meeting could not possibly take place at Federal Court. She knew she risked her reputation in Bronson's eyes because she planned to tell him her feelings without reservation. She took the chance because of her conviction that "they were innocent and only needed explanation to be cherished or rejected by him." At this meeting Bronson attempted to express himself, but Abby found "his communication was mystical. It seemed to me that the more he tried to explain, the more mysterious everything appeared to me." Once again the written word had to supplant the spoken. As a conversationalist Bronson was superb; as a suitor he was all but mute; but the pages he showed her on this occasion convinced her at last that their "tender, holy interest and affection"[32] were mutual.

They became engaged in August, 1828. She eagerly sent the good news to Sam, taking care to ensure that there was no mistaking her meaning. "I am engaged to Mr. Alcott, not in a school, but in the solemn, the momentous capacity of friend and wife." She went on to acknowledge that though he had been attached to her from the evening of their first conversation in Brooklyn, he had been reticent about pursuing his suit. Having realized, after much introspection, that she loved him, she had decided, she told Sam, that she must either "dissolve all connexion with him or give him that encouragement and promise which should secure to him my future interests." He was in every respect qualified to make her happy. "He is moderate. I am impetuous. He is prudent and humble. I am forward and arbitrary. He is poor, but we are both industrious. Why may we not be happy?" She asked Sam to use his influence and help Bronson out of his temporary pecuniary embarrassment by asking the organizers of his new school to pay him generously. Abby felt "the greatest security in his habits of industry and method" but was apprehensive as to whether an experimental school could succeed any better in Boston than in Connecticut. Nevertheless, she had never been so happy in her life. "I have something to love, to live for. I have felt a loneliness in this world that was making a misanthrope of me in spite of everything I could do to overcome it."[33]

Abby closed with hopes that Sam would continue always to be the sincere, candid friend, the affectionate brother she held so dear. He remained all three, but she now turned to Bronson as her "moral mentor, intellectual guide. He analyzes my mind with care and judgement, my character with discrimination and charity, my heart with love and confidence." In her zeal for perfection, Abby now looked to her lover for guidance in matters of mind and spirit. As her feelings of self-worth strengthened, however, she became more and more interested in the situation of women as a whole. In typically picturesque language she stated that no woman's intelligence should be "tramelled and attenuated by custom as her body is by fashion." Some progress had been made; reason and religion were emancipating woman from intellectual thraldom. "The irresistible force of merit" was at last beginning to place her by the side of man as his intellectual companion. Abby's conclusion, though couched in general terms, was of an immediate and personal nature. "What must we think of the husband who requires of his wife an unquestionable obedience instead of a sympathy of thought, taste, and feeling? Is it not true that a wife submits to conjugal authority just in proportion as she is ignorant and uncultivated?"

Abby did not marry to adore, idealize, and serve but to love, admire, and share. She strongly reasserted her belief that a woman should work for the improvement of society from within traditional roles. By virtue of her position as wife and mother, she insisted, a woman "is the most interesting as well as important member in the community."[34] By promoting moral excellence, good habits, and healthy living in her own family, she could contribute to the good of society in its entirety. Men and women had different duties but should converse on equal terms. She did not feel in any way subservient when she said it would be her responsibility as Bronson's wife to be unselfish, to "expect no more of him than he is ready and happy to bestow.... His obligations to society must be scrupulously observed, for it is society that he wishes to serve as a benefactor, a philanthropist, me as a friend and protector." Just as Bronson replaced Sam as Abby's intellectual mentor, he also replaced him as the reformer for whom she would act as helpmeet, but she by no means relinquished her independence. During their courtship she had taken the initiative, actively pressing for the engagement. She created opportunities for Bronson to declare himself and consulted no one regarding her course of action, not even Sam. It was a personal matter "to be decided solely upon principles and feelings which can be known and understood only by those immediately concerned in its issue, and upon which not the slightest external circumstance should be suffered to bear." It was Abby, flaunting custom, who informed her father of their engagement, after the fact. She did not want Bronson to seek the traditional interview requesting permission of his prospective father-in-law, more because of a desire to be in charge than because of concern that Joseph May would demur, though that was a strong possibility. Her diary entry reads like a series of commands as she enumerates what her father and friends *must* do.

> He must approve what I have done as a woman in whose judgement he has ever expressed a confidence. He must as the future companion and protector of his child become acquainted and familiar with Mr. Alcott, receive him as a son, make him acquainted with my relations and friends. And they must receive him as my friend, and of course as a worthy recipient of all their attention and kindness. They must cultivate his acquaintance for my sake; they will love him for his own.[35]

Her independent behavior led to the engagement both she and Bronson desired, but that very forthrightness soon began to trouble him. Abby copied into her diary a letter in which he cited "pride of opinion and obstinacy of will" as traits she must strive to overcome. "I cannot look with complacency," he said, "on exhibition of that spirit of individualism which sometimes assumes the form of pride. What security have I that the same spirit will not be connected with the events of our future life, with our friends, the inmates of the nursery, with me." Had she not been accustomed to hearing just such criticism she would have taken offense. As it was, she asserted that she valued it because it was offered "in the spirit of kindness and charity." She still felt her willfulness to be troublesome, although she could now hold her own in matters of reasoning and judgment. "I will modify if not wholly eradicate it," she said. "It shall become tame and harmless if not annihilated."[36] She wrote in her diary that Bronson's remarks showed that he had scrutinized her carefully and thought her capable of conquering this excess of spirit. This pleased her, at first. On reconsideration, she concluded that he was holding her up unfairly to the ideal woman of his imaginings. "He has delicately sketched what the object of his affection should be rather than what she is.... He thinks independence the prominent characteristic of my mind. I hope it is the independence of virtue,

for virtue is a higher power than knowledge.... What I think to be right
I pursue firmly, ardently, cheerfully. What I know to be wrong I avoid
obstinately, coldly."[37]

A convenient dream allowed her to give him the essence of her
feelings. In this dream, she told him, "I burst into tears and in a subdued tone broke a silence I could no longer endure. Will you forever
be picking out my moral excrescences. Only have patience till I have
time to recover myself. You will find me less faulty, though believe
my candor when I say, if you love me for my perfections you are loving
a creation of your own imagination." The dream ended happily, with a
tender embrace. Having gotten that off her mind, she told him that she
was finally beginning to enjoy an unusual tranquility. For the last few
years she had been so much disturbed by circumstances over which she
had no control and which had held her captive that "I seemed not to
have this ingredient in my temperament."[38]

The many circumstances to which she referred were her mother's
death and father's remarriage; the deaths of Eliza and Louisa; and
finally, baby Joseph May's death in December, 1828, only a month
after Louisa's. Abby's triumph of summer, securing her engagement to
Bronson while staying with the Greeles, was deeply shadowed by the
overwhelming sadness she felt in losing Louisa, who had been sister,
friend, and confidante. She could bear this, "the greatest affliction of
my life," only through a belief in a supreme wisdom. "Human wisdom
is here but of little use, for in proportion as it bestows comfort it repres-
ses feeling, without which we may cease to be hurt by calamity but we
shall also cease to enjoy happiness."[39] In the sad loss of her sister,
Abby realized more than ever that feelings were as important as reason.
In the fullness of her grief, she volunteered to take over the care of
Louisa's children. Because of her deteriorating relationships at Federal
Court, she arranged to bring them with her to Sam and Lu's, writing in
her diary that the trust weighed heavily on her mind. "It shall be discharged with fidelity if not success."[40] Despite good intentions, her
personal needs overwhelmed her, and her words became a
self-fulfilling prophecy. She depended upon Lu, now, as "nearer and
dearer to me than any female friend in the world, and I never needed
one so much."[41] The bond was mutual and went beyond ties of need
and affection. Abby characterized it to Lucretia as "an intelligent
friendship founded on those principles which time strengthens and circumstances confirm."[42] Lu's support helped her fulfill her responsibili-

ties towards Samuel and Louisa Greele as best she could, but Bronson was uppermost in her thoughts. She missed her almost daily contact with him and feared for their future together. "Circumstances may separate us 'til necessity become habit... now and then the fear of fate cries an alarm in my ears and makes me tremble."[43]

Bronson was doing his best to improve his circumstances so that they could marry. He stayed at the charity school just long enough to get it under way, simultaneously seeking out sponsors for a project more challenging to his intellect and more likely to bring notice to his theories. His goal was to teach children from well-to-do families which valued intellectual stimulation and independent thinking. There were many such in Boston, and under their patronage he soon opened a school for boys on Tremont Street. Abby's step-mother made a conciliatory gesture in paying it a visit. Abby professed herself glad but was cool in her thanks, dwelling on the nature of Bronson's educational methods. "His plan is not to be seen or heard but it is obviously felt by every recipient of his care. He makes no exhibition of his method, for it is the work of time."[44] For his part, Joseph May showed remarkable restraint and did his best to accommodate his daughter's unprecedented willfulness in forming her engagement without his prior knowledge or approval. He accepted Bronson into his home, writing Abby, "Mr. Alcott's visits to us afford us pleasure as we get more acquainted with him, but he is a man who must be drawn out. I wish we saw him oftener but believe he has no idle time." Mr. May began this letter with the statement that he had long wished to communicate but was prevented by "doubts, various feelings, and unsettled views of what I ought to write." She had withdrawn herself from him and his wife and formed an engagement which would determine the course of her future life, all without asking his permission or advice. He would try not to let her actions in this regard trouble him further, but he remained concerned about "the injuries done my *companion and friend*." He added that Mrs. May could only "forgive where she ought." He asked Abby to be a little more open. If he knew her plans, perhaps he could assist them. "Let us love one another with pure hearts fervently, and if we may not be allowed to strew flowers in the remainder of our path, at least we may be allowed to remove thorns from it."[45] Her father was remarkably indulgent towards her pursuit of Amos Bronson Alcott.

Abby replied to her father's letter within a week of receiving it and, as requested, obliged him with word of her plans. "It is Mr. Alcott's wish to be married as soon as he finds himself in possession of means sufficient to do so safely. This may be in the spring. It is my wish to remain here 'til within a few weeks of our marriage. I should love then to return to your home and make the few preparations that may be necessary, receive your blessing and the good wishes of all those whose connexion with you may make me relatively interesting in this trying momentous hour." She felt no need to ask his forgiveness for her independent actions, saying only, "I am fallible but faithful."[46] She felt affection for him and for the home of her youth, but she would live her life elsewhere. For the moment, her home was with her "good brother"[47] in Brooklyn, but the tranquility she thought was hers had fled. Mr. Greele arrived there for a visit, bringing Abby a letter from Bronson which reassured her as to their future together; but that future seemed too far off, and the present was wearing her down. The cares and anxieties of tending to "dear Louisa's orphans" was too much for her. She was unaccustomed to such full time demands, and the timing was wrong. Her heart, being elsewhere, was not in the task. "It was a responsibility and situation of my own taking, but like many of my plans, more perfect and desirable in design than execution. I am glad I have made the experiment. It was one founded on the principles of love and good will."[48]

Bronson and Joseph May agreed that Abby should be relieved, without delay, of the care of the Greele children so that she might attend to her health. Her father wrote, "To the children you have been faithful and your reward is in your own bosom." Both men agreed with her that she should not return to Boston until Bronson was able to undertake the care and expense of a family. They could then be married from Federal Court. When that time arrived, said Joseph May, he would cheerfully, with all his heart, see them united in the holy relation of marriage. "I am persuaded," he wrote, "that he and I have become more friendly as we become more known to each other. He improves upon acquaintance.... He is not a man of procrastination or indecision but considers well and then acts. I have told Mr. Alcott the sum that I promised you on your marriage and have so ordered in my will."[49] Her father acted very decently despite the circumstances, though Abby seemed to feel it was only her due. By return mail she thanked her father for his "assurance of kind feelings and benevolent intentions" and expressed her gratitude for the generous expression of his just opinion of Mr. Alcott. She prudently stated that she dreaded "pecuniary embarrassments"[50] but indicated, nonetheless, that they would not delay the wedding a moment longer than absolutely necessary. By February, 1830, Bronson's financial situation permitted of making tentative plans. Abby wrote her father that the return to Federal Court filled her with "doubt and apprehension," but she trusted in his sympathy and would return to him and his home "with the confidence of a child." She would meet with him and his wife as he desired. "Reason urges that it is right; religion that it is my duty; and affection that it is my pleasure.... I am commencing a new era, and with your blessing, my dear father, it will be a happy one."[51]

On May 23, 1830, Abby May became Mrs. Amos Bronson Alcott. Sam May officiated, and Abby's cousin, Samuel Sewall, was best man. By coincidence, the simple ceremony at King's Chapel was attended by Elizabeth Peabody, the educator with whom Abby was to have an uneasy and sometimes stormy relationship in the years to come.[52] There were many rain clouds in the skies of her future, some from within the marriage, some from without, but Abby loved her husband all her life and wrote Lu a few weeks after the wedding that her husband was all she expected, "and that is saying a good deal." She cherished his "moral and intellectual society" and reveled in having Bronson all to herself, fearing only that, given her distaste for society, they might become all too satisfied with their own company. The only mote in the "beams of the honey-moon"[53] was lack of money, a problem which was to plague her for most of her married life and keep her in conflict with her father. Right from the start they failed to anticipate a diminished income resulting from the fact that many of Bronson's students would soon leave for the summer break. Abby began to realize that a steady salary was necessary to relieve them of irksome and embarrassing financial concerns. Before the year was out they made a move which they believed to be the ideal solution.

# Chapter Two

---

# Motherhood

*She felt its sacredness, its beauty, and
its high responsibilities, accepted them
prayerfully, and found unspeakable
delight in fitting herself to bear them
worthily.*

Christie Devon on motherhood from
*Work* by Louisa May Alcott

After a modest wedding supper at Federal Court, Abby and Bronson
proceeded to his boarding house on Franklin Street.    There being no
funds, there was also no fuss about furnishing a home of their own.
Having successfully conducted her courtship in a spirit of independence, Abby now began her marriage unconventionally.  Daughter of a
May and a Sewall, she might well have been expected to move into a
home of her own, but she cared nothing for custom or show.  Making
little of financial constraints for the moment, she boasted that, unlike
other newlyweds, the early days of romance and promise had not
blinded *them* to the essentials needful for happiness.  Taking the superior tone she was all too prone to adopt, she added that for Bronson and
herself "love is and ever has been... a principle, not a passion."  How
easily she forgot the tenacity with which she had pursued him; how
smug she was in her pronouncement of ideals.

Mrs. Bronson Alcott at last, she was glad when the visits incumbent upon newlyweds were dutifully attended to so that they could settle down. They were not even disturbed by a servant to attend to the cleaning and washing. She had, in fact, looked for one but was predisposed to reject any and all applicants. Understandably, she wanted no intrusion into her cramped honeymoon quarters. Predictably, she wanted to be in charge. She was particularly hesitant to hire a mature woman because she believed love of power to be inherent in human nature, and a woman with experience of life would soon impose her importance and "thus become a despot... in the little domestic commonwealth." For all her idealism, Abby Alcott often dealt in stereotypes and did not have much good to say of humankind. She went so far as to conclude that even a girl, if city bred, would be undesirable because she would either be drawn to the shops or have "religious peculiarities." Later, with personal experience of poverty, her views mellowed for a time at least, and in the early 1850s she earned a living for her family by running an employment agency in Boston, placing a great many Irish Catholic females whom she would not herself have hired twenty years earlier.

Abby had waited to be married, albeit impatiently, until Bronson's prospects showed promise of supporting them. Now, only a few weeks wed, she wrote to Lu, "His school has diminished a good deal in consequence of families going into the country."[1] His prospects may have been good, but neither he nor she had the foresight to anticipate loss of tuition because of vacationing pupils. Financial concerns were not only irksome; they were becoming embarrassing and quite real. Throughout his life, Bronson's various failures were due not to idleness but to an excess of innovation and idealism. He did not shrink from hard work, and during this time of decline in his student body, he labored over a definitive essay on his theories, *Observations on the Principles and Methods of Infant Instruction*. He would have approved of today's language experience advocates, who emphasize the child's own imagery and imagination as the basis for learning to read and write. Unfortunately, Alcott did not place great emphasis on the acquisition of actual knowledge, stressing instead conversations on moral or abstract themes such as goodness. Though he undoubtedly schooled his pupils' minds to be active and inquisitive, on the whole he did not impart facts, thus failing as a teacher in the perception of all but the most patient parents. Abby recognized this from the start, when she wrote her step-mother that his method was the work of time. This was not a failing in *her* eyes; knowledge *would* follow in due course. Over the long term, the premise was valid. Alcott's expression of it in his essay, with emphasis on the child as human being, caught the attention of Roberts Vaux, a Quaker philanthropist from Philadelphia. Vaux wrote Alcott such an enthusiastic letter that Abby quoted passages to Sam in a letter dated July 25, 1830. Vaux's praise, she said, "is worth a 100 dollars to a man who expects to get his bread if not his butter by the labor of his brains." Vaux felt the work was "strongly marked by practical wisdom," more so than anything of the kind he had previously seen. He felt it should be read by parents and educators alike, and he offered to do everything in his power to have it published. The praise was welcome, as was whatever money publication would bring; but the Alcotts wanted to promote Bronson's theories in practice, and, besides, a regular income was required lest they "blush into obscurity and contemplate into starvation."[2] When the essay appeared in print in the fall, another Philadelphia philanthropist, Reuben Haines, came to Boston to offer Alcott the opportunity he had been looking for. Haines was willing to make a substantial investment and agreed to set him up in a school, enroll students from good families, and even provide a combined dwelling and schoolhouse. Here was justification for real hope; this was no chancy affair. Success did not depend upon the good will of a group of sponsors such as those in Boston who neglected to tide him over during the slack summer season. One man, Reuben Haines, had sought him out and would see that Alcott's theories were given ample opportunity to succeed.

Abby was six months pregnant when she and Bronson traveled to Philadelphia in December, 1830. Here they again lived in a boarding house, Mrs. Austie's, while Alcott and Haines discussed the proposed school and looked for a suitable location. They found just what they wanted in nearby Germantown, but as it would not be available until spring, Abby awaited the birth of her first child at yet another boarding house, Mrs. Stuckart's, also in Germantown. Anna Bronson Alcott, named after Bronson's mother, was born on March 16, 1831. Abby had conceived immediately upon her marriage. Though pregnant, she left family and familiar surroundings for Pennsylvania, not knowing but that her life, or the child's, or both might be forfeit. In a letter to Sam and Lu ten days after Anna's birth she wrote that even had Anna "not lived an hour after the pangs of birth, I still should rejoice that she

had been born. The joy of that moment was sufficient compensation
for the anguish of 36 hours." Bronson immediately began a diary
recording the babe's progress, but Abby did not entirely realize that his
grand plan was to use these observations on behalf of his theories of
early education. Instead, she remarked that all three would find the
record interesting if Anna were spared, "and should she be taken away
we shall be glad that her early infancy was recorded."

Bronson rarely left Abby's room during the ten days or so of her
recuperation, pleased with both his wife and his child, just as she was
delighted to have him nearby and to see him so absorbed in Anna. She
felt that his presence shed "tranquility on the scene," though he spent
most of his time at the desk, writing his observations of Anna just as he
was to do later for Louisa and Elizabeth. His first observations, of
course, concerned Anna's reactions to physical stimuli such as sound
and light, but they soon evolved into speculations upon her personality
and moral character. Contrary to a doctrine widely held at the time,
neither Bronson nor Abby believed that children were born with a
knowledge of evil, least of all a child of theirs. Such a belief would
have been manifestly out of character for both parents, though they
came to it from different approaches, he from theory, she from love.
Abby, so critical of so many, was blissfully content with her child and
her husband and said she felt Bronson inferior to none for domestic and
parental excellence. She was even well satisfied with the nurse, asking
her to move on with them as housekeeper when the new home should
finally be ready. Since Abby and Bronson shared the care of Anna
between them, a nursemaid was really not needed. The baby was
healthy and placid; she ate and slept on schedule, giving her parents
very little trouble. As was the custom of the time, Abby referred to her
confinement and delivery as illness, but she was certain that her current
happiness gave a sparkle to her looks and that in her husband's eyes she
had not "diminished in value for having become a mother." She made
a rapid recovery and couldn't wait to take the air, knowing that exercise
would "convert lilies into roses and thus restore all my former charms
and perhaps a little more." There would be no more thoughts of fune-
real lilies, and her sickroom pallor would soon be replaced by rosy
cheeks as she strolled in her Germantown garden.

Abby and her baby not only survived; they both thrived. She rejoiced and gave thanks that it was so. She was not alone in being fearful of child bearing. Women endured one pregnancy after another, notwithstanding the fact that birth control was understood if not widely practiced. Alcott's own cousin, the Dr. William Alcott who introduced Bronson's educational theories to Sam May, published a book called *The Physiology of Marriage*, and Sylvester Graham, whose spartan diet they approved, also wrote on marital sex. As it was, Abby was almost constantly pregnant for a full decade. Eight pregnancies, and perhaps a ninth, produced only four live children and undermined both her health and her spirits. Thoughts of her own individual death haunted her as much as the universal specter of miscarriage and infant mortality. She wrote Lucretia May, who had given birth to another boy, John Edward, that they both well understood the joy of being "a happy mother of a living, well child." It simply should not follow in the natural sequence of gestation and birth that so many mothers lovingly embraced their offspring, only to lay them in their graves within a year. She felt secure enough of Anna's health to jest that Lu might offer condolence since the baby was a girl rather than a boy, but Abby denied any such thought. "My happiness in its existence and the perfection of its person is quite as much as I can well bear.... I cannot conceive that its being a boy could add thereto."[3]

Both Alcotts read *The Health Journal* and endorsed modern practices which they believed would ensure Anna's good health and, of course, their own - fresh air, exercise, simple foods, cold baths. Bronson advised Abby to dress Anna in loose clothing in order to induce freedom of spirit through freedom of movement. He was indulgent in a philosophical sense. For her part, Abby adopted a laissez-faire outlook on child rearing which would later cause friction with Bronson, when her unwillingness to discipline led to noisy rows in the nursery. She wrote Lu and Sam, "I have no rules save one great one - to do what she indicates to have done - and she is so reasonable that I find no difficulty." For the moment, with only baby Anna, Abby's indulgence of the child's needs served those of her husband as well. He required peace and quiet for the comtemplative nature Abby found so appealing. When the Alcotts moved into their new home in Germantown, Abby was at the ready to satisfy Anna's wants; she left her with Bronson or the nurse only for the most pressing household

demands. "I never go out without her.... My own grounds are sufficiently extensive for exercise. I put her in her basket wagon and draw
her about morning and afternoon."[4]

Abby felt that Mr. Haines had given them a "little paradise." She
had a gardener for the spacious grounds, and trees shaded a pretty ser-
pentine walk.    Raspberry, currant, and gooseberry bushes abounded
as did fruit trees and flowers.   The nurse-cum-housekeeper was
cooperative and efficient; "an amiable girl" was hired as cook. They
expected ten of the students to board with them, and though Abby
anticipated cares and arduous duties, all began well.  She wrote Sam
and Lu that the amenities of their home rivaled Federal Court. Now all
she had to do was see it perfectly furnished, comfortable for their little
family and pupils alike.  To this end she applied to Sam and to her
father for funds, reasoning that the worthiness of the cause justified the
request. She insisted that she was not indulging herself. The students
would respond best to instruction given in attractive surroundings. The
expense, therefore, was justified. Using terms of phrenology popular at
the time, she declared, "The bump of acquisitiveness is nowhere on my
cranium. There is, rather, an indentation." The money expended on
furniture and books, she further reasoned, was not spent but deposited.
She hoped Sam could spare fifty dollars.  Her father had already
responded most kindly with one hundred and the promise of two
hundred more to come, payable with interest within a year and a half.
In truth, Abby was *not* acquisitive, but she had been brought up in just
such surroundings as she was now able to achieve with her "neat pem-
broke table," and her "little old-fashioned round-about sofa" uphol-
stered in French fabric of blue and yellow. As the schoolmaster's wife
she felt justified in her concerns for the comfort of the scholars. As a
bride she quite naturally wished to replicate the elegance of her childhood home. But Abby, though thirty, still lacked maturity and was burdened with the disadvantage of having been spoiled.   Since she
perceived her needs as reasonable, her husband's cause as worthy, she
expected their more affluent friends and relatives to come to their aid.
All was in the service of the greater good. A genuine idealism was ever
hers, and she wrote Sam, "I believe a little patience will put us in possession of this world's goods and that best of all pleasures, the pleasure
of doing good."[5]

Abby's hopes and expectations were immediately "prostrated," not through excesses of her own or of Bronson, but by the sudden death of Reuben Haines not long after the Alcotts took up residence in their little paradise. To Abby's dismay and disgust, Mr. Haines' friends did not rally to their support, and tuition alone could not carry expenses. She expected those who had encouraged his experiment to respect his memory by cherishing educational reform, but instead, she remarked with her usual flair for the dramatic, "with his body they deposited also his plans." Furthermore, her religious affiliation became known and the word Unitarian was affixed to the school. In consequence, she avowed with some exaggeration that it was avoided as a "pestilence, excepting by a half dozen rationals who seem to think if we are not sheep we must be goats like themselves."[6] So said Abby, displaying a no more Christian attitude than that of her detractors. Since, as she wrote Sam, Unitarians were "held in horror as being worse than infidels,"[7] she went to Quaker meeting, acceptable to both the community and to herself. She was comfortable with their religious belief that the mind was God's sanctuary; with their sectarian belief in liberal social principles; and with their industry and modesty despite occasional great wealth.

Abby's concession to religious niceties could do nothing to save the school, and personal problems began to intrude upon their contentment. Bronson was "suffering for intellectual society;"[8] Anna had been ill for weeks with a bowel complaint; and Abby was sleeping poorly, overly fatigued by the demands of running a household which included boarding students. Within a year of her marriage she had had to share her home with outsiders. This pattern persisted for the better part of two decades, first to implement their educational schemes, then to augment their meagre income, and finally to put into practice Bronson's particular philosophy of communal living. She learned from the outset, "It is a thankless employment to take care of other people's children."[9] Though she chafed at having to board students, she had been willing to adjust out of need. Now that funds were inadequate for even the most basic necessities, she came close to desperation. "We hardly earn the bread; the butter we have to think about."

Though fallen, they were not expelled from Eden immediately. They managed to remain in their paradise for two years, making do with only one servant for all the large household, trying to succeed on their own, existing on the simple food which was their preference even in the best of times. Fruit was an essential of their diet, then and ever after, but the apple became an instrument of moral instruction as well. Abby's paradise was Bronson's Eden. Early on, when Anna was three and Louisa two, their father produced an apple and from discussion with them drew forth their knowledge that they must not eat what was not theirs. As he hoped, in his absence they ate the fruit nonetheless. Whether his role was that of Jehovah or the serpent, he did not expel the wrongdoers, content that the little household drama had taught them the lessons of temptation, confession, and remorse.

There were apples enough for all purposes, but Abby had cause for concern beyond even the need to feed her family and her boarding students. She appears to have conceived again immediately after Anna's birth. This time she was truly worried that she might not survive, not merely apprehensive as during her first pregnancy. Writing in August of 1831, she urged Sam and Lu to visit in November so that Lu could "return the compliment of nursing." Abby had helped Lu at the birth of little Joseph; surely this comment referred to an anticipated confinement. Knowing a visit to be unlikely but hoping to impress her need upon them, she resorted to a familiar exhortation to duty and told them that the journey would be nothing once begun. With a despondent air of finality she added that the visit "may be the last you ever pay me."[10] Louisa's birth was more than a year later, in November of 1832, and there is no further mention of either a visit or a miscarriage in the fall of 1831. For a year and a half, there is total silence from Abby, no diaries, no letters. That is not to say there were none. In a bound volume of correspondence for the years 1828-1861, there remain, on average, six letters to Sam annually. Nothing exists from August 1831 to February 1833. On the flyleaf of the volume is the statement, "Some letters have been destroyed by family as unnecessary and unsuitable for others' inspection - reflecting hardships and troubles often of a very personal nature." Such excisions cannot be dismissed from the study of Abigail Alcott's life, for they appear at critical periods, signaling problems. She was as blunt on paper as she was in person, and the frankness with which she recorded her thoughts was often feared as threatening to the Alcotts' posthumous reputations.

Late in life, in her short, objective autobiography, Abby penned a meagre account of this year and a half. "We continued in this place two years with uncertain and vacillating prospects of success. Louisa May was born on November 29, 1832. The following April an agreeable proposition was made to Mr. Alcott to go into Philadelphia to open a day school which he cheerfully accepted."[11]   We know from Bronson's papers that Louisa was born a livelier and larger baby than Anna, but that she lost weight because Abby's milk did not come in until she was five days old.  The Alcotts managed to have a nurse for the baby, but the woman was incompetent, not bathing her for a week. As a result, Louisa cried incessantly, exacerbating Abby's already distraught state.  Prior to Louisa's birth she had suffered from "one of those periods of mental depression which women are subject to during pregnancy."  She later blamed this mental state for Louisa's childhood "peculiarities and moods of mind."  In writing of this favored child she could have been describing herself when she spoke of her daughter's "firmness of purpose and resolution," but also, at times, "the greatest volatility and wretchedness of spirit, no hope, no heart for anything, sad, solemn, and desponding.  Fine generous feelings, no selfishness, great good will to all and strong attachment to a few."[12]

Abby's depression while awaiting Louisa's birth was unusually severe, and Bronson tried to buoy her spirits with a poem which he felt would both acknowledge the anxieties attendant upon pregnancy and focus her thoughts on the miracle of life.

> .  .  .  .  .  .  .  .  .  .
> The primal soul, a semblance of thine own,
> Its high abode shall leave, and dwell in clay,
> Thyself its shaping parent.  A miracle, indeed.
> .  .  .  .  .  .  .  .  .  .
> Firm faith may rest in hope.  Accordant toils
> Shall leave no time for fear, nor doubt, nor gloom.
> Love, peace, and virtue are all born of pain,
> And he who rules oe'r these is ever good.[13]
> .  .  .  .  .  .  .  .  .  .

It was some time before Abby felt fully well following Louisa's birth.  Her eyes bothered her on top of everything else. The problem besieged her intermittently throughout the rest of her life and threatened her with "unknown evils."[14]  Letter writing was a pleasure she had to forego for a while.  When she did write Sam and Lu in February, 1833, her babies, at least, were thriving.  Louisa, at three months, was "a sprightly, merry little puss."  Anna was "an active pantomimic little being, loving everything to death and often smites her sister from pure affection." A mother sees what she wants to see in her children. It did not occur to Abby that Anna might be jealous.

In anticipation of the move back to Philadelphia, the cherished new furniture was sold, and arrangements were made to board with Mrs. Austie once again. It was with relief that Abby anticipated the prospect of withdrawal into her own family. "I find in my contact with the world so much selfishness and so little brotherly love that I am very much disposed to hug my own and revolve in as small a circle as possible."[15] She never warmed towards the general run of people and continued to exaggerate human shortcomings, but she had the grace to admit that not *all* of Mr. Haines' friends had deserted Mr. Alcott. True, they allowed the establishment in Germantown to fall of its own weight; but it was expensive beyond reason. A day school in Philadelphia was another matter, and Roberts Vaux was particularly helpful. In a letter to Mrs. Haines, Abby put aside her previous animosity and gave due credit to those "discriminating" and "philanthropic" friends who wished to encourage her husband, "a quiet unostentatious individual who is ready to give the results of deep and earnest thoughts, careful observations, and the experience of ten years to the advancement of early education." Abby told Mrs. Haines that for the most part she passed the two years in Germantown "delightfully" despite "some moments of fear and distrust." The place would always be dear to her in any case because Anna and Louisa were born there. At present, their humble rooms at Mrs. Austie's were at least consistent with "the measure of our pockets,"[16] and the children, she related, were enjoying the variety of the city and thriving upon the improved health of their mother.

Permanence, however, was not to be theirs. Although they remained in Philadelphia, it was not at Mrs. Austie's. She had to give up her boarding house only two months after the Alcotts settled in, so they removed to Mrs. Eaton's establishment, opposite State House Square. Their rooms were open to the Square, airy and shaded, altogether very pleasant, the more so as there was no servant. Though their future was far from secure, Abby's letters reiterated the theme that Bronson's prospects were good. For her part she claimed, "When I stick to my little family and my round of little duties I am brave and invincible as a lion."[17] The care of her children both occupied and preoccupied Abby. Bronson gave her advice in general terms, but she saw to the details of their daily care, and it was a matter for constant thought. When she was not seeing to the girls' physical needs, she was either observing their mental development much as her husband did, or worrying about whether her methods of child rearing were appropriate. Anna was irritable, "yet so intelligent as to be making inferences and drawing conclusions about every thing which is done for her or said to her." Abby said she lived in constant fear of mistaking the motives of the child's actions. She knew there were those who thought her a slave to her children, but she could not be otherwise. "If I neglect every thing else, I must be forgiven." Responsibility for "these little mortal beings" weighed upon her, and she worried incessantly. "Am I doing what is right? Am I doing enough? Am I not doing too much?"[18] By the time Louisa was crawling inquisitively about, she and Anna were rivals for the affection of a mother who now had *two* children and a daunting task. It was all very well to do for the infant Anna, "what she indicates to have done," but how could she oblige both little girls when each wanted the other out of the picture! The squabbling grew worse and worse.

Abby was a bit wiser with regard to her own well being. It was her conviction that "cessation from labor" was impossible for a mother, and that the only way to get rest was "by change of occupation." In the fall of 1833, therefore, the Alcotts made a trip from Pennsylvania to Connecticut to visit Sam, Lu, little John Edward, and the new May baby, Charlotte. In her thank you note for the visit, Abby wrote with good news for a change. The enrollment at Bronson's Philadelphia school was increasing. In a well chosen analogy, she described parents' growing confidence. "We do not make much noise but shed some light - which travels faster and more direct and its influence is more effective."[19] Always adept in her choice of words, she was particularly attuned to symbolic language just then, for Bronson was immersed in writing a book of parables, allegories, and fables for young people. He did not confine his use of these to domestic play acting. Moral lessons were as much a part of his teaching method as were the conversations he used to draw forth innate knowledge. He was challenged by his writing and, happily, no longer suffered from want of intellectual society. The Reverend Dr. Karl Follen, Unitarian minister and ardent abolitionist, was visiting Philadelphia and spent many hours in deep discussion with him. Dr. Follen was no better off financially than Bronson, but they were both "bold thinkers," wrote Abby, philosophers

who "soar high and dig deep, but such minds are somewhat solitary in
this world of folly and fashion when a man's hat is the most essential
part of his head."[20]

Abby seldom missed an opportunity to berate the worldly. She
herself had been disappointed in several Philadelphia matrons and took
the whole of society to task as a result. Its gentility was evanescent,
she said, and "of the mushroom order" which "disgusts by its strong
smell." Damask cloth and Brussels lace did not intimidate her. "I am
more familiar with those things than they are aware of,"[21] she countered. Her childhood home at Federal Court had been well appointed, of
course, but the pretensions of these new acquaintances could not help
but remind her of a great-aunt on her mother's side, Dorothy Quincy,[22]
whose first husband was Governor John Hancock of Massachusetts.
Bronson drew the old aunt's portrait in words one evening after he and
Abby dined with her during their courtship. He described her as fancy-
ing herself superior because of her fine marriage, a woman who was
thus "a good subject for moral philosophers, showing the influence of
station upon weak and ignorant minds." Her manners were abrupt, said
Bronson, but her sincerity and amiability made her interesting, "even in
her foibles."[23]

Though Abby didn't give much actual thought to the matter, a consciousness of notable forebears underlay the self-assurance with which
she criticized "folly and flummery."[24] There were no sour grapes to
choke on. She could have lived a life of social calls but chose to avoid
those who, like Great-aunt Dorothy, were guilty of temporal pride. She
sought, instead, those who were concerned with moral and ethical
truths, and the abolition movement began to engage her attention as
actively as did educational reform. Her brother, Sam, was already
much involved as was her friend, Lydia Maria Francis, now married to
David Child. Both Abby Alcott and Lydia Maria Child endorsed the
view that women best served moral authority by supporting involved
husbands and by nurturing future citizens, the children. Abby remained
committed to that position, but early on her friend found herself unable
to stay out of the fray. Mrs. Child planned to limit her active participation to writing when, in 1833, she published the first of her many anti-
slavery articles, "An Appeal in Favor of that Class of Americans called
Africans." The piece became a rallying call, and she suddenly found
herself committed to action. Mrs. Child became one of the first female

members on the executive board of the American Anti-Slavery Society, and she edited a weekly newspaper, the *National Anti-Slavery Standard*.

Abby's efforts were not public, but her mind was certainly active on the subject of abolition. She attended speeches and read anti-slavery literature gathered for her by Sam and Mrs. Haines, informing herself further by means of *The Emancipator* and William Lloyd Garrison's *Liberator*. It was through Abby that both the Quaker abolitionist, Lucretia Mott, and Lydia Maria Child entered into correspondence with Sam May. Abby wrote her brother that she had joined the Society, not specifying whether the American, the Philadelphia, or the Female Anti-Slavery Society. As she well knew, Mrs. Child had her doubts about all-women societies, commenting to Mrs. Mott, "They always seemed to me like half a pair of scissors."[25] These two agreed that for the greatest success of the movement women were well advised to be equal members in organizations which were not sexually segregated. Just as there were male and female, local, state and national societies, there was great and heated diversity about the means and the speed with which to address the problem of slavery. Mrs. Child was for immediate emancipation and against colonization in Africa as was Abby, who noted that bad financial management in the Philadelphia Colonization Society had dealt it a death blow there. She was perturbed by the human error but not by the demise of the chapter. Many blacks, she had been told, would rather "be sold into Georgia"[26] than go to Liberia.

Since her children were young and she was loath to engage herself in anything apart from them, Abby did not attend many meetings of the local Society. She did not consider herself passive in this important matter, however, because her mind was so active, her reading and her correspondence so copious. It was wisest to remain somewhat sedentary in any case, for she was again pregnant. Their financial outlook was bleaker than ever as lies and slander began to undermine Bronson's new efforts; and her own relationship with him was becoming troubled. Beneath the need to economize fifty percent or "go aground," lay the darker necessity of preserving her marriage. Bronson's temperament was as intractable as hers, different though they were. She had reveled in his comtemplative habits when newly wed. Now that reality was upon them, his need for quiet was leading to their alienation. The household was in turmoil. With every physical advance made by baby Louisa, big sister Anna felt a keener rivalry, and their mother could not control the girls' squabbles. In the resulting hubbub, their father could neither work on his book of allegories nor concentrate on his exhaustive studies of Platonic idealism.

In his journal, Bronson acknowledged the deterioration of the marriage. Separation, he rationalized, would give them both new perspectives. Abby was less candid. Asking Sam to find a place near him for herself and her girls, she gave health and economy as her reasons. A friend offered Bronson the use of a basement room, and Abby acquiesced, for what else could she do? "This would be an excellent thing for my husband," she wrote Sam, "and reconciles my leaving him more than anything else could do."[27] She wrote of the contemplated separation as temporary but asked her brother to look quietly for a place, telling no one. There was no question but what it was financially expedient. She could afford only one large or two small rooms, she told him, hoping to board for five dollars a week rather than the twenty she was presently paying. She relied on Sam who was "good enough for heaven, and great enough for earth,"[28] and she was bound she would press on despite her cares. Abby Alcott was maturing of necessity, using her dogged determination to good effect, acknowledging as much when she said to her friend, Mrs. Haines, "for with all sorts of external oppression and failure I rise with the necessity and am stronger in theory and practice at every blow."[29]

Friends in Philadelphia got wind of the Alcotts' personal and financial problems and began offering everything from advice to dwelling places. Mrs. Haines was to Abby an invaluable counsellor who "knows where to say kind and candid truths and when to say them."[30] Another friend, having gotten wind of her intention to move, offered Abby, *free*, her choice of two houses. Ever aware of her children's health, she refused one place because it had a marshy exposure, the other because it was in a poor and thickly settled neighborhood. Mrs. Morrison did not take offense and continued to support Abby with her friendship. Meanwhile, Mrs. Eaton seemed "determined we shall not leave her yet on account of expense. I sincerely believe the woman would keep us for nothing rather than have us go. And should my children continue well, I think we may as well remain, at least for the present."[31] Feeling somewhat her old self with the rallying of friends, Abby turned around and disparaged Mrs. Eaton's boarders, if not Mrs. Eaton herself. She pronounced them to be literary despots who insisted upon hearing their own opinions echoed. "You must say what they like or say nothing so we choose the nothing and it is very stupid work."[32]

Abby retrenched and settled into the routine at Mrs. Eaton's, literary despots notwithstanding, but it did not work out. Bronson needed a time apart from his noisy children. In April, 1834, Mrs. Alcott, with Anna and Louisa, moved to Mrs. Sheppel's boarding house in Germantown, where she awaited the birth of her baby. It was an unorthodox arrangement, particularly because it was instigated by a man who believed, before his time, that a father should play an active role in the care and upbringing of his children. Bronson moved into the attic at Mrs. Eaton's and visited his family on the weekends, unable to live with them, unwilling to forsake them. Once the new living arrangements were accomplished, he wrote in his journal, "I am now alone. My mind can work on itself. Reflection, the Saviour and interpreter of the Soul, cannot now escape me."[33] Like many brilliant men, Bronson was able to compartmentalize his life, living each segment in its own sphere, with little or no overlap. Lydia Maria Child observed this and empathized with Abby when she wrote, during a time of personal marital stress, "Mr. Alcott would consider this shameful weakness; but the woman greatly predominates in me. I cannot live without being beloved."[34] Bronson did love his wife. Abby was as yet unable to fathom love on his terms.

The temporary separation, the distance, did give them a respite, and the short periods spent together with the children were happy enough. He and she spent a pleasant day together in Philadelphia in early May, visiting abolitionist friends, William Lloyd Garrison among them, but on the night of May 19, Abby had a miscarriage which nearly cost her her life. Only her immense will to live saved her, for the landlady, Mrs. Sheppel, did nothing but wring her hands until Abby begged her to fetch a doctor.

The near tragedy brought them up short. Acknowledging that the Pennsylvania experience was anything but a success, they resolved to return to Boston where Bronson anticipated more general acceptance of his ideas, more intellectual stimulation, and where Abby could recuperate at Federal Court. She had no alternative, though such a move could only stir up old animosities. She remained on uneasy ground with her father and was still hostile towards her step-mother. When first at Germantown, Abby wrote "Mother" a personal, respectful letter at her father's request, but in telling Sam about it she said that, given past experience, they would all have to be very careful in word and deed because the slightest of incidents led so easily to "misunderstanding and unkind thoughts."[35] Only the distance between them had kept the peace; returning to New England would undoubtedly destroy it; but, seriously unwell, she had no choice. As for the future, she said, "I try to suppress all emotion but that of hope for I have always been woefully disappointed in my expectations and I mean this time to keep on the safe side. My health is far from good."[36] Abby was not accustomed to failure and, though she had been ill from time to time, she had never been so near to death. Such an experience sometimes opens one up, in gratitude, to the joy of being alive. It was not so with Abby, nor would it be as she struggled through the remainder of the decade.

# Chapter Three

---

# Marital Discord

*Married life is very trying, and does
need infinite patience, as well as love.*

Meg March from
*Little Women*

The Alcotts changed lodgings more than half a dozen times in the first
four and a half years of their marriage. Abby's resolve not to reopen
hostilities at Federal Court pressed her to a timely recovery, and as
soon as possible they moved to Mrs. Wheelright's at Morton Place,
boarding for fifteen dollars a week. This move proved to be no more
permanent than the others. Bronson's future as an educator now rested
upon his hopes for the school he planned to establish at the Masonic
Temple on Tremont Street. In order to have their dwelling place
nearby, Abby agreed to pick up yet again and go to Mrs. Whitney's, at
21 Bedford Street.

Bronson's good fortune in establishing the Temple School was due
largely to the efforts and admiration of the educator, Elizabeth Peabody, who recognized his talent after reading some remarkable letters
and diaries written by his Pennsylvania pupils. She realized that his
advocacy of student introspection and journal writing related directly to
the skillful use of language and initiated both moral and intellectual
thought. She generously gave him the scholars she had gathered for a

proposed school of her own and then scurried about helping him recruit additional children and solicit sponsors. Bronson rented comfortable rooms on the top floor of the Temple, borrowing money to purchase books and pictures and hiring a carpenter to build desks specially constructed to accommodate the pupils' books and slates. With Abby's help they arranged the pictures and placed busts of Socrates, Shakespeare, Milton, and Scott in the four corners of the spacious main room. On the top shelf of the bookcase behind Bronson's desk they placed his head of Plato, and they fixed a large bas-relief of Christ onto one of the shelves.

The Temple School opened in September of 1834 and was to be both his greatest success and his greatest disappointment, his most fulfilling experience and his most devastating. Abby, dubious after their experiences in Pennsylvania, said of Miss Peabody that she was almost as much a hoper as was Bronson, and she was insightful enough to recognize that *their* hope was founded on faith whereas *hers* was born of despair. Miss Peabody, though she had very little money herself, offered to work for what Bronson could afford, thus agreeing, in effect, to volunteer her services. She was to teach Latin and be his assistant, acting also as recorder of his conversations with the children. Abby told Elizabeth it was a good thing she would be in the classroom, bringing substance to the curriculum by providing book learning. Convinced by previous experience that parents could not wait for an education that was the work of time, Abby was quite frank in stating that some acquisition of actual knowledge was necessary and Mr. Alcott "would never put his mind to that."[1] As usual, she was exaggerating; there was substance to the curriculum. Besides the conversations and the journal writing, there were spelling, reading, poetry, Bible study, geography, geometry, and even drawing. The students did acquire knowledge, and they learned to think for themselves as an added and unique benefit. One student said in wonder, "I never knew I had a mind till I came to this school."[2] Critics and patrons alike focused public attention on his innovative methods of instruction; but, as the months passed, the critics became increasingly vocal when Bronson began to use lessons less for knowledge and more to elicit moral conclusions. Miss Peabody herself became aware of his excesses but dared not, as yet, speak her mind to this man who had no self-doubt and little tolerance for the opinions of others. In explanation of his goals he told his students, "You have taken the knowledge and used it to govern yourselves, and to make yourselves better. If I thought I gave you knowledge only, and could not lead you to use it to make yourselves better, I would never enter this school-room again."[3]

Although Abby watched over the organization of the Temple School, there was little else of interest to her in Boston, which she described as "more like a sepulchre than a home to me. There are few here that I care anything about and fewer that care anything about me."[4] Sam often came to Boston to further his efforts in the cause of abolition, and while his visits revived her spirits, she desperately wanted Lucretia and the children to come, too, and board with them for a while at Bedford St., for she needed a friend near at hand. The two mothers, she suggested, could enjoy pleasant hours together while little Charlotte May and Louisa played; John Edward could go to school with Bronson as could Anna. Such companionship was wishful thinking, of course, and did not come to pass, but Abby was trying to take the responsibility for her own well being because, as she was learning, neither her mental nor her physical health was automatically assured by marriage to Bronson.

Association with individuals of intellect and moral worth invariably raised Abby's spirits. Miss Eliza Robbins, her childhood teacher, was still in Boston. She had written a series of books for her students, little volumes which pleased Abby inasmuch as "elevated moral sentiment" was conspicuous. Though she wanted content in the classroom, she wanted the improvement of society no less than Bronson. Abby particularly liked Miss Robbins' history of Greece because it not only informed, it instilled love of peace through its account of "the horrors of barbarous man." Abby rued the fact that, though the series was used in New York, Miss Robbins found it all but impossible to get it into popular use in Boston. Abby carefully composed a letter to those in charge of Boston's Educational Institute, urging them to encourage the moral education of children. Receiving no reply, she suggested that it must have been used to light their cigars. Refusing to give up so easily, she went to one of their meetings only to hear the appalling philosophy that teaching consisted of "breaking the will" and "subduing the spirit." Returning home, she wrote Sam that educational reform, more than ever, was crucial and that Bronson was at the forefront. "I believe that my husband is to be the Messiah to announce to the world a new revelation."[5]   It was not unusual, from time to time, for her to ascribe Christ-like attributes to her husband, sometimes in admiration, sometimes in awe of his unwavering "fidelity to the pursuit of truth."[6]

She knew that few shared her faith in him, and though she continued to advocate his reforms, she soon had to defend both Bronson and herself on a practical level which had nothing to do with either educational idealism or moral perfection.  Joseph May could no longer contain his anger about what he viewed as the Alcotts' economic profligacy.  Bronson's request for a loan of fifty dollars triggered an outpouring of pent up criticism.  He wrote a scathing letter to Abby, telling her she must cease her habit of "thoughtless expenditure," the consequences of which should alarm her.  He preferred her to owe him rather than anyone else, but she should owe no one at all, should not "yield to expenses... which you cannot afford, cannot pay for."  She must not persist in such a course.  He was convinced that Bronson's new school would succeed no better than his others for it was too intellectual and commended itself only to thinkers, who, needless to say, were not in the majority.  And while he was pointing out her present shortcomings, he took the opportunity to enumerate her past misdemeanors as well.

> You have made several important mistakes since you began to manage for yourself, and *without* or *against* the advice of your friends - Marrying without possessing the needful to keep house - and without having tried the success of your Friend's pursuits to obtain a support - changing your places of residence - removing to Germantown - furnishing a large house there to accommodate boarding scholars - selling your furniture at auction - and removing to Philadelphia - all of which have consumed four and a half years of the best part of your life - nearly all of your property - and left you burdened with a debt of $1,000 or more - to be provided for and paid, and besides yourselves two children to be maintained and educated.[7]

Her father hoped Abby would receive his advice in the knowledge that he wrote with deep concern for her future and with the kindest of feelings.  He should have known better.  Her anger steams from the pages of her reply.

If my husband were a spendthrift or had a single habit of personal indulgence that led to an unnecessary expenditure; if I indulged in dress, in public amusements, or after five society, the charge of 'thoughtless expenditure' could be proven.... But the case is wholly different. My husband is a peculiarly sober, temperate man, neat and unostentatious in his personal habits, dress and manners, visits only those who by their intellectual and moral superiority can benefit him, or those only whom he thinks he can benefit. .... But the admonition is more directly for *me*. Let me then enlarge a little on my own merits. They are few, and can be the more briefly enumerated. Extravagance in dress is not my sin. I am barely decent. I am this moment (as I showed my brother) wearing the clothing of my mother, my two sisters, and articles given me by... friends in Germantown and Philadelphia.

Abby demanded that her father tell her how they could get along on less. He should show her, without delay, "the superfluous expenditure" which was causing him so much anxiety. Who was he to criticize, when those to whom she and Bronson owed the thousand dollars were treating them with complete confidence, inasmuch as they were spending the money judiciously. None of the misfortunes were of their own doing. Was it their fault Mr. Haines died? Didn't her father understand that suitable furniture was essential in Germantown and reputable lodgings necessary to the success of their school in Philadelphia? They had been led to believe that there would be sufficient pupils, but the enrollment did not meet expectations. Was this their fault, too? They had lived one year almost literally on hope. Should they abandon that as well? The "debilitated state" of her health required their return to Boston where her husband, beloved by some of the best people, if not by Joseph May, was "solicited to remain." Their bedchamber at Bedford Street was so small that Mrs. Whitney included another small one, free of charge. Yes, Bronson had a study. That was as indispensable as the girl she had hired because the children couldn't eat with the boarders and couldn't be left alone. Didn't he appreciate the fact that her health required relief from her duties and that there were days when she was "wholly incapacitated for the care of my children?"

A tone of righteousness pervaded her letter. None of their misfortunes were of their own making, she insisted. Quite the opposite. They had acted wisely and prudently. Being themselves blameless and their cause so worthy, those connected with them and their ideals were duty bound to maintain them as necessity required. "Would you have me take in washing?" demanded Abby. She acknowledged her father's desire to be helpful in his criticism, but she was unable to take his advice or accept his blame. His letter, she said, was cruel and unfounded, Bronson much maligned. "Ever since this excellent man was connected with my family, discouraging predictions, questionable civilities and querulous surmises have been made to and about him and me which, had our connexion not been founded on the most disinterested affection and devoted principles, it would have been dissolved into annihilation."[8] She had defended her courtship; now she defended her marriage. She was fast becoming adept at defending her husband's idealism and was soon to do so beyond reason.

Throughout the winter of 1835, Abby continued to do her utmost to convince Lu to board with them at Bedford Street. She was tenacious in her urgings, all the more hopeful because Sam was so often in Boston, now considering the post of general agent for the Massachusetts Anti-Slavery Society. Abby reported that there were those who thought him a fool if he intended to give up the ministry in favor of proselytizing the reluctant, often antagonistic, Bostonians to the cause of abolition; but Abby defended her brother as ardently as she defended her husband , pointing out that too many in the ministry were respected but self-centered, comfortably wrapped up "in the ghostly folds of a black silk gown,[9]" preaching once a week to a sleepy congregation which attended for form, not reform. In Connecticut, Sam was well known for supporting a woman named Prudence Crandall, who was jailed for teaching colored girls. In Massachusetts, he was one of the founders of what Bronson called the Preliminary Anti-Slavery Society and had been threatened by Boston mobs several times. In 1830, the two brothers-in-law, with Abby's cousin Sam Sewall, had met with William Lloyd Garrison following a speech this fiery abolitionist delivered at Julien Hall. The four men believed ardently in the need for *immediate* emancipation; Bronson and the two Sams vowed to help Garrison in his efforts to this end although few in Boston at that time believed in such a drastic step.

Always compassionate towards suffering humanity, even when she herself could be considered a needy case, Abby agreed wholeheartedly with the abolitionists. Every day she heard some new example of vice or prejudice "connected with the sin of slavery," and she was horrified that "the slave mother is not protected in her conjugal or maternal rights."[10] Mincing no words, she was indignant that black women were subject to the lust of white masters and did not even have rights to their own children, who were often taken from them and sold.

Not feeling well and burdened with her fifth pregnancy in four years, Abby was somewhat diverted from preoccupation with herself by this flurry of anti-slavery activity in her small but influential circle. Furthermore, she began to believe that Bronson was at last succeeding as an educator. His young pupils, boys and girls from the ages of five to ten, were the children of some of Boston's leading liberals and wealthy professionals, who remained undaunted by either Bronson's attitude on slavery or his educational theories. Not knowing or not wanting to know the opinion of the general public, Abby felt it was only his due when converts praised Bronson's "unique and transcendent" conversations with students. Miss Peabody kept a record of them as planned, and Abby believed it would no doubt be published "to aid in the further development of Mr. Alcott's methods and principles."[11] Spelling and vocabulary words had become vehicles for student self-analysis through discussions which Bronson often led towards moral conclusions. The word "blind," for instance, evoked the idea of spiritual blindness, and the word "spot" led to the observation that inherent innocence of children could become spotted through disobedience. One of the older students, a ten-year-old girl, wrote about "atom" in her journal. "The word atom was the most interesting word we talked about. Mr. Alcott said that we were all atoms once that could not be seen, but love formed our bodies, and when we die our spirits leave us, and without them we crumble away into the air, and help form other bodies."[12]

Bronson had indeed come into his own. Abby was not alone in extolling his Christ-like attributes, for he did so himself. As his prophecies of success unfolded into reality, he felt a unique wholeness and believed himself to be his students' Saviour. He felt he imbued them with spirituality just as Jesus did his disciples. Like Christ, he taught morality through the use of parables and emblems. This allegorical approach, he told Miss Peabody, stimulated minds which otherwise would be untried. As he saw it, "From neglecting this mode of instruction, we have shorn the young mind of its beams! We have made it prosaic, literal, worldly. We have stripped truth naked, and sent her cold into the world, instead of allowing her to clothe herself with the beautiful associations in which she presents herself in infancy and childhood."[13]  As for discipline, it was not a problem, for not only was Bronson very strict, but by probing his students' inner thoughts he elicited from each the desire to behave appropriately.  Words from their own mouths tended to carry the weight of authority.  The behavior of his own children was another matter.  Abby confided to Lucretia May that although Bronson's quiet but firm disciplinary methods worked "most successfully with others,"[14] he was not entirely effective with his own offspring.

There was parental rivalry at Bedford Street, just as there was sibling rivalry, and it was Bronson's observation that Abby allowed her fondness for the children to interfere with "the delicate and yet necessary work"[15] of remediating their bad habits.  He felt it his duty, as father and husband, to relieve her of the task, peremptorily taking over the supervision of the girls' morning and evening routines.  He allowed them to begin their day by playing in the bath, and he told them bedtime stories, often weaving their own little adventures into fanciful tales.  While these practices were unusual in their day and served to bring some peace to the home, Abby was excluded from participation.  Child rearing can be divisive, and so it was with the Alcotts.  All the complex dynamics of family life were at work including, unfortunately, adult rivalry for the affections of the children.  As parents, the Alcotts were more competitive than cooperative in raising Anna and Louisa.  Bronson, who observed them so closely, complained in his journal that both girls preferred their mother.  This, of course, further strained his relationship with Abby, especially as he could not understand this preference.  After all, it was he who fashioned toys for them and made their daily routines more pleasurable.  To add to the complexities, he was partial to Anna and was annoyed that Abby seemed to prefer Louisa who was, like herself, obstinate and of an uneven temperament.  He called his wife to task for misunderstanding their eldest child, who was overly sensitive to events around her and who, like himself, was introspective.

Bronson's careful observations of his children did not inform him of the selfishness inherent in his less than spontaneous relationships with them.  He often used them more to prove his theories than to supervise their well-being or participate in their pleasures.  Small wonder they preferred their mother when their father turned home into a laboratory.  He set scenes and provoked responses, whether physical, mental, or moral.  When they were infants he recorded their reactions to physical stimuli such as color, light, sound, and pain, experimentally exposing them to one or the other. As they grew into toddlers, he used them to test his theories on innate morality, conversing with them on goodness and then placing before them the tangible temptation of a shiny red apple. When the next child was born, he proceeded to even loftier and more abstract planes, avowing that they and, in fact, all children, brought him to knowledge of the Divine, "from the radiance of their simple spirits."[16] Although some of his work in teaching, whether at home or in the classroom, anticipated what is best in today's give and take between students and teachers, his goals were too lofty. He truly saw himself as a messiah come to redeem the world from sin and selfishness through education of children. His pupils benefited from their unique relationship with this inspired teacher, but his children, his family, often did not. Abby, with good reason, accused him of being too metaphysical. One can not help but agree when reading a typical entry from his journal.

> He who kindles the fire of genius on the altar of the young heart unites his own prayers for humanity with every ascending flame that is emitted from it through succeeding time.... But here come my two children to spend an hour with me in the study, and I resign my thoughts to their spirits whence, if I do my part, shall soon shoot forth branches to heal and bless the people. For genius is the endowment of every spirit, and parents are its supervisors while on its terrestrial mission. May I fulfil [sic] my divine behest.[17]

Bronson, to his credit, was not entirely without self-knowledge. He understood that he dealt excessively in abstractions but felt that his domestic life saved him from total absence of "the sentiment of humanity."[18] So it did, but only on a relative scale. His thoughts tended always to transcend consideration of the mundane. He cared about his family, but Abby was well aware that intellectual stimulation was his obsession. Consuming philosophical interests had excluded wife and daughters in Philadelphia and would do so again. Bronson met Ralph Waldo Emerson at about this time, and the two became fast friends, seeing one another in both Boston and Concord, each admiring the outstanding mental capacities of the other. They were both members of the Transcendental Club, an informal group of the brightest liberal minds in Boston. Their meetings gave Bronson access to stimulating ideas which Abby, to her frustration, could only hear of second hand.

She knew she and the children were "less to him than the great ideas he is seeking to realize"[19] but, for the very reason that he never wavered in the pursuit of his ideals, she admired and defended him even when his intractability brought them near to destitution.

Because they were in debt after equipping the Temple School, the Alcotts had no alternative but to reside in lodgings. Since others must be part of their living arrangements, and since Abby craved congenial company, she persisted in trying to convince Lu to come to Bedford Street with her children. Sam had indeed taken up official duties with the Massachusetts Anti-Slavery Society and planned to board there. Abby, who was not willing to concede that Lu was not going to join him, used the best argument she could muster, that separation from Sam would be a great loss to them both. She knew whereof she spoke, remembering her own separation from Bronson. In one last effort to entice her, Abby pointed out that the landlady's family was obliging and kept much to itself, thereby assuring the boarders' independence. Elizabeth Peabody, she informed Lu, was established there in comfortable, though small, rooms which suited her meagre pocketbook. So far, Abby had nothing but good to say of Miss Peabody. She fit in admirably, was sociable and pleasant, and she read to the children to their mutual pleasure. Abby spoke of her as "truly good... very poor but hopeful and resolute. She is not the first genius that has craved bread and received a stone. Her death would be celebrated in marble and eulogy but her life is almost forgotten and her peculiarities vilified." Elizabeth Peaboody was generally considered peculiar. The enthusiasm which she brought to her various good works was apt to be rather overwhelming, but her unselfishness endeared her to Abby, who valued that trait perhaps more than any other.

Spring, and Abby's confinement, were fast approaching. Her feet had become so swollen that she found it misery to walk, and sitting in the house all day "benumbed"[20] her faculties. She was unfit for getting about and felt her mind was atrophying for lack of stimulation. Inaction left her too much time to dwell on her pregnancy, and what's more they were about to move yet again. In May,[21] the Alcotts and Miss Peabody left Bedford Street for Miss Beach's at Somerset Court, where Abby gave birth to a healthy baby girl, Elizabeth Peabody Alcott, at sunset on June 24, 1835. The name was Bronson's suggestion and unmistakably a tribute to his assistant and recorder, but at the time Abby did not object inasmuch as the woman was her friend if not con-

fidante, and the first name was that of her sister, Eliza. Later, given
what she felt was ample provocation, she angrily crossed the Peabody
from the family Bible and replaced it with Sewall.

During the first year of the Temple School's existence, Bronson
was at the height of his powers as an educator, and he brought his mes-
sianic ardor into the nursery, chronicling not the physical and moral
growth of Elizabeth as he had done with Anna and Louisa, but her
spiritual life, the unfolding of her soul. "I shall endeavor," he wrote on
the day of her birth, "to give some representation to the inner life as it is
enacted in the spirit of childhood."[22]   He called the work *Psyche* and
often referred to his newest daughter by that name. Elizabeth, it turned
out, was very much the prototype of Beth in *Little Women*, meek, willing, and loving, with an inner light even in infancy. As Bronson
watched her at her mother's breast, he believed she manifested "a
oneness with the Divinity."[23]  He was not alone in feeling this although
his expression of it was, as usual, metaphysical. Elizabeth Peabody's
sister, Sophia, found Lizzie to be "an angel of love and peace."[24] From
the beginning, she set an example of goodness recognized even by her
quarrelsome older sisters, and her very existence had a soothing effect
on Alcott family life. Everyone, family and friends alike, loved Lizzie.
She was such a good baby that Abby was able to regain her strength in
relative peace, especially since Bronson had begun taking Anna to
school every day, separating her from Louisa and thus effectively cur-
tailing the girls' squabbling. What is more, Abby did not conceive
again for over a year and a half, giving her a respite from pregnancy
simultaneous with a somewhat improved economic outlook. She began
to yearn for a home of her own. Alas, she was disappointed. Although
they moved within two months of Lizzie's birth, it was to lodgings with
Mrs. Perkins, at 6 Beach Street.

Abby continued to turn a blind eye on reality. Her ups and downs
were partially due to the fact that her desires exceeded her means. She
was ready to put boarding house life behind her, but improved finances
did not mean solvency, so she did what she was accustomed to do. She
applied to friends for help. When they failed to follow through on
negotiations for a house, she accused them of equivocating and of causing her embarrassment. Although abdicating responsibility for her own
affairs, just as she had in Germantown, she felt put upon and angry.
Ignoring any possibility that she might have brought the situation upon

herself, she solicited Elizabeth Peabody's sympathy, telling her, "I am growing selfish and misanthropic. I began life tender, affectionate, free. I shall, I fear, close it hardened, selfish... broken in spirit."[25]

She should have known her next move would not improve her temper. Incredibly, she asked her father for the loan of five hundred dollars that they might rent a house big enough to accommodate not only her own family but four to six boys as boarders. Forgetting another lesson of Germantown, she again proposed to install other people's children in her private dwelling place. Later, in copying Abby's request of her father, Bronson annotated it at the bottom, "He did nothing."[26] Small wonder. The Alcotts' relationship with Joseph May was tenuous, at best. Abby dared not appear at Federal Court for fear of an encounter with his wife, and he, therefore, would not call upon her. Abby likened the situation to the dripping of water which wears imperceptibly but irretrievably. Joseph May visited a month before Lizzie's birth, however, prompting Abby to send him "a few thoughts." He meant well, she acknowledged, "but the one thing needful is lacking, that is mutual confidence." The mere act of visiting for the sake of appearances would never satisfy her. Her life was of too serious a nature to be wasted "in the forms and ceremonies of living."[27] In any case, she could not and would not spend an evening with him until assured of the good wishes of his wife. Matters did not improve. On her birthday in October, Joseph May penned just the kind of platitudinous statement she despised. It was thirty-five years ago that they "began to sojourn together," he said, and he offered "deep gratitude to heaven for our favored lot."[28]

The joint birthday celebration of Louisa and Bronson, for they were both born on November 29, was by contrast a happy and memorable occasion. It was held at the Temple School, at the height of its success. Bronson's pupils lavished fruit and flowers upon him and crowned him with laurel. Louisa wore a wreath of flowers upon her three-year-old head and had the honor of giving out the little celebratory cakes. Unfortunately, there were not enough. If she offered one to the last child, she would have none herself. Recounting the incident years later Louisa wrote, "As I was the queen of the revel, I felt that I ought to have it, and held on to it tightly, 'till my mother said, 'It is always better to give away than to keep the nice things; so I know my

Louy will not let the little friend go without.' The little friend received the dear plummy cake, and I, a kiss, and my first lesson in the sweetness of self-denial."[29]

The account is well known. It was Louisa's tale, of course, an important event in her formative years, but it was her mother's story as well. Abby Alcott practiced the unselfishness she preached and taught her children the virtues and pleasures of sacrifice from their earliest years, setting the example herself, often despite near poverty. This characteristic endeared her to many who would otherwise have found her haughty moral stance wearing. An unremitting seriousness of purpose was as much a hallmark of her personality as was her willfulness, and her sarcastic jabs did little to win friends or to cheer herself. Letters and journal entries for the first dozen years of her marriage give little indication that there was any joy in her life, but despite all, there was. Her family was her pleasure. From the time Anna and Louisa were toddlers, they sang in the evenings and performed little plays, simple fables such as Bronson used in his teaching. Marmee in Louisa's *Little Women* was a distillation of all that was good and generous and gentle in her mother and in their family life, a loving tribute, but only half the story.

Abby Alcott was quick to anger, especially in these years during which she had little or no control over events. The beams of the honey-moon having dimmed, her need now was for a separate, functioning identity. She had not expected to be smothered under the weight of Bronson's presence. He did not overwhelm her by design or desire but simply by being himself. During their courtship he had been concerned about possible negative effects of her willfulness upon their marriage; but she had not imagined that his gentle, philosophical self could threaten her independence. The time had come for her to take charge of her life within a marriage which she had not dreamed would be confining, but circumstances were not auspicious. Elizabeth Peabody was still sharing rooms with them and, worse, sharing the daily rewards of assisting Bronson at the Temple School. Abby felt she should be grateful since Elizabeth was willing to forego a salary, but the anticipated sharing in her husband's grand design was thus diminished. She occasionally played the piano for Sunday hymn singing at the school, and the students acknowledged that she had a fine voice, but her health did not always permit her to enjoy this pleasure, and it was but peripheral participation at best. At home, Bronson had preempted her maternal prerogative by taking over the children's bath and bed routines. True, the move restored temporary calm to the household, but in November of 1835 Anna sprained her ankle badly and could no longer go to school with her father. Abby felt she required constant care, and Louisa, jealous of the attention shown her big sister, was "noisy and boisterous," more demanding than ever. Between them, Abby had "little time for thought." She was "tired of living in other people's houses,"[30] and the dismal winter days were at their shortest. Always affected by the weather, as 1835 froze into 1836, she felt the combined weight of darkness without and doubt within but vowed to arm herself with the hope so much a part of Bronson's makeup. "I *will not* be overcome,"[31] she wrote in her diary. She knew she must cultivate the habit of cheerfulness or both she and the children would suffer.

It was strange that her spirits were so low when the Temple School was thriving, but there was much more than the weather underlying her malaise, and her concerns were real enough. She was a woman beset by the weakening effects of pregnancy and miscarriage, a mother unequal to the task of keeping peace in the household, a daughter alienated from her father, a wife supplanted as helpmeet by her husband's assistant. She sought perfection in her relationships, just as she did in herself, but now, powerless to achieve it, she turned her energies inward against all she could not change and succumbed to fatigue and depression.

It is significant that no letters remain between Abby and her brother for two years, from April 1835 to April 1837, leading to the conclusion that their contents, in the retrospective opinion of Bronson, Louisa, or Alcott heirs, would have been damaging to the family. Other documents attest to the fact that Abby displayed an irrational temper during that period. In the fall of 1835, she lashed out against a woman whose opinion she believed would undermine the Temple School, Harriet Martineau. This English reformer spent several hours at the school and became persuaded that Bronson was manipulating his students' responses as well as giving them an unhealthy sense of self-importance, concerns which Elizabeth Peabody herself was beginning to share. Merely to inform Bronson of her thoughts, wishing neither to criticize nor suggest changes, Elizabeth wrote him a carefully worded note in which she observed that he was liable to injure his pupils' modesty "by making them reflect too much upon their actual superiority to others. For though they may theoretically believe that there is no essential difference between individuals, this is not enough to balance the effect of a constant reference to their actual superiority."[32] She also suggested that his method delved too deeply into the philosophical. Abby's ire was raised. She had, in essence, said the same thing when she referred to Bronson's manner of raising his own children as too metaphysical, but she could allow no one to raise a similar cry against his teaching practices. Elizabeth voiced her thoughts modestly and in private, but Miss Martineau had no restraints against speaking out. The word transcendental was in the air, and she had no patience with it. She was avidly in favor of social reform and felt strongly that nebulous, transcendent idealism played no part in reality. She had no hesitation about saying so, and Abby launched into an irrational attack against this English woman who was "incapable of appreciating a moral subject." She delivered her tirade to Miss Peabody, knowing that her husband's assistant agreed with Miss Martineau, and her words were all the more intemperate for the knowledge. In describing Abby's wrath to her sister, Mary, Elizabeth wrote, "If this is the state in which she intends to go on - I think it will be more comfortable to live on the top of a whirlwind than to live with her."[33]

Bronson was convinced that his emphasis on moral and spiritual development was entirely appropriate in the classroom. Although he could not abide any criticism, much less that of a woman whose censure could adversely affect his school, his response was a haughty silence. A teacher and friend of the Alcotts, Anna Thaxter, spent some time with Miss Martineau at Bronson's request and reported that while the English woman shared Bronson's "undoubting faith in humanity"[34] and had no doubt tried to be objective and impartial, the two differed in practice if not in principle. Abby was not soothed by her friend's attempt to put the matter in perspective, especially since she believed that the book Miss Martineau planned to write once back in England would further damage her husband's reputation. Her explosion towards Miss Peabody testified to the seriousness of her fears for their future and was the beginning of a serious rift. Nonetheless, the two women calmed down to the extent that Elizabeth followed along when, in the early spring of 1836, the Alcotts moved to their next dwelling, a rented house at 26 Front Street. It was "an old-fashioned wooden house with a garden and large yard to it,"[35] but its very size dictated that they take in boarding students, which in turn required the hiring of two servants. Abby was no longer living in someone else's house, but she certainly was not alone with her natural family.

In anticipation of being able to call the kitchen their own, at least, Bronson wrote in his journal, "We shall then be able to modify our dietetic habits more in accordance with physiological laws than we have been able to do heretofore."[36] In accordance with the doctrine of Sylvester Graham, they planned to exclude flesh and live on the simplest and purest of natural foods. At the dinner table soon after they were settled in, the Alcotts and Miss Peabody had a quarrel concerning Graham's opinion of physicians. Bronson peremptorily forbade her to discuss the matter as she was not of the same opinion as he. At suppertime the next evening, when Elizabeth attempted to make conciliatory remarks, Abby jumped in with the statement that the topic was not suitable for their boarding students, unjustifiably silencing a guest in their home. Abby, had she not been inwardly seething about Miss Peabody's ubiquitous presence, might have remembered her Germantown days and her contempt for fellow boarders at Mrs. Eaton's who would hear nothing but their own opinions. She and Bronson were becoming no less despotic than they.

There is no doubt but what emotions ran high at Front Street. In general, Bronson smouldered over criticism while Abby raged. Elizabeth wisely took some time off during the summer of 1836, securing for Bronson the services of her sister, Sophia. Time away from total absorption with the Temple School gave her a fresh perspective, and she began to realize how much her own feelings on the subject were in accord with Miss Martineau's. Bronson was courting disaster with his daily conversations. They now revolved around the life of Christ as found in the Gospels, including, of course, the annunciation and birth. Each session began with a reading from the Bible and was followed by discussion, with Bronson asking leading questions. "What does love make?" The children gave such responses as obedience, happiness, and holiness. Bronson suggested, "Love begets love, and is not a baby love made flesh and shaped to the eyes?" Many of the pupils thought that angels brought babies. Bronson persisted. "What is birth?" He wanted metaphysical answers but was treading on dangerous ground. One boy was attuned enough to suggest that birth was "putting the spirit into a body." Perhaps, mused another, "the goodness from bad people is taken by God to make into little babies." This was not enough for

Bronson who wanted them to "account for the origin of the body." Some of the children thought that it was made out of dust and others that it was made by God to make manifest the spirit. Bronson then gave his opinion. "The spirit makes the body just as the rose throws out the rose leaves. I cannot tell you how the rose leaves come out of the rose. But I think the spirit throws the body out. The body is the outside of the spirit - the spirit made visible."[37] He certainly did not go into the sexual aspects of conception and birth, nor was that his purpose, but parents of his scholars began to get restive, particularly those whose children were little girls.

Bronson was proposing a new volume to be patterned upon his and Elizabeth's successful *Record of a School*, to be called *Conversations with Children on the Gospels*. Elizabeth, armed with objectivity after her vacation, demurred. These new conversations went beyond the bounds of propriety, and she wished to disassociate herself from them. She resigned her position and "in the spirit of friendship"[38] dared to enumerate her objections and to caution him that publication of such a book could endanger his school. Abby could not forgive her either for criticizing Bronson or for abandoning him and angrily crossed baby Elizabeth's middle name out of the family Bible, substituting Sewall for Peabody. As time went on, the Alcotts and Miss Peabody resumed a friendly relationship. In the meantime, Sophia Peabody had become fond of the family while living with them in her sister's stead and wrote her impressions to their mutual friend, Mrs. William Russell. She said she felt at peace in the calming presence of Bronson's "melodious repose and accord," and she revered Abby's energy, trueness, and "quick sympathy with all suffering." Elizabeth she described as "an angel of love," but she had more sympathy with Anna than Louisa, who had a "whole heart" but also a *force* which "makes me retreat sometimes from an encounter."[39]

A second edition of *Record of a School* was meeting with success, but Elizabeth Peabody had alarmed Abby with her caution about publication of *Conversations*. In November, 1836, Abby wrote her brother-in-law, Chatfield Alcott, that the new book would "build up his school or pull it down forthwith." Times were bad, she said, and new ideas were anathema. Merchants and bankers were "tottering and trembling,"[40] and the moral health of the nation was in jeopardy as men grabbed for wealth and earthly possessions. Bronson, she was convinced, would one day be acknowledged a benefactor of mankind for his cultivation of moral truth. Already, he was her "savior" as she groped, "weary and heavy laden,"[41] to find her way. Pregnant again, hard pressed to look after the large household of fourteen, and worried about the future, she found that her duties "far exceeded"[42] her strength and ability.

Abby was right in giving more credence to Miss Peabody's words than did Bronson, who was reviled in the press and mocked by children in the streets upon publication of *Conversations with Children on the Gospels*. Though many defended him, Elizabeth Peabody among them, the volume led directly to the demise of the Temple School and the loss of the rented home on Beach Street. In April, 1837, they settled "sweetly and quietly" into a small house in Cottage Place, in Boston's South End. It was with relief that Abby sent the news to Sam. The worst had come, and they had survived it. She wrote that it was "a perfect luxury to be thus alone and quiet." No students boarded with them, and she no longer had to contend with brazen servants, women she called "humbugs in the form of help." True to her dictum at the time of her marriage, she still preferred a young girl to a matron for household help. Now she had just what she wanted, "a clever little girl to assist me with the children." Claiming that the gridiron no longer held any terrors for her, she assumed all the household work herself though she was neither accustomed to nor skilled at it. With buoyant spirits, at least for the moment, she invited Sam to stay with them when in Boston so that he could sample her meals "a la Graham with Alcott improvements." Mimicking Dr. Graham's prose style, she referred to her cookery as a "combination of nutritive substances."[43]

When public opinion and the subsequent loss of students forced Bronson to leave his spacious quarters at the top of the Masonic Temple, he sold the books, busts, and furniture so lovingly assembled and moved to a room in the temple's basement, where he taught the few pupils who remained. Abby, despite her temporary high spirits, feared that extreme poverty awaited them; but instead of blaming her husband for the disaster, she admired him all the more for sticking to his principles. She knew that, though a quiet sufferer, he was a sufferer none the less. He was stung by the vehemence of the criticism unleashed by the publication of *Conversations* but was equally determined to remain silent on the subject inasmuch as he had "committed no offence nor stepped from the line of my duty."[44] Abby wrote Sam, "I rail - he reasons."[45] In his rationalization he was able to find solace in the hope that he might still be able to dispense "virtue and wisdom"[46] by means of paid formal conversations with adults on "subjects connected with the nature and destiny of man."[47] The final success of his doctrines need not, after all, depend exclusively upon the instruction of children. He was correct in envisioning successful and moderately remunerative conversations with adults, though it would be many years before he devoted himself fully to this occupation.

Despite the efforts of the Alcotts to put the best possible face on the decline of their fortunes, both succumbed to ill health in the summer of 1837. Abby went to visit Sam and Lu at Scituate in June, hoping the country air would refresh her and enable her to endure this sixth pregnancy with equanimity. Bronson's journal entries at the time show but surface sympathy with her efforts to be the wife he wanted. As he saw it, she threw herself into her duties with excessive ardor in order to acquit herself worthily, thereby wearing herself out unnecessarily. Admitting her cares to be many, her health poor, and her days spent "without satisfaction or solace," he nonetheless complained because she was "a learner late in the school of discipline."[48] He regretted that her upbringing had not provided her with the practical qualities necessary for the life she was now leading. He did not feel critical of himself for their current situation, having always been open concerning his uncompromising singleness of purpose. Observing the materialism of the times, unable to further his moral influence upon the young through teaching and unwilling to comply with "vulgar aims and pursuits," he said he was "an Idea without hands.... The age hath no work for me."[49] Better to be poor than to be false to one's self. As for his wife's ill health, had she not pressed for marriage in full knowledge of his idealism? Should she not have been prepared for hard times? Soon after she arrived at Sam's in hopes of restoring her well being, Bronson wrote her a letter which brought little solace. He seems not to have understood the physical and mental toll taken by almost constant pregnancy and fear of miscarriage or worse. The time would come, he said, when her darkness would turn to light, her distrust into faith, and her anxieties into peace. Her destiny was bound with his, and God, in His providence, was fitting her for great duties. All she need do was submit gracefully and wait. Such comfort as his words may have brought was short lived, for instead of regaining her health she suffered her fourth miscarriage. Again, Bronson urged her to have faith, writing that God had a divine charge for her, and in His time she would find her way.

Fortunately, he voiced compassion as well as complacency, beginning
the letter with unaccustomed warmth, addressing her as "My good
wife" and going on to say, "Again have you been called upon to the
mother's trial of suffering, yet without her reward." He told her to
remain with Sam and Lu as long as necessary. He would be fine at
Cottage Place. Anna, at age six, was quite the little housekeeper.
Louisa flitted about with her customary abandon and was "as good an
Abolitionist as the lady whom she calls her mother. And little Psyche
carols her sweet ditties all day long."[50]

Mrs. Anna Alcott, Bronson's mother, came to Boston to help out
upon Abby's return. Abby was genuinely fond of her, and the household benefitted from her caring heart, but Abby was not reconciled to
the trials and vicissitudes of her life. "I would not say a word if I could
feel submission, but oh! this rebellious spirit."[51] She was not pacified
by Bronson's belief that she need only wait for God's grace, and very
soon watched with dismay as his own faith was sorely tried. He
thought he had rationalized away his personal defeats, but his body told
a truer tale. He, too, fell ill. She feared that in giving life to his philosophy he might well cause the death of his body. No sooner had she
returned from Scituate than Bronson repaired to the Mays' for the same
purpose, recovery. Hearing of his friend's plight and grieving over his
"continual illness and weakness,"[52] Ralph Waldo Emerson sent Bronson money with which to pay his current bills and invited him to recuperate at Concord, a kindness readily accepted.

At this time, Abby sent an interesting letter to her niece, Elizabeth
Willis. It was reminiscent of her thoughts as a young woman, exhorting this child of her dead sister to cultivate friendships with pure
minded girls and to influence society for the good by her actions.
Never mind if in doing what was right Elizabeth offended others or ren-
dered herself unpopular. If her actions resulted from a sense of truth
and love of duty, public opinion was of no consequence. Abby was
proof of that. "Many think your aunt is odd," she acknowledged, attrib-
uting it to her need for perfection. Though she would rather not have
Elizabeth thought odd, if that was the price she must pay, so be it.
Better to be an influence for the good than to be pleasing. Abby certainly practiced what she preached. She was also still true to her belief
that women's influence on men was immense, that there would be more
hope for society if only they would use it. She did not stop to analyze
her own situation, however, making no mention of the fact that

although Bronson was already in a state of grace and she therefore had no need to minister to him in that regard, moral rectitude such as his was not conducive to a comfortable family life. Instead, she was at the ready as his defender, ending the letter to her niece by asking whether she had read Miss Martineau's book. The English reformer was deaf, and Abby underscored the fact in her sarcastic comment, "She is unsparing in her crucifixion of Mr. Alcott's school, which she never saw because she could not *hear*."[53]

Now, and for the rest of her life, Abby placed excessive blame for their downfall on Miss Martineau and her book. Years later she still insisted that the woman had taken the bread from their mouths. There was no question but what the Alcotts did need help following the failure of the Temple School. In thanking Sam and Lu for a gift of apples and potatoes she told them, "We are as poor as rats." Dr. William Alcott helped out in the fall by renting half the little house at Cottage Place while he attended meetings in Boston. His wife came as well, and Lydia Maria Child visited often, enlivening Abby's solitude "by her brilliant and joyous mood." The Childs were not much better off than the Alcotts, and Abby shared with her the produce sent by the Mays. This time became a brief respite, an interlude of some pleasure, not because life was easier but because she had sympathetic companions in the house. The women talked endlessly about those of their sex who might one day hold positions of power. "A great revolution is coming," Abby wrote Lu. "Women are to be preeminent in settling all these great moral questions now in agitation."[54] She did not modify the guidelines she set for herself as a young woman, however, and continued to play a modest role, believing she could best serve the cause of reform by seeing to it that her own family set an example of selflessness.

Life settled into a routine for a few months. Abby was as well as could be expected inasmuch as she was again pregnant, at age thirty-seven, having barely recovered from the miscarriage suffered at Sam's. The Alcotts rose at 5 a.m., and Bronson readied the children for the day while Abby prepared the morning meal. It was something of an effort. Although the potatoes could be peeled the night before, this meal was the equivalent of dinner and the leftovers were, in fact, the basis of lunch and supper. They used butter, cheese, and honey sparingly; ate but little flesh or fish; and drank neither coffee nor tea. Their Grahamite diet consisted largely of rice, potatoes, bread, pies, fruits, and vegetables. Unbolted, or unsifted, flour was used exclusively. Anna and Louisa helped their mother clean up and at 8:30 went off to the Temple basement school with their father. The mid-day meal was at 1:00, "remnants of the dishes of the morning."[55] They stayed at table until 2:30, conversing upon the topics of the day under Bronson's direction, and then each member of the family was occupied with work, reading, or leisure as appropriate. Supper was at 5:30, and Bronson put the children to bed immediately afterwards. Abby tidied up and joined her husband in the parlor on the nights when he remained at home, but his public conversations frequently took him from the house, and he often attended lectures. Once in a while Abby's evenings were enlivened by visitors, but by and large she passed a quiet hour or two in reading or sewing and then went gratefully to bed.

Abolition remained a strong focus in her life, and though she joined the Boston Anti-Slavery Society, household cares prevented her from attending many meetings. News was most apt to reach her through Bronson and Sam, but also through newspapers and periodicals and from visitors such as Mr. Garrison and Lydia Maria Child. Despite increasing ill health, Abby's zeal for the emancipation of slaves never abated or faded into the background. She did not understand how churches could send missionaries all over the world and at the same time condone the actions of all who denied literacy to slaves. "Why?" she asked. "Because it is thought best to keep them as near the condition of brutes as possible, and because no one can read the Scriptures intelligently and not soon discover that God has made us all of one blood and in his own image."[56] Two South Carolina women she met in Philadelphia, Sarah and Angelina Grimke, had freed their slaves and were now in Boston, major voices in the movement. Their writings commanded national attention, and so compelling was Angelina's presence that she was soon dubbed "Devilina." Abby's condemnation of hypocritical clergymen was fully justified when many of those in Boston denounced Angelina for the offense of espousing immediate emancipation and worse, of being a woman abolitionist who crusaded for her cause on the public lecture platform.

In February, 1838, Angelina delivered an impassioned speech at the Odeon Theater, an anti-slavery event notable for being held in such a large hall as well as for raising the issue of women's rights. In the same month Abby was delivered prematurely, again without a mother's reward. The route to the salvation of society through family rather than through social activism was, it seemed, the more hazardous course. Childbirth nearly took her life once again. So near to death was she that Dr. Windship[57] slept at Cottage Place for a fortnight. It was seven weeks before she made perceptible improvement; and when she was finally able to write Sam, her words attested to the fact that a greatly diminished will to live had slowed her recovery. "I am getting hardened, toughened, indifferent. I care less for this world than ever and when for 24 hours I was balancing into another, I felt a serene satisfaction which I may never know again and which I could not account for." In retrospect, she found this feeling of serenity incomprehensible because it was coupled with a simultaneous and poignant sense of loss at the thought of "leaving my excellent husband and my darling children." In her delirium, she constantly voiced fears for her girls' future, much moving Lydia Maria Child, who spent hours at her bedside.

In a monumental effort of will, Abby overcame the lethargy which caused her to hope "the strife of mortal things will cease ere long, for I am tired and weary, and would gladly lay me down."[58] In April, she resumed her household duties and showed unusual resolution in assuming the care of her children. She took over with an authority which brooked no interference from her husband. In his journal he showed an unusual bitterness, indicating a serious problem in their relationship. Though he aimed his barb at *those whose duty it is*, he was clearly writing of his wife.

> Even in my own home and at my own fireside is my vision marred by unsightly manners which I cannot soften and passions which I cannot exercise without reproach from those whose duty it is to co-operate with me in the sacred ministries of parental discipline. I am denied the means of realizing my ideal in the souls of my own, or the children of others.[59]

In the delirium and in the reality of her illness, Abby's visions of her children destitute gave her strength to assert herself on their behalf. Though "scantily supplied with food"[60] and sustained only through the generosity of friends, she refused to give in. Bronson was considering an itinerant ministry on behalf of his gospel, which would require her to live without him for the most part. Despite their differences, this prospect was not to her liking, so she tried to convince him to seek further in Boston for a position which would not compromise his ideals. Besides, with uncharacteristic warmth towards her fellow beings, she wanted to remain near those who had been so kind to her. She and the girls would have been welcome at Mother Alcott's in Wolcott, but she did not want to leave her friends. Elizabeth Peabody, hearing of their plight and forgiving past offenses, suggested that Abby and the children come to live with her in Newton, Massachusetts. They vacillated long enough to do what they had wanted to do in any case, spend the summer in Scituate, boarding with a farmer who lived near the Mays. Abby's health remained indifferent but Bronson was well and busy, giving conversations in Boston and surrounding towns on topics such as free will, conscience, and faith. The first of the children's extant diaries, Anna's, appears at this time and attests to the fact that she and her sisters thrived on country life.

The Alcotts were five thousand dollars in debt, living on the barest of means, still greatly dependent upon others. In the fall they returned not to Cottage Place but once again to 6 Beach Street, their final residence in Boston during this decade. Bronson placed an ad for day scholars and taught a few students in his home, but, increasingly, conversations became an important source of income, his new mode of teaching. Though he sometimes had audiences of up to fifty people, there was little money to show for it, and Abby became convinced that only on the other side of the Atlantic would he find the sympathy lacking at home. An English educator, James Greaves, wanted copies of both *Record of a School* and *Conversations*, and showed great interest in Bronson's teaching methods. It was through Abby's enemy, Harriet Martineau, that Bronson's work became known to Mr. Greaves, but Abby neither noticed the irony nor softened her views. She was in no condition to forgive; her courage all but failed her. She had conceived again, not half a year after the premature birth which had brought her so near to death.

By Christmas she was so wasted that Bronson had to hire a young girl to help out. Death seemed ever present, but there was one loss which wore the garb of hope. Mary Ann May died in January of 1839. In this death Abby saw a final opportunity for reconciliation with her father. The relationship had become worse than ever, largely because of the intractability of the two women. Abby had barely recovered from the loss of her baby the previous winter when Mrs. May sent her a packet containing unsettling notes for herself and Bronson, seeking reconciliation. Abby had heretofore adopted the strategy of silence as the safest course, believing that anything she had to say would be misconstrued and widen the breach. As she surely would have been all too blunt, silence was indeed wise. However, lest not responding should "give tacit assent to a misunderstanding" or be misconstrued as indifference, she broke her resolution and replied. It was a mistake. As usual, she was too outspoken. Her step-mother and father wished them to pay a visit? Fine, but Mother May must realize that it would be at great inconvenience because they had no one to look after the children in their absence. The Mays wanted reconciliation? Good. Abby did too, but she could not refrain from imputing all blame to Mrs. May, writing her that she was exposing her girls to gratuitous hatred. The note to Bronson apparently contained explicit complaints about his character and behavior. He would have left the matter to time and "mutual forbearance,"[61] but Abby followed a now familiar pattern and hastened to his defense. In the certain knowledge that her father would share her comments with his wife, she wrote him that she could not dwell long on the subject because of "delicate health" and "precarious state of mind." However, he should know that she had written Mother as respectfully as she could, "though I could speak volumes on the spirit and character of her note to my husband, both of which were neither respectful to me as a wife or judicious to him as a husband." She wouldn't belabor the point lest "the progress of our reunion be impeded."[62] He replied immediately that they would call upon the Alcotts in a few days' time. It made no difference that the Mays accepted the conditions and considerately went to the Alcotts. The attempt was to no avail.

The winter of Mrs. May's death was altogether a low point in Abby's life. Though this next to last pregnancy left her physically and mentally depleted, extreme poverty and her domestic relationship with her husband were of themselves cause enough for depression. Though she would not countenance criticism of Bronson by others, she was beginning to speak up to him on her own behalf. As was his custom, he read aloud to her from his journal one evening in February, 1839. The portions pertaining to her, she complained, were pure caricature, and she threatened to scissor the passages. Though he replied that he meant no injustice and was simply recording her as "one of the facts to be noted in the history of my domestic life,"[63] she would not be placated. She was not a mere fact. She was a human being with interpersonal needs which, she was finally realizing, his perpetual objectivity could not satisfy. It was a reality she had to come to terms with, rationally, emotionally, and on the practical plane of redefining herself in the context of such a marriage. At the moment, all her available energy was devoted to self-preservation on the most basic of levels, but she was beginning to acknowledge the truth of her situation and would eventually evolve strategies to preserve her integrity, minimize mutual bitterness, and promote some happiness. Many pages have been cut from this portion of Bronson's journal. Whether it was done by Abby or another, their deteriorating personal relationship was deemed unfit for the eyes of posterity.

Mary Ann May's illness and death were the cause of further destruction of Alcott documents. During her final days, Mother May destroyed most of Abby's letters so as not to leave evidence of the hostility between them. Though her action could have been construed as self serving, Abby chose to see it in a favorable light and did likewise, following her "wise example." She had not been informed of Mrs. May's final illness and professed regret at not having been able to speak kind words to Mother on her death bed, an act which she felt would have lessened their mutual animosity and eased the future of her relationship with her father. Though she was no longer privy to "the wishes of his heart," she truly wanted his friendship and believed their reunion would bring him "sweet satisfaction"[64] equal to hers. Their reconciliation was hastened by another loss, this one beyond Abby's comprehension. In early April, she gave birth to a stillborn son, "full grown, perfectly formed, but not living. Mysterious little being.... Oh, for one vital spark of that heavenly flame to rekindle, reanimate its cold and quiet clay!!!"[65] She could not understand God's will in pressing upon her this heavy sorrow after nine months of patient anticipation and many hours of difficult labor. Joseph May accompanied Bronson to the May family tomb when he went to "deposit the body of our dead baby - a beautiful boy."[66] A tenuous reconciliation was the only light in this time of deepening shadows.

Bronson, when collecting his papers years later, penned an enigmatic notation on an early letter to his mother. Rereading it brought back vivid memories of the joyous anticipation with which he had expected the birth of a son, and on it he noted, "But my thrill of hope proved a pang of grief - a true son of its mother - a joy in a winding sheet."[67] Whether he was referring to his wife's many miscarriages and

premature births or alluding to failed hopes for the success of his marriage, the comment, *joy in a winding sheet*, speaks to a deep and enduring loss.

Abby had no strength to spare to set matters aright between them.
Her primary need was the recovery of her health. Again she considered
going to Mother Alcott's; again she went to Scituate. Joseph May volunteered to pay their expenses, an unexpected kindness gladly
accepted, and Abby continued her recuperation with temporary peace
of mind. She loved the country; she enjoyed the ease with which she
could visit Lu and Sam; she was delighted when Mrs. Morrison came
from Philadelphia to visit, bringing her little girl. One day the children
picked whortleberries for supper and, after the meal, gathered wild-
flowers for their mothers. Abby was proud of Anna who was becoming
a little homemaker and liked to put her mother's chamber "in fine
order."[68] Anna and sister Lizzie loved order, Anna wrote in her diary,
implying by omission that Louisa did not. Bronson gave lessons to his
children throughout the summer, a treat Anna looked forward to. She
enjoyed the multiple meanings of words and never minded when conversations with her father led to discussions of her faults, being eager to
have them pointed out to her that she might correct them. She attended
Miss Briggs' school while in Scituate and reported that she knew the
definitions of words whereas the other students merely spelt them without understanding, a true testimony to her father's methods.

To Abby's gratification, Joseph May was attentive in sending
occasional gifts of fruit as well as paying their expenses. As autumn
neared, however, concern for their livelihood again became uppermost
in her mind. She had once haughtily demanded of her father, "Would
you have me take in washing?" With new humility she began to take in
sewing, a more genteel but nonetheless servile means of supplementing
the meagre returns from Bronson's conversations. He no longer had
paying students in his home because he bravely refused to dismiss a
little black girl, Susan Robinson, and parents of his other pupils therefore withdrew their children, leaving him with only William Russell's
children and his own girls to teach. The Russells lived with them at
Beach Street and shared the rent, giving Abby at least some assurance
of shelter. A place of her own was no longer thinkable. Unchar-
acteristically embittered, Bronson wrote in his journal, "O stupid and
ungracious generation! Patience, my heart, thy hour of action shall
come."[69] Ever the hoper despite his setbacks, he was sustained in part

by the letters which continued to make their way slowly back and forth across the Atlantic and in part by Emerson, who offered encouragement as well as financial help.

The previous year Abby had written, "It never was so dark with us."[70] Now, in the fall of 1839, it was even darker as they prepared to return to Boston. She had conceived for the last time during the waning days of their summer idyll. The future was uncertain, and she did not know by what means her family would be clothed and fed. Bronson's belief, "God shall provide a way in his own due time,"[71] was inadequate to say the least; but she loved him. She lauded his ideals and his adherence to them and did not think the less of him for being tenacious in pursuing the life his intellectual needs demanded. Unfortunately, there was an aspect to that life which was undermining their marriage. Whereas she needed companionship, he required solitude. In seeking it to excess in Philadelphia, he all but abandoned her by remaining in the city when she returned to Germantown. Now, financial constraints dictated that he remain at Beach Street, but he withdrew into himself as best he could, getting away from the crowded household by taking long walks and reading at the Athenaeum. Unable to communicate his feelings, he unintentionally denied Abby the emotional support she badly needed. Nine years after their marriage, in matters of deep personal importance, he was no more able to express himself through the spoken word than he had been during their courtship, when he assured her of his affection by giving her his journal to read. Following the same pattern, he tried to show understanding during her pregnancies, composing poems expressly for that purpose. Writing "To My Wife" in 1839, he wished to reassure her that all would be well between them despite "The noiseless solitude in which I'm rapt." Though his companions were so frequently ancient philosophers such as Plato, he wrote, "Still are the friend, the wife, the child and home / The cherished objects of my busy thought."[72]

Abby needed the reassurance of these lines more than ever when Bronson's philosophical idealism committed him to a communal way of life which threatened the very existence of her natural family. Early in the next decade she copied "To My Wife" into her diary as a reminder that she and the children *were* important to him. Meanwhile, in mud season during the spring of 1840, pregnant with Abby May but not dispirited, she prepared to move to the town of Concord with Bronson, Anna, Louisa, and Elizabeth under the patronage of Ralph Waldo

Emerson.    Rising to the occasion in a spirit of hope not unlike Bronson's but mingled with typical irony, she packed up her goods, as she put it, in preparation "for another experiment in the great art of living."[73]

# Chapter Four

---

## Con-sociate Family

> *'Are there any beasts of burden on the place?'  Mrs. Lamb answered, with a face that told its own tale, 'Only one woman!'*
>
> *Transcendental Wild Oats*
> by Louisa May Alcott

Abby was hopeful that country life would restore her health and vigor as well as Bronson's, after so many sorrow-filled years in the city.  She wanted to bear her new baby without mishap and bring it up as she had wanted to bring up all her children, in a place of her own.  Bronson had other ideas.  Utopian communities, he was beginning to realize, held promise as models for the perfection of society.  His new plan for the great art of living was the antithesis of Abby's ideal and self-contained nuclear family.  A year's respite was all the grace period she had before uncertainty and conflict arose anew.

In March, 1840, though feeling "enfeebled," Abby began preparations for the move to Concord, hoping that the coming of spring would promote "a more vigorous state of mind."[1]  For fifty dollars a year the Alcotts were to have the use of a small cottage and large garden.  They sold the remaining schoolroom furniture and some household articles in order to pay for their transportation to Concord as well as for the purchase of the spade, hoe, and rake which signalled Bronson's return to his agrarian roots. On the fifth of April, settled comfortably into their new home, Dove Cottage, she wrote her father, "A spirit must, indeed, be weak and weary that cannot be renovated by influences such as these."[2] An early spring snowstorm had left the air bright and crisp. Fantastic, ice-coated trees sparkled in the sun. Anna, Louisa, and Lizzy were in raptures over the fairy-like scene, and Abby experienced a lifting of the spirits which even pregnancy could not quell. She took heart as Bronson immersed himself in various projects, satisfying "his love of neatness and beauty"[3] by fixing the doorstep, laying a drain, building a trellis in the little flower garden which she and the children proposed to make gay with bloom. Before the month was out he had dug, raked, and planted his acre of arable land - the philosopher-farmer returned to his plough but in the congenial society of men such as Emerson and Thoreau, who shared "liberality of sentiment on all subjects he is interested in."[4]

Abby wrote her friend, Hannah Robie, a spinster relative who lived in Boston, that she loved to hear the philosophers "talk mystical things." She was not intimidated by their intellectual prowess, however, as evidenced by her well phrased comment about an endeavor which was currently engaging their literary and editorial efforts, establishment of an intellectual, transcendentalist quarterly. Said Abby, "Mr. Ripley and Miss Fuller are about starting a new periodical entitled *The Dial*, by which I suppose we of the sublunary world are to be informed of the time of day in the Transcendental regions." Further elaborating her celestial metaphor, she told Miss Robie that whereas the transcendentalists could be sustained "only by bread from heaven,"[5] she was content with food from the earth. Abby spoke her mind to this confidante, with whom she felt a kinship beyond the loose familial tie inherent in Hannah's sister's marriage to a Sewall. Miss Robie, for her part, cared deeply about Abby. As a woman, she understood, even more fully than Sam May, the complexities of Abby's relationship with Bronson. Though Joseph May might criticize Abby, Bronson, or both, Hannah Robie knew that, no matter how just the criticism, Abby's love for her husband was secured by admiration of the very characteristic which was making them dependent on friends and relatives, his refusal to compromise his ideals. Abby wasn't naive. She readily acknowledged that his principles were the cause of their poverty, but she continued to give him her support and understanding.

No one will employ him in his way; he cannot work in theirs, if he thereby involve his conscience. He is so resolved in this matter that I believe he will starve and freeze before he will sacrifice principle to comfort. In this, I and my children are necessarily implicated; we make and mean to make all the sacrifices we can to sustain him, but we have less to sustain us in the spirit, and therefore, are more liable to be overcome by the flesh. He has, for a long time gone without everything which he could not produce by labor, from his own place, that no one could in truth reproach him with wantonly eating of the fruits of another's labor.[6]

Bronson gave occasional conversations, for which he earned small sums, "slight compensation for the benefit they [his audience] felt he had conferred upon them."[7] Abby wrote Sam, who had dared to offer some harsh truths about her husband, that she would refrain from forwarding a note which Bronson received along with twenty-three dollars earned for a conversation he gave in Hingham.

I should like to copy the note accompanying it, but you never care to see how his fellow fanatics rave on these holy themes, life, duty, destiny of man. Thus he occasionally finds a market for his thoughts and experiences, which, though inadequate to our support, is richly prized as the honest gains of an innocent and righteous labor. You spoke of his 'poetical wardrobe' whether in satire or in a worthier spirit, I cannot tell. However spiritual he may have become, there is still enough of the carnal to feel the chills of winter, and the chiller blasts of satire. His tatters are the rags of righteousness and keep him warmer than they would anyone whose spirit was less cheered and warmed by the fires of eternal love and truth.[8]

Bronson had no aversion to manual labor despite years of commitment to matters of the mind. By working ten and eleven hours a day, he was prepared to chop wood for fuel and grow food for the table. For the moment, Abby continued to defend him, proud to be the wife of a man who clung so tenaciously to his solitary path. No matter that he was called fool and visionary, she boasted that he would "never sell his principles for bread, nor his soul for that which perishes."[9] If he and his family must suffer the consequences, so be it. When there was enough food on the table, even she tended to sound like a transcendentalist, professing to believe that only the intuitive and the spiritual were real. Shortly after their move to Concord, she wrote her father, "Life is within us, all without is temporary and passing away. The real is in no wise subordinate to the will and ways of men. The only source of happiness is to bring the spirit in harmony with its lot."[10] Consistent with this philosophy was her continuing belief that little could be done towards the reformation of society until love and self-denial were well established in the natural family. Once this was accomplished, a communal family was the logical progression. This was the new focus of Bronson's hopes, but not of hers.

Abby balked at the notion of a con-sociate family. She had had her fill of living with others and wanted no influence but her own brought to bear upon her children. Alarmed, she exchanged books and articles with Miss Robie, driven to discover all she could about the matter. Albert Brisbane's proposals for Associationism in his 1840 volume, *Social Destiny of Man*, did not appeal. "I should not often want a dinner from the great Golgotha of the public kitchen,"[11] declared Abby. And although twenty cradles might be all very well when twenty babies were sleeping, one per household was preferable. The last Alcott baby, Abigail May, called Abba, was snug in her cradle at Dove Cottage, having been born on July 26, 1840. Bronson did not begin an infant diary as he had done for Anna, Louisa, and Elizabeth. This child, much loved by all, was more pampered, less rigidly observed than the others had been. It was Abby, not Bronson, who commented that her existence strengthened the moral qualities of the family. The older girls' awareness of baby's helplessness, she was certain, would make them less selfish, more alert to the needs of others. At age nine, Anna was capable of assuming some of the care of little Abba. Indeed, she loved doing so and tried all the harder to be kind and gentle; for if she were not, she would be forbidden to tend baby, and any other punishment would be preferable to that.

Relatives rallied round during Abby's confinement, for the families of the May sisters remained close even though Catharine, Eliza, and Louisa were in their graves. Louisa Windship, the daughter of Abby's brother-in-law by his second wife, went to Dove Cottage to help out for a week, followed by Abby's niece, Elizabeth Willis, who lent a hand for several additional days. Though not strong of body, Abby maintained her strength of spirit for yet a few weeks. Bronson's garden was doing well, and she eagerly awaited the ripening of their melons so that she could invite Miss Robie to come and share a dinner of fruit and bread. Abby wrote her, not without humor, that she was vigilant in sending her father specimens of "transcendental farming," and she noted that Bronson took pride and pleasure "in carrying little offerings from his garden of Eden to confound the false prophets in the neighborhood."[12] As Abby was well aware, not all Concordians were transcendentalists, or even Grahamites. Indeed, she herself gave up milk, butter, and cheese as much for the sake of economy as for philosophical conviction. The staples of their diet were water, bread, potatoes, apples, squash, and oatmeal puddings, with fruits, vegetables, and nuts in season. Miss Robie was a liberal and an abolitionist, but she was no Grahamite. A visit to Dove Cottage did not pose a problem, however, for with Abby's concurrence she brought along her own tea and a bit of cooked meat. The tea was prepared over Bronson's objections, but otherwise Miss Robie chose to live as they did, finding the simplicity of their lives more agreeable "than the usual way of the world."[13] She had not the heart to take out her beef, but for the sake of the children she eventually convinced the Alcotts to resume drinking milk.

Abby had to take up her household duties less than two weeks after her confinement; and although Anna was taken from Mr. Thoreau's school to be near at hand, she began to experience "an exquisite sense of weariness." She felt that life's toils were ruining her peace of soul and health of body. "I cannot get rest. I feel like a noble horse harnessed in a yoke and made to drag and pull instead of trot and canter." Fortunately for her mental health, she began to speak her mind to Bronson and to confide in both Sam and Miss Robie, for "the world of want" was before them. She was not at all certain they would succeed in living on the produce of their own land. In the past she had "furnished a good many pairs of shoes and paid many little debts" with her needle; but she now had neither time nor strength for sewing. With uncertainty always before her, she could not be the placid creature her husband would prefer, nor could she sustain her own brief truce with transcendentalism. Instead, "re-established in [her] household traces, dragging and pulling for dear life,"[14] she put her plight to her brother. Could he find Bronson some lucrative employment which would not compromise his principles? Sam responded in the negative. There was no such work. If only Bronson would keep the kind of school people wished, he could be a teacher, but visionaries were not wanted. In a letter to Hannah Robie, Abby acknowledged as much. Bronson would willingly take a district school, she said, but none was to be had, so much mystery and controversy surrounded his opinions.

Abby claimed that the adverse circumstances of her life were narrowing her outlook, fostering what she called "don't care-ism," an indifference to subjects which previously filled her with passion. In an unusual mood of resignation, she began to bemoan her fate rather than rise to its challenge. She contented herself with doing only as much as health permitted, trying to put out of mind what was left undone; but the more chores she neglected the more dispirited she became. Facts were all that interested her, she said. Baby, stove, broomstick, and needle were her realities; those and lack of money. Joseph May and nephew Hamilton Willis promised to see them through the coming winter, and though it galled, she had no choice but to accept their help. But for Abba May's infant innocence, she feared she would have forgotten that there could be laughter and poetry in life. The older girls were as dear to her as ever, and she stretched her strength to the utmost "that life shall bring no doubtful times to their young hearts just yet."[15] Concerned that their care might be taken out of her hands if Bronson were moved to act upon his growing interest in con-sociate living, she wrote urgently to Sam, asking his opinion of such schemes in general, and to Miss Robie, seeking information about Brook Farm in particular. Located in West Roxbury, Massachusetts, and founded by *The Dial*'s George Ripley, this community was, for a while, very attractive to Bronson. Abby conceded that life in a communal society would put her mind at ease regarding food and shelter, but what would become of her family? At best, the interests of the natural family would be subverted to the needs of the whole. At worst, she feared family members might actually be separated, an unthinkable possibility. In trying to sort it all out, she acknowledged that her children were everything to her, "the threads wrought in the texture of my life, the vesture with which I am covered."[16]

Along with her desire to keep her family intact was a second and equally compelling reason to remain at Dove Cottage, her need for independence. Sharing chores and thus lightening her housework was not sufficient reason to live either communally or with another family. She preferred controlling her "own little sphere" to moving "in the orbit of another."[17] Even when the Emersons offered to let them share their home, rent free, Abby refused. So weary was she that she wanted to turn her back to the world and try to "annihilate"[18] anything unrelated to her natural family and her little cottage. She expressed her feelings to Sam in a familiar beast-of-burden analogy. "I cannot gee and haw in another person's yoke." Fatigue, she claimed, was so befuddling her that if asked the way to Boston she would reply that it was in the oven. If asked whether she had read the most recent *Liberator*, she would say it wanted darning. When she expressed her anxiety to Bronson, he calmly replied that all would be well; the ravens would feed the prophets. She retorted that they must have forgotten the way, it had been so long since last they came.

Bronson was willing to barter labor for goods and to accept cash for his words, spoken and written. For *The Dial* he was composing epigrams, "Orphic Sayings," each of which compressed an idea into a few pithy sentences. Unfortunately, most were too obscure, and eventually even his fellow transcendentalists at *The Dial* refused to publish them. They certainly did not put much bread on the table. Anna and Louisa sewed and mended with their mother to bring in a little money. Mrs. Savage and Mrs. Shaw, Temple School patrons who continued to have the Alcotts' interests at heart, saw to it that they did not want for work with the needle. Often, one or another read aloud while the others sewed. The family favorite was *Pilgrim's Progress*, but Krummacher's fables remained popular, and Maria Edgeworth's novels were much cherished for her moral family themes and love of nature. At Christmas, Hamilton Willis made the girls the gift of a Mother Goose, an alphabet of natural history, and a history of the scriptures. The children's own writing was fostered through journal keeping, and into these diaries they frequently copied birthday and holiday messages from their parents. Abby's notes took a strong moral tone. When Louisa sent her one expressing love, her mother wrote of a kiss upon the lips in return, and prayed that Louisa never speak with hers but "in kind words and sweet sounds for us all."[19] To Anna on Christmas Eve, 1840, Abby wrote much as Joseph May had written to her young self, "Love your duty and you will be happy."[20]

There still remained more duty than love in Abby's attitude towards her father, but since the death of her step-mother, their relationship had been cordial if not warm, and the Alcott girls frequently dined with him while they were still living in Boston. Anna wrote of enjoying his "queer stories"[21] from olden days. Louisa, during her mother's confinement with Abba May, lived with him for a full six weeks. In truth, Abby used him more than she loved him. He was a source of sustenance and child care rather than an object of affection. When he died at the end of February, 1841, she wrote in her diary that his life had been one of frugality and decorum, that he was "loved by many, regretted by many, understood by few." In his public life, she said, he had lived a life of philanthropy; in his private, a life of meanness, at least with regard to her. She still held the irrational belief that since she was in need, her father owed it to her to help and should have left her more than a seventh share in his estate. She voiced no praise for the scrupulous impartiality with which he bequeathed $15,000 in equal sums to herself and her brothers, Sam and Charles; to the three guardians of his dead daughters' children; and to an adopted daughter, Louisa Greenwood. Her portion was wisely secured to her sole use, specifically excluding Bronson. Mutual dissatisfaction had certainly embittered her relationship with her father since her marriage, but she thought he had, for the last two years, evidenced "something like confidence and affection." Perhaps, she surmised, he had not softened his severe judgment of her after all; perhaps her husband and children had not truly become objects of his care and regard. Though she was convinced he did not love her, she claimed to hold his memory no less dear. Having so said, she did some honest introspection and admitted that, in fact, she might be found wanting "if weighed in the balance of filial duty."[22] If so, she would make up for it by being an exemplary wife and mother.

Though her concept of marriage had never included the notion that a woman must be subservient to her husband, the reality had nonetheless been that her life revolved around Bronson's needs and her pregnancies. She now began to separate herself, loving him not less but with more objectivity. She said as much to Sam. "We have in no wise been aliens in affection, but our diversity of opinion has at times led us far and wide of a quiet and contented frame of mind.... I have been looking for competence and rest, he for principle and salvation. I have been striving for justice and peace, he for truth and righteousness."[23] Since "wisdom must be fed and clothed, and neither the butcher or tailor will take pay in aphorisms or hypotheses,"[24] Abby realized that she must be the one to carry the financial burden. Heretofore, that usually meant she was put in the uncomfortable position of asking for help, though she lamented this dependence on others as "the worm gnawing at the vitals of my tranquility."[25] So deep were her feelings on the subject that she vowed her girls, as adults, would have trades. Though sewing was all she could do at the moment, she began to consider what she might be able to undertake when her babe was more out of her arms. Almost anything would do, just so it made her independent of the charity of relatives and friends.

Abby carried the responsibility of her children's care, without Bronson, for much of the summer and autumn of 1841. Having decided Brook Farm was too worldly, he was a frequent visitor at the communal society of Holly Home in Providence, Rhode Island. Abby made a journey there as well and said she found greatness in the simple goodness of the men, reassurance in the sweet kindness of the women. Some of the Providence people visited Dove Cottage in return, and the Alcotts were particularly taken with a young educator by the name of Christopher Green. Her good will towards these strangers was in direct contrast to Abby's opinion of her Concord neighbors, Emersons and Thoreaus excepted. Most Concordians, she complained, had neither aptitude nor desire for enlightening conversation. All they could talk about was the latest new frock or Irish maid, "anything that is temporary and unimportant to the salvation of the body or soul."[26] This view of her neighbors, in combination with her straightened means, inclined her to take a chance on communal life, especially when the Providence community offered a few acres and a cottage to themselves. The family would not be separated and, Abby concluded, it would be more agreeable to reside "with those who are free to live and die for their principles than be compelled to conform to the world, all of whose ways are so false."[27]

The dutiful wife rationalized her acceptance of communal life only to find that Bronson once again held hopes of resuming his role as educator, this time at a school in England patterned on his philosophy and named Alcott House in his honor. Harriet Martineau, still his nemesis in Abby's eyes, brought back to her native country a copy of *Record of a School*, despite her differences with Bronson's theories. In England, it was read by James Greaves, who invited Bronson to his school, Alcott House, in Surrey. The purpose of this visit to the so-called English mystics was unclear to Abby. Was Bronson to be offered a position? Was he to share his insights regarding the process of education as the ideal means for the reformation of society? What *was* the most effective means of reform - education or a model community based on cooperative living? Bronson's discussions with transcendentalist friends at home, it appeared to Abby, had little to do with practical matters pertaining to important and immediate needs. She soon had her fill of the mystical conversation she once admired; and worse, she resented Bronson's apparent lack of commitment to his family. In her diary she made a statement couched in general terms but reflecting increasing personal dissatisfaction with her marital relationship.

> Why are men icebergs when beloved by ardent natures and surrounded by love-giving and life-devoted beings. Why so much talk, talk; so little give! give! Women are certainly more generous than men. They endure, they give, they love, they live. Man receives, enjoys, argues, forsakes. Man reasons about right. Woman feels right. Love is with her instinctive, eternal.[28]

Bronson did express his love for her in a birthday note on October 8, 1841. The Alcotts observed birthdays with warmth, enthusiasm, and simple tokens. Spiritually significant cut-out pictures, which they called emblems, were a favorite gift. Along with Bronson's emblem to her, a draped female figure carrying a cross, he wrote, "Accept it as a token of your husband's love, his satisfaction in you, and hope in the changes that await us." He acknowledged that their pathways had been diverse but assured her that they would soon be one and the same, that they would walk together, hand in hand. Heretofore, they had been aware of the means rather than the end, "losing the view of the summit in the windings that led to it."[29]

By December, neither Abby nor Bronson could dwell very long upon summits. When Miss Robie arrived for a visit, she found Bronson unwell and the entire family poorly clothed. Abby's toes were out of her shoes, and although Miss Robie brought several pairs with her, an offering from Mrs. Savage, there were none that fit. There were frocks for all, however, and yards of flannel from which to sew garments for baby. The ravens had found their way to Concord at last, as Bronson pointed out. Never one to hold her tongue for politeness' sake, Miss Robie demanded of Bronson what he was doing towards their well-being. When he replied that he chopped wood for his neighbors and received in payment a portion for himself, she commended him and commented, "it was the only way to show people he was willing to work to do what he could."[30] Abby owned some family silver, her mother's tea pot and some Sewall spoons, which she asked Miss Robie to sell for her. Not only would this bring in needed funds, it would eliminate false appearances which were doubtless causing tradesmen to believe them more recalcitrant than poor. Abby also desired her friend to sell the warm merino cloak the Sewalls had pressed upon her at her father's death, but Miss Robie happened to see Sam soon after, and he foresightedly asked her to keep it a year or two for the time when Abby would, no doubt, be glad of it.

The following month, Emerson presented Bronson with an elegant cloak, which was also put away for the time being. Abby said his old one, worn and faded, better suited "the color of his condition." He was unwell in the extreme, and she wrote Sam she feared he could not long survive as matters stood. "[If] his body don't fail his mind will. He experiences at times the most dreadful nervous excitation, his mind distorting every act, however simple, into the most complicated and adverse form." He brooded excessively and was too much alone. She knew he must involve himself in the affairs of life, or perish. There were, after all, two opportunities open to him. He could accept Greaves' invitation to Alcott House, or he could accept the Holly Home offer of land and a cottage. Neither course was to her liking, but no course at all was even worse. She knew Bronson inclined towards going to England and began to judge it the better plan herself, though fearing for his safety during the dangerous ocean voyage and apprehensive about a prolonged separation. She was not ready for communal life and doubted that she ever would be. Adding strength of argument to knowledge of self, she suggested that congenial as the Providence people might be, her husband was too much "their senior in wisdom and life."[31] When Emerson offered to finance the trip abroad, Bronson accepted Greaves' invitation and Abby, able to take action at last, began to prepare her husband's wardrobe.

Firm plans made, she confronted the reality that her children's welfare might be in jeopardy no less through Bronson's absence than through con-sociate living. His brother, Junius, would be living with them at Dove Cottage but could not teach Anna, Louisa, and Lizzie as Bronson did, nor could Junius replace "the fostering care of his gentle spirit."[32] She questioned whether it was robbing the girls of their birthright to separate them from their father's daily influence. Was this really the best decision, she wondered. Having put aside earlier jealousies and differences with Bronson regarding child rearing, she now feared the responsibility of guiding them entirely on her own. Unsure of herself, she also feared the judgment he would render upon his return but hoped it would be "one of mercy if not approval."[33] At least she could foster her children's health and innocence if not advance

their knowledge. In any case, Bronson was going; she was in charge.
With an objectivity born of increasing understanding, she wrote in her
diary, "Wife, children, and friends are less to him than the great ideas
he is seeking to realize." As the time for his departure approached, she
made a mental list of all the justifications for the journey and found
among the most persuasive "the belief that these trans-Atlantic worthies
will be more to him in this period of doubt than anything or anybody
can be to him here."[34]

He left Concord for Boston on May 6 and embarked for England
on the *Rosalind* on May 8, spending the two intervening nights with
Abby's Uncle Sewall. Hannah Robie, who was also there, wrote Abby
a letter of reassurance and spoke her mind as usual, for Abby wrote in
her diary that this dear friend remained "lenient to his infirmities of
judgment"[35] and was ever willing to help them out with charity and
wise words. She was a woman of substantial good sense who promoted "reality in her life and conversation."[36] During the half year of
Bronson's absence, Miss Robie made many a visit to Dove Cottage and
took her tea without enduring the discomfort of Bronson's frowning
countenance. Abby wanted for female comfort immediately after
Bronson's departure, however, and wept uncontrollably for several
days, unable to eat, seeking comfort in walks and cold baths, resolving
to cheer up for the sake of her girls. Once more she echoed one of her
recurring themes, that strength emerges from defeat. "How elastic is
the nature of woman," she said. Just as the oil of seeds is obtained by
pressure, so is the worth of a woman's soul obtained by the weight of
outward circumstances. "Some flowers give out little or no odour until
crushed."[37]

Knowing doubt to be "a death knell to repose of mind" and anxiety
"a shroud for all joyousness,"[38] she vowed to put aside both just as she
would also banish sorrow, which was but selfish indulgence. She
reminded herself of Bronson's love by rereading his journal of their
courtship days and tried to direct her thoughts to the time ahead when,
the dangerous voyage safely accomplished, she would receive in his
own hand further reassurances of his well-being and affection. She
prayed that God would restore him to her and discovered the trite but
true commonplace that one values a treasure the more for being
deprived of it. Her affection for him was deepening as they shared the
difficult circumstances of their life together, as their souls merged with

the lives of their children. The existence of her daughters sustained her in his absence, and she wrote in her diary that she lived, moved, and had her being in them.

Two months after Bronson's departure, assured of his safe arrival and warm welcome at the hands of his English friends, Abby wrote a surprising line in her diary. "I am enjoying this separation from my husband." She went on to explain that his letters gave her the "full melody of his rich words"[39] beyond even the grandeur of his voice. As it turned out, she liked being entirely in charge and found she was fully capable of it. Cousin Samuel Sewall, executor along with Sam May, sent her a draft on the bank for one hundred dollars from her father's estate, and with it she paid her outstanding bills. She was annoyed with the merchants of Concord, who treated her as though she had no intention of paying up. Once her money was in their hands, she was of the opinion *they* ought to thank *her* for "circulating so much among them,"[40] and she hoped they would use it rightly, for the real wants of life. It is not out of the question that she said as much to their faces, annoyed as she was that they seemed to have no charity and would rather let the Alcotts starve than give them credit. Kind to those in more dire straights than she, benevolent in sharing food from her own meagre table, she was less than generous towards those whom she deemed uncharitable. Sam May, charity itself, gave her another fifty dollars, thus allowing her an unaccustomed freedom from want.

With neither Bronson's brooding presence nor habitual debt to worry her, Abby *was* enjoying the separation. Junius Alcott, himself as gentle a man as Bronson, did not intrude upon her newfound authority and was content to follow her lead. Cheerful, amiable, and patient, he was especially dear to her for his loving way with the children. Abby, whose moods were always susceptible to season and weather, was buoyed up by fine summer days as well as by her new sense of independence. They all rose early and, waxing poetic, she compared the purity of early morn to the "unmarred condition" of her children's souls. God, she said, educated children in the morning by harmonious sounds and sweet odours. Communing with nature was, for her, a form of worship, and summer birthdays celebrated its bounty and beauty. Lizzie's was on June 24. They decorated the barn with green boughs and flowers, invited Mrs. Emerson and a few others to share their simple meal of nuts and fruits, and the children declaimed a ditty written expressly to give their absent father a place in the celebration. "Father

dear/We wish you here/To see how gay/ On this birthday/We are."[41]
For Abba May's birthday in July, Uncle Junius rowed them on the Sud-
bury River in his little boat, *Undine*, to a favorite haunt, the Cliffs,
where they picked berries, spread a plaid blanket, and made a fine meal
of fruit and cake. This time the jingle was composed by Mother, who
laid no claim to being a poet but who knew sound often pleased the
young as much as sense. The important thing was that she communicate to them "the joy I feel in their birth and continuance with me on
earth."[42]

The Alcotts, though separated, were strengthening their ties, Abby
and Bronson for each other, both parents for their children. The girls
regularly decorated a miniature of their father with everlasting flowers,
emblems of their love and remembrance. Abby prayed that each gar-
land placed around his head would form a bond in their young hearts.
Bronson wrote the girls a fond letter, describing them much as they
appear years later in Louisa's *Little Women*. Anna was graceful and
fair, cherishing beauty and mystic shapes. Louisa was agile of limb
and boundless in curiosity, her penetrating mind and sympathetic heart
sensitive to all living things. Elizabeth was gentle and serene, blessed
with deep contentment. The little Abba, still a toddler, was happy in
"frolick joys and impetuous griefs." It was their mother, he told them,
"whose unsleeping love and painstaking hands provide for your comforts... and is your hope and stay."[43] His family was more dear to him
than ever; Abby had been his constant companion since their separation
and had grown ever more precious as the *Rosalind* carried him across
the ocean. For her part, she felt bound to him by "indissoluble
chains."[44]

Incredibly, in August he wrote Abby of his renewed hope for a
communal society, to include several of the Englishmen from Alcott
House, the Christopher Greenes from Providence, and maybe even the
Emersons. He seemed to see no inconsistency in writing paeans to his
natural family while at the same time proposing a con-sociate family.
Abby was taken aback. Idealism and reality seemed poised for confrontation. Emerson wanted no part of such a scheme and was apprehensive that Bronson's friends would find themselves in a barren field,
without sun to cheer them or shade to shelter them. He told Abby, "Mr.
A. lives in such a region of high hope that he does not feel the atmosphere of less elevated humanity, who are perishing in the chills of a
cold and selfish world, or who are lulled into extreme forgetfulness of

others by their excessive interest in themselves."[45] Abby had a brief reprieve when Bronson decided to delay his return by two months, but she used the time not to strengthen her arguments against the idea but to adjust herself to it. First and foremost, she wanted to be certain that the well-being of her children would not be in jeopardy. Assured by Bronson's letters that he loved them as much as she, she summoned up her old self-denying demon, duty, and was reminded that the proposed communal society, based upon simple living and self-denial, would mean the realization of his hope at last. She reread his journal for 1838 and copied his prophetic words into her diary. "My hour shall come.... My deeds as yet are enfolded in my Idea, and shall spring into light when the sun shineth."[46] Now that he had found the long-awaited stimulus in new friends and coadjutors, now that his detractors would see him take action, Abby had not the heart to put her own desires ahead of his fulfillment.

Nonetheless, she did not enjoy the same sun as he; clouds obscured her light. She was not at all certain that her capabilities were equal to the demands of a "united scheme of life,"[47] but as long as Bronson and his English companions returned safely she would be "content with anything."[48] Her natural family was already accustomed to plain living, and she agreed with the premise that unselfishness was essential for the reform of society. On the other hand, she knew that Dove Cottage had insufficient house-room for additional inhabitants. Having demonstrated her own subjugation of self by agreeing to go along with the idea, she took the practical step of looking for a suitable house and land, for these transcendental educators planned to join Bronson in becoming philosopher-farmers. Abby herself waxed philosophical in diary entries telling of her searches for property in nearby Stowe and Lincoln. "My mind to me a kingdom is,"[49] she wrote. Location should affect an individual but little; intellectual freedom and minimal creature comforts were all she needed to thrive.

Growing physically stronger over the summer of 1842, Abby reentered the kingdom of her mind and resumed her reading, which was no less prolific and diversified than it had been under the tutelage of Sam and Miss Allyn so many years ago. Some volumes she enjoyed and contemplated in solitude, others she read aloud to her girls, continuing to select uplifting voices such as Frederika Bremer, who felt as Abby did, that while family should be the basic unit of goodness and beauty, it must not deny women their mental birthright, intellectual equality

with men. John Bunyan and Maria Edgeworth remained favorites, and
she introduced Anna and Louisa to Goethe's *Bettina*, Samuel Johnson's
*Rambler*, and the novels of Mary Howitt. Howitt's works transcended
the mundane and suggested that those who live in the country but who
do not revel in its glories deny themselves the rich life which is their
potential. Abby copied an illustrative passage, one of many, into her
journal. "If he sees in Nature only the potato field which gives him
food, then is this golden vein closed to him, and he himself stands like
the potato plant, fast rooted in the earth." Her views in this regard
clearly coincided with Bronson's, and in copying some lines from Plato
she showed herself as pure a transcendentalist as her husband. "All is
received directly from the Divine Ideal, flowing into the soul of man
when he is obedient and still."[50]

Abby owned books of her own and also borrowed from Miss
Robie or Sam, following up her reading with discussions about current
religious thought, botany, biology, and physiology. Works on health
served mostly to confuse her with contradictory theories. One advised
a diet of bread and fruit but forbade water, as it distended the stomach
and weakened digestion. Another insisted that bread ossified the system and shortened life and should be avoided. She concluded that
moderation was the wisest course, along with plenty of exercise in the
fresh air, unaware that her own table was sadly wanting in protein.
After reading of widespread mortality among children the previous
winter, she took a rather superior tone and reproached other mothers for
"stupid inattention to the dietetic habits of their children." These
women, she lamented, believed sickness fell from heaven, alike on the
just and on the unjust, and did not trace it to their own habits and tab-
les. She suggested they look to causes and at the very least be temperate and simple in the quantity and quality of their food. "Graham," she
declared, "is not sufficiently valued as an apostle of light on this
momentous subject."[51]

Abby maintained the Alcott household on Graham's principles;
and Bronson, upon his return to Dove Cottage at the end of October,
found his family in good health. Their reunion was everything Abby
had wished for and, in a state of euphoria which usually foreshadowed
a letdown of equal extremity, she wrote in her journal, "Happy days
these!! Husband returned accompanied by the dear Englishmen, the
good and true. Welcome to these shores, this home, to my bosom!"[52]
Arriving with Bronson were two adults, Henry Wright and Charles

Lane, and Lane's son, William, who was about Louisa's age. They all went for a walk the first morning, and Abby spoke of experiencing pure joy in the presence of her husband and sympathetic new friends and, in the spirit of Mary Howitt, in contemplating the divine essence of the natural world. A mere month later, on Bronson's and Louisa's joint birthday, she wrote in her diary that circumstances were driving her cruelly from the enjoyment of domestic life. Predictably, her decision to accommodate herself to Bronson's plan proved to be a mistake. All nine beings remained crowded together in Dove Cottage, where she felt "frowned down into stiff quiet and peace-less order,... almost suffocated in this atmosphere of restriction and form." Though she was able to rouse herself to observe her daughter's birthday, she felt she was unfit company, even for the children. Her gift to Louisa, a pencil-case to encourage her love of writing, belied this notion, but she was justified in accusing the adults of being "stupidly obtuse on the causes of this occasional prostration of my judgment and faculties." She hoped their atonement for the invasion of her rights as a woman and a mother would not come too late for her recovery. Forced from her by despair, her words no longer denied the depth of her disillusionment. "Give me one day of practical philosophy; it is worth a century of speculation and discussion."[53]

Henry Wright was as disillusioned as she. He left, claiming their existence was too spartan and Alcott too despotic. There is no doubt that life at Dove Cottage was austere, especially in winter. The household rose at dawn and bathed in cold water, sometimes having to peg a hole in inch-thick ice which had formed on the basin overnight. At seven or seven-thirty they all gathered around the fireplace and warmed themselves while eating a breakfast of water, unleavened bread, apples, and potatoes, which Bronson often prepared. According to Lane, the meal was usually served into small red napkins, in order to save washing up. He failed to notice that although there were no dishes, the females were burdened with laundering the linen. Profitable conversation upon domestic topics engaged their attention until Lane took out his violin and gave William and the girls their music lesson. Lane then wrote or studied while the senior Alcotts did chores. The children either helped or played until ten o'clock when they commenced their studies - diary writing, spelling, arithmetic, reading, thinking, and paraphrasing. The noon meal was much like the morning's except that they sat at table. Lane gave William, Anna, and

Louisa lessons in French and geometry for an hour or so in the afternoon, and everyone came together for a simple supper about six, after
which they sang and sometimes danced to the accompaniment of
Lane's fiddle. The children retired at about 8 o'clock, the adults following after an hour or so of conversation, during which Abby knitted
and Bronson peeled potatoes for breakfast. Only occasionally did they
pass an evening with the Emersons or go to a lecture.

Bronson found himself displaced, unwelcome in his own daughters' classroom, when Charles Lane insisted upon taking over most of
their lessons. Both Alcotts were taken aback by Lane's overwhelming
need to dominate, with the result that a three-way struggle began at
Dove Cottage in the winter of 1842 and was resolved only by the final
failure, a year later, of all their attempts at con-sociate living. In addition to the constraints affecting life and liberty at Dove Cottage, Lane
was convinced that celibacy was essential to spiritual fulfillment.
Bronson was undecided on the issue, whereas Abby saw it as a threat to
the very structure of family. Lane claimed not to be "that devil come
from Old England to separate husband and wife,"[54] but Abby began to
see him in exactly that light. She had gone out of her way to make him
comfortable, giving him a bedroom-study with a cheerful wood fire.
He repaid her with words which countered all courtesies of hospitality.
"Mrs. A. has passed from the ladylike to the industrious order but she
has much inward experience to realize. Her pride is not yet eradicated
and her peculiar maternal love blinds her to all else."[55] It did not take
him long to discern that mother love was as much an antagonist as the
mother herself.

At Christmas time, Abby left Dove Cottage to visit relatives in
Boston, taking Louisa and William. Bronson wrote Junius that she was
in need of a change, as indeed she was, her moods continuing to rise
and fall with unsettling rapidity. In the company of Sam May, Miss
Robie, assorted Sewalls, Windships and Willises, she regained not only
her spirits but also her interest in issues of the day. She went to a lecture on physiology and was taken with the speaker's lifelike mannikin,
which had removable parts designed to expose the muscles, nerves,
veins, and arteries. She was not much taken by the speaker, however.
Henry Wright's lecture on the early years of childhood was more
dynamic and evoked the kind of lively conversation she considered a
hallmark of worthy company. Warm friends and interesting talk stimulated her, roused her from depression even though the festive rounds of

the season reawakened her distaste for the vain show and selfishness of society in general. Buoyed up by her intimates, however, she returned to Concord and her chosen life on New Year's Day, "glad to resume the quiet duties of house and love... quickened by a new spirit of confidence and love."[56]

Bronson's influence over her experienced a rebirth with every separation. He wrote her a note in which he assured her that she was in the arms of a benignant Providence which would sustain her, and she responded that she was filled with "unusual quietude... truly quickened into spiritual life."[57] She likened the feeling to that of life quickening in the womb. All but past her child bearing years and sleeping apart from Bronson - he shared a room with Elizabeth and she with baby - she carried within her the seed of his idealism and was strangely at peace.

Notes to one another were a commonplace with the Alcotts, whether to express feelings too difficult to speak or to remind the children of their duty to be good and kind, but in January of 1843 Abby formalized the custom by establishing what she called the household post office. It was to be a daily opportunity for the exchange of feelings and criticisms, "a pleasant way of healing all difference and discontents."[58] Letters were placed in a basket hung in the entry, and the children took turns distributing them after supper each evening. Anna and Louisa, still occasionally unkind to one another, found in the household post a convenient means of reconciling their own small differences. Charles Lane used it for the much more serious purpose of placating Abby. So important to her were two of his letters that she pasted them into her diary, commenting at the same time that Bronson thought it a weakness to need reassurances and words of appreciation for her labors. She was but human, she said, and toiled in the world of reality.

Though as self-serving as Bronson, Lane was more aware of personal interactions and less certain that Abby would willingly participate in plans for the establishment of a larger con-sociate family elsewhere. He therefore deliberately set about winning her confidence. He assured her that her "excellencies"[59] were not unnoticed. He suggested that she rest herself and then openly state her feelings and views. Of course, resting herself was not possible, but his words had a salutary effect and were enough to appease her, if not convince her of the wisdom of such an experiment. Lane knew that no progress could be made without Abby's approval and told her plainly that all must agree on both plan and property. Abby acquiesced because she could not bear the burden of refusing Bronson the chance, as he expressed it, to put hands to his idea. Bronson, in accepting a site fourteen miles from Concord, bowed to Lane, who wished to remove him from Emerson's influence. Since Lane held the purse-strings, he was able to deny Alcott his wish to establish their New Eden at the Cliffs, location of many a happy family picnic and birthday celebration. During the late winter and the spring of 1843, the search for house and land beyond the confines of Concord began in earnest.

Though the location was yet to be determined, the aims, nebulous enough, were set down on paper. Bronson was seeking converts to his New Eden from among those who found the spiritual life at Brook Farm inadequate. One of these was a man who craved an ascetic existence and who was later to found the Paulist order within the Catholic church, Isaac Hecker. Bronson wrote a letter which began by outlining the most tangible of his goals, the desire for self-sufficiency on fertile land, "with benignity toward all creatures, human and inferior." They would follow a regimen of simplicity in all things and act with refinement and charity. All individuals with similar aims were, by definition, suitable for such an association, and Bronson hoped to attract men, women, and whole families "desirous of access to the channels and fountains of wisdom and purity." Providence, he was certain, would use them for "beneficial effects in the great work of human regeneration."[60]  Hecker left Brook Farm for Bronson's con-sociate family in July, 1843, a month after it was established, but he did not stay long, citing precise reasons. Alcott was not frank; he tended towards separateness rather than cooperation; his family ties prevented plans for reformation; his property had little fruit on it, though he proposed fruit as a staple of their diet; and, finally, Alcott and the others tended too much toward literature and writing to guarantee the success of the enterprise. In later years he added that he would have been better pleased if the hereafter had been of as much concern as human perfection.

While Alcott and Lane continued to seek out members for the proposed con-sociate family and a site for its location, Abby tried unsuccessfully to keep her mind open and at peace. Sam May had moved to the neighboring town of Lexington, where he pursued his interest in education as head of the normal school there. A visit to him left her more uneasy than ever. Since the Alcotts could not leave Concord without paying their debts, Abby hoped Sam would be able to help or at least to suggest some acceptable course of action. Instead, he told Abby some home truths. Bronson was unwilling "to be employed in the normal way,"[61] causing even his friends to doubt his self-proclaimed righteousness. It was wrong of him to be indifferent towards his financial obligations. If he would not support his family, why should others? Sam, much as he admired his brother-in-law's mind, was distressed by his intransigence. Abby returned to Dove Cottage in an unsettled frame of mind. Sam's plain speaking provoked an unwelcome acknowledgment that her husband was, indeed, improvident. The future of her family was in jeopardy, not only because of the imminence of communal living, but also because Bronson would never be a good provider. Other than sewing for a pittance, she had not yet found a way to earn money herself and doubted that she ever would. Such thoughts prompted her to cut out an emblem and send it in a prophetic note to ten-year-old Louisa.

> I enclose a picture for you which I always admired very much, for in my imagination I have thought you might be just such an industrious good daughter and that I might be a sick but loving mother, looking to my daughter's labors for my daily bread. Take care of it for my sake and your own because you and I have always liked to be grouped together.[62]

Love for her children, determination to see them safely through childhood and into productive womanhood, gave Abby strength where she might otherwise have faltered, but she was not yet confident enough to act in outright opposition to Bronson. All too often she submitted to his admonition that she put herself in the hands of divine Providence. In a birthday message to twelve-year-old Anna, she echoed her husband and offered advice she knew in her heart could not possibly prepare the child for healthy, active participation in life. "Then humbly take what God bestows and, like his own fair flowers, look up in sunshine with a smile and gently bend in showers."[63]

A product of her time and upbringing, Abby had no model for taking charge of her life. Furthermore, Bronson's ideas and her own choice of reading reinforced her powerlessness, blinding her to the positive possibilities of self. In the wet, cheerless days of New England's early spring, she was more bowed down than gently bent by the weather and her burdens. She was sensible that knowledge of her sufferings was a principal part of the sufferings themselves; but as the days lengthened and bud became bloom, she rallied, packed up her household goods, and set off on yet another new experience in the art of living.

The problem of money had once again been resolved by others. Charles Lane paid the Alcotts' Concord debts, and Sam May reluctantly co-signed the note Lane took on the property, a secluded hundred acre parcel of land in the town of Harvard, Massachusetts. The owner agreed to allow them use of the farmhouse rent free for a year, and well he might. The building was shabby and dilapidated, though not "scarcely tenantable"[64] as Lane had stated when attempting to describe it honestly to Abby. It was at a remove from the traveled road, accessible only by a cart path which descended diagonally downhill for half a mile. A family by the name of Lovejoy shared the path with them, but the con-sociate family were to live at its end, isolated and remote. The plans they had for subsequent construction of "tasteful buildings in harmony with the natural scene"[65] came to nought, though the beauty of the scene remains to this day. Anna described it in a composition entitled "Fruitlands," for that was the name chosen by the ever hopeful inhabitants of this New Eden.

> It is a beautiful place surrounded by hills, green fields and woods, and Still River is at some distance flowing quietly along. Wachusett and Monadoc Mountains are in sight, and also some houses and fields of grain. The house itself is now very pleasantly situated. It has a vegetable garden behind it and some fruit trees. On the left a hill on the top of which are pastures and a road. In front is a small garden, and fields and a house at some distance. On the right is a large barn, grain and potato field, woods and mountains. There are many walks about Fruitlands, and berry fields, though the berries are not yet quite ripe.[66]

The con-sociates planned to make fruit the mainstay of their diet, and the land seemed compatible with that objective. Mr. Wyman, previous owner of the hundred acres, agreeably allowed them the crops already under cultivation; and even before June 1, the day of their arrival at Fruitlands, coadjutors were already working the soil. Joseph Palmer, a well-to-do farmer of a philosophical bent who lived in a town nearby, gladly gave of his time and expertise. Samuel Larned, twenty-year-old son of a wealthy Providence merchant, left Brook Farm for Fruitlands earlier than Isaac Hecker and was there to greet the Alcotts. A cooper by the name of Everett was also there in advance of the others. An anomaly inasmuch as he had no spiritual pretensions, Everett was a conscientious worker and spent his time in useful physical labor. One of the tenets of the association was that each should do as seemed best at any given time, whether that meant engaging in philosophical discussion, cultivating the land, or traveling in order to garner recruits and spread the so-called Newness. It was this vagueness of approach which sowed the first seeds of failure along with the oats and wheat, corn and beans. They planned to secure a Graham diet by their own labor and, initially, were industrious in the tilling and planting of their acres; but the enthusiasm wore off and their methods were hostage to their principles. They did not use manure, as it was unclean; and they used but little animal labor, as they would not deprive beasts of their freedom. As Louisa was to write years later in *Transcendental Wild Oats*, a gentle, fictional parody of the Fruitlands experiment, the mother was the only beast of burden on the place. Cultivation could have been a common purpose for the disciples of the Newness, but they would no more deprive one another of freedom than they would oxen and horses, and so selfish interest crept in to undermine the community. There were only a dozen or so in residence at any one time; and the arrival of Samuel Bower, an English mystic, further undermined the credibility of the undertaking. Bower advocated nudity as the ultimate freedom. Fortunately, he confined himself to nightly wanderings modestly clad in a sheet.

Abby had chosen not to see, much less challenge, the impossibilities inherent in the proposed community. She convinced herself that Bronson would attract "true men and women" who would find contentment by "putting away the evil customs of society and leading quiet exemplary lives." She wrote in her diary on the day of their arrival that, though their labor must be arduous, "there is much to strengthen our hearts and hands in the reflection that our pursuits are innocent and true, that no selfish purpose actuates us, that we are living for the good of others, and that though we may fail it will be some consolation that we have ventured what none others have dared."[67] The communal society they ventured to form was indeed unique, certain to fail if only because of their insistence upon lack of structure. Only Abby followed any sort of productive routine, that of cleaning, washing, and cooking.

Like the workhorse she was, she wore blinders until it was almost too late to gain control of her life. She toiled at the household chores with only Anna and Louisa to help, although Bronson sometimes baked the con-sociates' unleavened bread. Hannah Robie visited from time to time, warm in her love for Abby, though looking on skeptically and choosing to board nearby rather than live at Fruitlands. Abby confessed to her that she was living an exhausting "public tavern sort of life"[68] which provided precious little satisfaction. The only compensation was the beauty of the place. Looking westward from the top of their hill she could see across the intervale of the Nashua River to the mountains of southern New Hampshire, which were sublime in all moods and which transported her from petty cares and concerns. Wandering about wood and meadow, she collected chips for fuel while her children gathered flowers for delight and berries for the table. Nature itself was one of the celebrants at Lizzie's eighth birthday party on June 24. The con-sociates built a bower in the woods, trimmed hats with leaves, placed little gifts and notes on a small pine tree, and made symbolic flower offerings. Anna and her father chose the rose for love and purity; Louisa, the lily-of-the-valley for innocence; Mother, the forget-me-not for remembrance; Mr. Lane, moss for humility. They all sang to the accompaniment of Lane's fiddle and then recited original odes fit for the occasion. Only a thunder shower prevented them from passing the late afternoon hours, as well as the morning, in this delightful glade.

Christy Greene gave Lizzie a trailing arbutus, symbol of perseverance, as his flower gift. He taught in nearby Tyngsboro that summer of 1843, and was not long at Fruitlands, but while there he gave lessons to the children.[69] Lane and Alcott also presided in the classroom, and Anna supervised the younger ones during their frequent absences. Abby continued her practice of reading aloud to the children but had little time for browsing in her personal library. Her intellectual stimulation was further hampered by the men of Fruitlands, who allowed her to participate in their discussions only when worldly matters were under consideration. She wrote of them sarcastically as "higher intelligences who admit me sometimes at their debates when the carnal things are to be discussed."[70] Annoyed beyond measure, Abby absented herself from the table until Anna wrote her a note telling her she was missed and, besides, ought to sit down with them and eat the food she went to so much trouble to prepare.

The household post continued as a way for Abby and the children to smooth over little differences and encourage one another. Abby wrote Anna, "I am sure I feel as if I could fold my arms around you all, and say from my heart, 'Here is my world within my embrace.' Let us try, dear Anna, to make it a good and beautiful world, that when we are called to leave it we may be fit to join the good and beautiful of another sphere."[71] Though Abby continued to feel a special love and concern for Louisa, her relationship with Anna was becoming more and more companionable as this eldest daughter matured. Louisa remained volatile and still quarreled with Anna, vowing afterwards to try and love her better, always succeeding until the next time. The two youngest girls were adored by both older sisters. On little Abba's third birthday in July, however, there was no woodland celebration such as was given Lizzie in June. A few small gifts were put in her stocking, but Lane, Hecker, and Alcott hastened off to Boston after breakfast, leaving the females to the chores. Anna did the wash and set the dinner table while Louisa took the two youngest girls for a walk. In the afternoon Anna helped Abby and the few remaining men with the haying and then joined Louisa in picking berries for supper.

They were not sorry when another woman joined the community. Ann Page, who came from Providence as did Larned and Greene, arrived at the height of the summer, and Abby was for a time "somewhat relieved by [her] aid and presence."[72] Miss Page took over some of the classroom duties, but the children came to dislike her, and Louisa claimed she was too fussy. Abby welcomed her at first and was especially grateful for her help during an unexpected crisis. Bronson returned from Boston with a severe case of dysentery. When the worst was over, Abby wrote Sam that she had feared for his life. Bronson kept saying that his faith would heal him, but she favored common sense, insisting upon spearmint tea, blackberries, and a bath twice daily. If he had not improved, she planned to send for Emerson, who "has good sense enough not to be afraid of human aids for human ends." Bronson remained debilitated for some time, but worse, he became nervous and excitable, his mind "too morbidly active." Again, just as during the winter of 1841, at Dove Cottage, Abby worried about his mental stability. "I do not allow myself to despair of his recovery, but oh, Sam, that piercing thought flashes through my mind of insanity, and a grave yawning to receive his precious body would be to me a consolation compared to that condition of life."[73]

Concern was uppermost in her mind when Bronson, still weak, went off with Lane and one James Kay, a reformer, for a day of conversation with the elders of Harvard's nearby Shaker Village. Lane was particularly drawn to the Shakers, attracted by their prosperity and their practice of celibacy. Male members of the two communities became well acquainted with one another; and when Lane and Alcott encouraged the two women to see the Shakers for themselves, Abby and Miss Page agreed to go. The men were to regret having so urged them, as it resulted in an unfavorable first-hand look. Productive and efficient as it was, Abby had no use for the Shaker way of life. There was something very much amiss, even beyond segregation of the sexes and denial of family life as she knew it. Despite the professed equality of elders and eldresses, brothers and sisters, she and Miss Page found servitude. Abby wrote in her diary, "There is a fat sleek comfortable look about the men, and among the women there is a stiff awkward reserve that belongs to neither sublime resignation or divine hope. Wherever I turn I see the yoke on woman in some form or other." Though ostensibly continuing to comment on the Shakers, her words clearly struck closer to home. A woman, she said, may live for truth and righteousness, but she lives neglected and dies forgotten. Man speculates about his beliefs, but woman lives hers and, in her embodiment of goodness, is the greater of the two. To this Miss Page added a succinct comment. "A woman may live a whole life of sacrifice and at her death meekly says I die a woman. A man passes a few years in experiments on self-denial and simple life and he says 'behold a God.' "[74]

Abby's will, as woman and as self, was in the ascendency. As the situation at Fruitlands deteriorated, the sympathetic understanding of Sam May and Hannah Robie encouraged her impulse towards independent action. Curiosity had enticed a constant stream of visitors to Fruitlands, increasing her labors and diminishing her stores. "People have been and devoured our substance," she wrote Sam, "and turned round to scoff at our efforts. Well, never mind. We set up for a mark. Strange if nobody dared to fire and nobody to hit."[75] Not only were the con-sociates criticized for impracticality in the cultivation of their crops, they were considered peculiar in their refusal to wear either wool or cotton. Sheep must not be deprived of their wool; and since cotton was the product of slave labor, garments must be of linen. As for bathing, Bronson rigged up a sort of shower so that they could begin each day with a cold dousing, to the amazement of neighbors who also considered their Graham diet extreme and their refusal to eat flesh unreasonable. In *Transcendental Wild Oats*, Louisa blamed the casting out of Ann Page's fictional counterpart to the eating of the tail of a fish. In reality, Abby could no more endure intrusion into the household sphere at Fruitlands than she could in Boston or Concord. Lane unequivocally put the blame for Miss Page's departure on Abby, describing it as "little short of a kicking out of doors chiefly on the part of Mrs. A. who vows that her own family is all she lives for or wishes to live for."[76]

The truce between Lane and Abby was fast coming to an end. In September, he and Bronson abandoned the harvest and left on a prose-lytizing trip to Providence, New York City, and thence for a visit to Bronson's childhood home in Wolcott, Connecticut. Abby's friend, Lydia Maria Child, saw them in New York and was quick to recognize the danger of Lane's personal magnetism. "Perhaps Lane is one of the best and greatest of men; but his countenance pleased me not. In the first place, it looks as if the washwoman had caught it and scrubbed it on a washboard; and in the second place there is an expression which would make me slow to put myself in his power."[77] Bronson, not so perceptive, was increasingly in Lane's thrall. Between Abby and Lane there was much more at issue than the differences which had under-mined her well-being at Dove Cottage. His outlook on communal liv-ing now threatened her very marriage. In his zeal to help Bronson realize his potential as a fully spiritual being, Lane was urging him to renounce the bondage of matrimony, leave his family, and join him in uniting with the local Shakers. Until Lane's underlying plan became clear to her, Abby persevered in her duties, doing what she could to help Bronson realize his hopes for Fruitlands by fulfilling obligations from which she reaped but little reward. Determined to get to the bot-tom of Lane's motives, which she called equivocal, she vowed to sift matters to their depths, "for I will know the foundation, centre, and circumference."[78] She made it clear to him that his will was not unop-posed. Lane, for his part, correctly saw her as a substantial hindrance. "Mrs. Alcott has no spontaneous inclination towards a larger family than her own natural one. Of spiritual ties she knows nothing, though to keep all together she does and would go through a good deal of exte-rior and interior toil."[79]

Lane's divisive influence brought the Alcotts' marital relationship to the point of crisis, threatening their natural family and ending what little hope remained for a con-sociate family. By late autumn, all but the Alcotts and the two Lanes had fled Fruitlands, the experiment in renunciation either too much or too little for the few who resided in the community for any length of time. As Abby observed, "The right people, with right motives and holy purposes, do not come."[80] Unhappy as she was that Bronson's search for human perfection was once again thwarted, the failure of the Fruitlands experiment came as no surprise and was insignificant compared to the family separation urged by Lane. During the month of November, the three adult players in this triangle tugged and pulled at one another, proposing options, urging decisions. Lane thought of selling the land, freeing himself from financial ruin but throwing the Alcotts on their own. Bronson would thus be prevented from pursuing the only suggestion satisfactory to Abby, that of building a cottage for the family on a few of Fruitlands' acres. Should the worst come to pass, should Lane and Alcott go to the Shakers without her, Abby would have to consider accepting Sam's offer of a refuge near him in Lexington. Alarmed that even the children's peace of mind was being disturbed by discussion and innuendo, she was the first to take action, forcing Bronson to make a decision by peremptorily announcing that she would go elsewhere with her girls as soon as she could see her way clear as to the most suitable place. By two further measures she effectively ensured that neither Lane nor Bronson could remain. She told them she was taking her furniture, and she asked Sam not to honor the note for the property he had co-signed with Lane, thereby necessitating its sale.

Faced with Bronson's possible defection, Abby showed a healthy assertiveness and innate common sense. She loved him despite his impracticality; she admired his tenacious pursuit of truth as he saw it. She wanted the Alcott family to remain intact, but she was up against an unprecedented obstacle and was taking a chance in forcing Bronson's hand. Society might censure her for leaving him, but she had little use for society. More to the point, Bronson was unlikely to exercise his legal right to take the girls from her on the grounds of abandonment. Holding fast to his prior professions of tenderness towards herself and their children, she pursued her course. Christmas was bleak. Few families celebrated the birth of Christ as a gift giving holiday, though the Alcotts were accustomed to exchanging handmade tokens and emblems. Bronson was not a part of the observance this year, as he was attending a convention in Boston. Abby invited a few local children to join her girls and William Lane for an attempt at merry-making in the evening. Though there had been a constant succession of snow storms, Mr. Lovejoy, their nearest neighbor, kept the cart path open so they would not be completely isolated. As snow and night descended, Abby suggested to the young people that they try song "to cheer the scene within, to render the cheerlessness without more tolerable."[81] It was all the more difficult for Abby to set an example as her mood matched the weather, chill and unsettled.

She spent the days of Bronson's absence trying to determine where best to go, for go she would. When, on January 1, he returned from the convention, she told him that she was dissolving all connections with Fruitlands and sending her goods and furniture to the Lovejoys, who had offered them three rooms and use of the kitchen for fifty cents a week. Her decision taken, all was action. Lane and William visited the Shakers on January 3 and 4 to see about joining the Harvard society, making their actual removal on January 6. When Abby and the children left for the Lovejoys' the following week, Bronson went with them. She sent the news to those who had most strongly urged her to independent action. "All Mr. Lane's efforts have been to disunite us," she wrote Sam. "But Mr. Alcott's conjugal and paternal instincts were too strong for him."[82] To Hannah Robie she confessed that the last six months had been "tedious beyond bearing," but she had done her best to fulfill her commitment and was not troubled by guilt. "My satisfaction is great that Mr. Alcott comes away cheerfully and is convinced that Mr. Lane and he were never truly united." Not for the first time she acknowledged inexpressible comfort in being alone after living too closely with others. With her burdens lightened, she could give time "to some employment by which the future needs of the little group are to be met."[83] In the meantime, Sam sent her ten dollars and for another ten she reluctantly sold a silver fish-slice which had been a gift from Miss Robie. "Several calls for money without visible means to answer them impelled me to part with it. I am sure she did not think hardly of me for it. I have been driven to many of these straits during these last few years but I hope we shall be settled soon to some mode of life which shall either be more independent of the aid of others or less irksome to ourselves. Mr. Alcott cannot bring himself to work for gain, but we have not yet learned to live without money or means."[84]

Joseph May, circa 1820

Charles Lane

Fruitlands farmhouse, circa 1890

Catalogue of my books — 1844

| | Vol | | Vol |
|---|---|---|---|
| Shakespeare | 12 | American Commonplace | 1 |
| Homer | 4 | Young's Night Thoughts | 1 |
| Wakefield's Testament | 2 | More on Education | 1 |
| Darwin's Botanic Garden | 1 | Fashionable world | 1 |
| Pope's works | 1 | Bulwer's Pompeii | 1 |
| Taylor's Holy living | 1 | England & English | 1 |
| Madame Guion | 1 | Thomas a Kempis | 1 |
| Bolingbroke | 1 | The Disowned | 1 |
| Bigelow's Botany | 1 | Married Life | 1 |
| Eaton's Manual | 1 | Art of being happy | 1 |
| Letters from New York | 1 | Enfield's Prayers | 1 |
| Vegetable Diet | 1 | Mrs Barbauld's work | 1 |
| — Cookery | 1 | Frederika Bremer's work | 4 |
| Cheering views | 1 | Nina | |
| Addison's works | 2 | Presidents Daughters | |
| Fenelon's Thoughts | 1 | Neighbours | |
| Philothea | 1 | Home | |
| History King's Chapel | 1 | Bible | 1 |
| Mrs Child's Appeal | 1 | | |
| Zimmerman on Sol. | 1 | | |
| Queen's name | 1 | | |
| The Nurse | 1 | | |
| Calebs | 1 | | |
| Gilmans Election | 1 | | |

Mrs. Alcott's personal books, 1844

Graham Bread.

3 pts warm water
1. tea cup wheat flour
1.         indian meal
1. tea spoonful of yeast.
1. spoonful of molasses
  "        Saleratus
  "        salt.

Stir them together, then
add as much graham flour
as will easily stir with a
spoon. Do this over night.
in the morning stir it again
a few minutes and pour
it into two deep pans. let
it rise again, and bake
an hour and a half.

Mrs. Alcott's recipe for Graham bread

Brick Ends, Still River

Hillside, drawn by Bronson Alcott

Waterford, from Mrs. Alcott's diary

# MRS. ALCOTT

Will re-open her books at No. *88 Atkinson Street* for the purpose of Registering the best American and Foreign Help. Families provided, at the shortest notice, with accomplished COOKS, good PARLOR and CHAMBER GIRLS, NURSERY MAIDS, SEAMSTRESSES, TOILETTE WOMEN, and DRESS-MAKERS.

Any person paying the Subscription of $1 shall be furnished with a Ticket, entitling her to a choice of Help for six months from Mrs. ALCOTT's Rooms.

Subscription Papers at Miss PEABODY's Book-rooms, No. 13, West-street; and at Mrs. DAVID REED's, No. 1, Bedford Place.

*Boston, August* 14, 1850.

Broadside for Mrs. Alcott's Intelligence Office

Bronson Alcott, by Mrs. Hilldreth, 1852

Samuel May, circa 1850

Lizzie Alcott,
circa 1855

May Alcott,
circa 1850

Anna Alcott,
circa 1860

Louisa May Alcott,
circa 1858

The Alcotts in front of Orchard House, circa 1865

# HEAR US FOR OUR CAUSE!
## A CONVENTION
—— OF THE ——
### MIDDLESEX COUNTY
## Woman Suffrage Association
WILL BE HELD IN THE
### TOWN HALL, CONCORD,
At 2 1-2 o'clock in the Afternoon, and 7 1-2 in the Evening,
### WEDNESDAY, May 19.

Eminent Speakers will address the Convention, among whom will be

WM. LLOYD GARRISON, JULIA WARD HOWE, H. B. BLACKWELL, LUCY STONE, Rev. GEO. H. VIBBERT, MARY F. EASTMAN, A. BROWNSON ALCOTT, and others.

### THE HALL WILL BE FREE TO ALL
### AND ALL ARE INVITED.

☞Supper will be provided for those in attendance from out of Town, and there will be ample time between meetings to see the old battle ground and the new statues.

Broadside, Woman Suffrage Association

May Alcott, by Rose Peckham

Mrs. Alcott in the parlor at Orchard House

May Alcott's Frontispiece for the first edition of *Little Women*

# Chapter Five

## Natural Family

*Do you remember how you used to play Pilgrim's Progress when you were little things?... Our burdens are here, our road is before us, and the longing for goodness and happiness is the guide that leads us through many troubles and mistakes to the peace which is a true Celestial City.*

Marmee
from *Little Women*

When Abby challenged Bronson by taking the initiative in the move to the Lovejoys', she showed considerable progress in her lifelong effort to govern emotion through reason. She was angry; she was resentful; she was hurt; but she discovered that the better she controlled herself, the greater the power she had over others. Emotional outbursts served no useful purpose in efforts to keep her family together; deliberate, rational moves succeeded. She withdrew her personal support from the Fruitlands community, saw to it that Sam withdrew his financial backing, and announced that she would act altogether independently, removing herself, her children, and her furniture. As a result of the experience she was, in the future, less compliant, more vigilant to all ramifications of Bronson's schemes for ideal living. Her objectivity increased in proportion to her reliance upon reason, the one an integral part of the other. In gaining distance from Bronson, she exchanged an unrealistic, romanticized attachment for mature caring. She continued to love him but complained that a little industry on his part, more effort towards financial integrity, would relieve them from "disagreeable dependencies." The aid of friends and relatives was still necessary; and though these gave of their abundance, they were vocal in their censure. Abby agreed with them. "Should like to see my husband a little more interested in this matter of support..." she said. "Mr. Alcott is right in not working for hire if thereby he violates his conscience; but working for bread does not necessarily imply unworthy gain."[1]

Their sojourn at the Lovejoys' was but an interim measure. Abby wanted Sam May and Samuel Sewall, as the trustees of her father's estate, to purchase for her a house and several acres of land. For the time being, they declined to do so. "Soul-sick,"[2] unable to earn the family bread herself, Abby was willing to undertake any reasonable scheme but insisted upon an informed and influential voice in the shaping of her family's future. For the last fifteen months she had felt herself "allied to a shadow."[3]   It was time her needs received the consideration due them.    Bronson still spoke hopefully about con-sociate living. Communities did, Abby admitted, "have advantages over common social life;" but unless she could find one ready-made with women, children, and reasonable duties, she would not "move an inch."[4]   Determined to judge merits and drawbacks first hand, she warmed herself at unfamiliar hearths during the month of February, visiting communities in Milford and Northhampton, Massachusetts, even reconsidering Brook Farm at the invitation of its founder, George Ripley. So recently liberated from bondage, her observations were not without prejudice, and she returned with the predictable conclusion that none of the groups suited her family. She found "no sphere in which we could act without an unwarrantable alienation from our children." Abby's predisposition to find fault was furthered by the bleakness of winter, and at Northampton she was depressed by what she considered to be desultory, aimless lives. She was further disappointed by the mediocrity of the Hopedale society in Milford; and although she found "more neatness, order, beauty, and life" at Brook Farm than at either of the other communities, she nonetheless discerned "no advance on the old world." It was a foregone conclusion that she would find little favor with communal "association in labor."[5] Clearly, she preferred to avoid con-sociate living at all costs, though in so doing she might "perish under dependence."[6]

Bronson, after a visit to Northampton in March, agreed with Abby that no community, as presently constituted, would suit. In his view, those currently established in Massachusetts aimed at too little and were not sufficiently noble of purpose. For the moment, Abby was spared agonizing decisions and confrontation. Relieved, she wrote Hannah Robie, "Quite satisfied that I am not ready for community life; or it is not ready for me. I intend to look out for a little cave and take my cubs and retreat."[7] She continued to bear all responsibility for her family, husband as well as children, for Bronson was not well, nor had he been for any significant duration since the failure of the Temple School. During this winter of 1844 he had a clairvoyant experience, not necessarily a sign of illness but a matter for concern in view of his continuing physical and mental weakness. There is extant no contemporary record with which to document his mental health during either the Fruitlands months or those immediately following, but he wrote about it in later reminiscences. In *Tablets*, a rambling metaphysical work of 1849, he wrote that at Fruitlands, tormented by demons, he had feared insanity. In his journal for February, 1851, he recalled being transfigured and tasting mannas during the winter of 1844. "I enjoyed this state for a couple of months or more, but was left somewhat debilitated when spring came, and unfit for common concerns."[8]

It was under these circumstances that Abby searched both Harvard and Concord for an inexpensive refuge, a dwelling place exclusively their own. Thanks to the Lovejoys,[9] she found a temporary home only a mile or so distant from Fruitlands, in the village of Still River, a hamlet within Harvard's boundaries. Here they had five rooms in half of a house, including their own kitchen for cooking a la Graham, and permission to construct "a little bathing room"[10] so as to continue the custom of cold shower baths. At a cost of twenty-five dollars a year, they were by themselves as Abby wished to be. Bronson, better in health if not fully well, industriously began to turn the stone and stubble of their half acre into neat, rectangular gardens, promissory plots for food to come. Abby did not believe that faith alone would sustain them, as Bronson all too often proposed; but she believed fully in God and in His intercession on behalf of those who help themselves. She was confident that the divine in nature would reward her husband's

honest labor. "What a holy calling is the husbandman's. How intimately he relates himself to God. Placing his seeds into Earth's bosom,
he calls upon sun and dew for their divine agencies; he plants and
waters, and the increase is from God alone."[11] These words, written in
her diary on April 24, the day of their move to Still River, were not
those of a passive woman hoping for the best but were, rather, an
expression of the interrelatedness of her spiritual and worldly values.
The theme was much on her mind, for on the same day she wrote Sam
that they hoped to "bring forth abundantly of spiritual as well as material food."[12]

Abby saw helping those in need as her Christian duty and was
committed to easing human suffering. She found limited opportunities
in Still River, sharing clothing sent to her family by Miss Robie and
Mrs. Savage, exhorting local residents in uncertain health to regimens
of Graham diet, daily bathing, and vigorous scrubbing. She remained
deeply concerned about the plight of slaves and asked Sam to send her
a packet of newspapers, particularly Garrison's *Liberator*, pasting into
her diary a clipping about "a hero *worth* immortalizing," Moses
Grandy, a former slave. "See this great, noble heart *three times* achieving its freedom, being twice balked by the diabolical wickedness of the
white man - robbed of his beloved wife and children - treated with
every indignity which soul and body could endure, yet, still preserving
his sweet, patient spirit, loving his masters when it was possible, faithful till the death, not even *taking* the freedom which with his intellectual capacity he could have easily have achieved, but preferring to *buy*
it by extra toil. Here's a *man* for you."[13] Immediate emancipation, she
felt, was a moral imperative, so when the citizens of Still River and
Harvard held a festival to further the cause of abolition, she participated
with all her heart.

Clippings, as well as passages from her favorite works, continued
to reflect Abby's thoughts and opinions. In July of that Still River
summer, she sought moral and mental enlightenment from the sermons
of the Englishman, James Martineau,[14] copying excerpts into her diary
and writing Sam of their inspirational effect. Abby, staunch advocate
of Bronson's unique qualities, gained new insight into her own through
reading these sermons. Since she agreed with Bronson's ultimate aim,
the reform of society, she had mistakenly placed herself too much
under his influence in seeking its accomplishment through communal
living. Martineau's sermons made the point that no matter how well

one individual knows another, only the self can have true knowledge of personal needs and motivations. Morally worthy individuals must therefore be guided by purposes suited to the peculiarities of their own characters. She knew herself to be morally worthy. She now understood more fully that her own means and motives were equal in worth to Bronson's. Both he and she could press onward, each in accordance with personal revelation and each willing to accept the consequences. Bronson remained a seeker, seeing "in the spirit's deepest darkness... the stirrings of a mystic energy [wherein] the haze may be gathered together and glow within the mind into a star, a sun, a piercing eye of God."[15] She left the mysticism to Bronson, but in order to awaken the divine which was uniquely her own, she vowed to rededicate her life to the duties and aspirations which sprang from the deity within.

Family, of course, was Abby's microcosm for an unselfish society guided by love, respect, and duty. She nurtured hers from the depth of her devotion, ever mindful that she must prepare her girls to replace her one day as moral examples for the improvement of society. Even in family recreation Abby set a tone of honest simplicity, creativity, and concern for the oppressed. Under her guidance, on Lizzie's ninth birthday the girls decorated their Still River home, Brick Ends, with evergreen boughs and invited neighbors to an amateur theatrical, one of many, many more to come. Louisa, with headdress and burnished skin, recited a lament for Indians killed by the white man. Her dramatic sense developed early under her mother's tutelage, as did her sympathy for the down-trodden and the persecuted. Abby watched approvingly as rapt faces attended while Louy recited lines from "Geehale - An Indian Lament." "I will weep for a season, on bitterness fed,/For my kindred are gone to the hills of the dead;/But they died not by hunger, or lingering decay;/The steel of the white man hath swept them away."[16]

Summer passed pleasantly enough. Anna and Louisa attended Miss Maria Chase's Still River school, and each of the four girls had at least one particular playmate, even four-year-old Abba May. Picnics and hay rides were a common occurrence, and Abby packed luncheon baskets and climbed into rustic carts right along with the children. For four weeks, Hannah Robie and Mrs. Savage boarded nearby, affording her sympathetic female, adult company for which she was thankful, inasmuch as Bronson was away once again in search of "a field of action free from the complications of society and trade as now instituted."[17] Communal life, it seemed, remained the focus of his thoughts. Abby wanted him to pursue his hope, and she knew he must seek fulfillment in his way, not hers. The irony of the situation was that, having determined her motives to be of equal worth to his, she was compelled to compromise. He was an integral part of the natural family of her ideal; to assure his place in it she would in all probability have to welcome others to her hearth. It would be no easy task to balance her needs against his, but because the purpose of this particular trip was to recruit Junius and Chatfield Alcott, she was, for the moment, sanguine. These were blood relatives, not untried strangers, and Junius had earned her respect at Dove Cottage in 1842. Bronson had been unable to attract his brothers to the con-sociate family at Fruitlands, but he was now determined to convince them of the advantages of this mode of living. For himself, he said, forming a union with his brothers and their families would avoid the narrow selfishness inherent in living solely for and with his immediate family. Without too many misgivings, Abby packed Bronson's trunk and one for Anna as well, for she was making the journey with him, and the two set off for Oriskany Falls, New York, "the West." After a pleasant but inconclusive family visit, Bronson extended the trip by a week in order to inspect communal societies in nearby Mottville and Marengo. Abby was not mistaken in expecting that her husband would continue to find distasteful the idea of joining an established community. He was constant in his unique ideals and disparaged the New York communities just as he had those in Massachusetts. It remained to be seen what would come of his efforts to recruit Chatfield and Junius.

Emerson was aware of Alcott's restless discontent and urged his friend to return to Concord, encouraging him to do so with the promise of buying a few acres and building him "a plain house."[18] Because Abby dreaded the thought of Bronson's falling once again into the dangerously solitary way of life which had consumed his body and spirit the previous winter, she went along with the scheme, acknowledging that living in Concord would return him to the society of kindred spirits and might "help to mature a wiser and broader scheme of action than can be concocted in Mr. Alcott's celestial cogitations." She knew Emerson could be relied upon to "keep a rational view in sight;" and she was tired of the endless moving about, which consumed "time, life, and money." Knowing that Bronson was not yet through with communal living, however, she could not restrain herself from commenting sarcastically to Sam,"The great idea will be realized before a thousand years, I hope, and we shall all be transfixed in eternal marble."[19]

In October, they found temporary quarters in Concord, thanks to a cousin of the Hosmer from whom they had rented Dove Cottage. Abby was correct in judging "the great idea" not yet put to rest. Bronson insisted that he could not consent to live solely for one family and sent a letter off to Junius, earnestly desiring his participation in a union. "If we perform wisely our parts," he wrote, "Providence will send us worthy company in due time."[20] Thoreau might join them now and again, and their friend and cousin, Dr. William Alcott, might be interested. Meanwhile, the Alcotts set up housekeeping in half of the Hosmers' house while they sought permanent arrangements elsewhere in Concord. The two families were much thrown together, with the result that Abby was less enthusiastic than ever about communal life. The Hosmers did not live up to her high standards of selfless living, nor did Mr. Hosmer give his wife her rightful place as wife and mother. She felt them "a sad illustration of self indulgence and *paternal* rights! Oh no, *maternal* wrongs!!"[21]

Abby suffered in close proximity to the Hosmers for but a few months. She and Bronson decided that the Cogswell house, near Emerson, could be adapted to their needs, unspecified though those were as yet; and Abby recorded in her diary on New Year's Day, 1845, that the two Sams, May and Sewall, were willing to provide a thousand dollars from her father's estate towards its purchase.[22] Wasting no time, Abby took a quick and firm hand, dispatching Mr. Hosmer to Worcester to negotiate the deal as soon as her brother and cousin approved it. Bronson believed the dwelling, which they named Hillside, was large enough to accommodate two families, and he proposed to convert a wheelwright shop into a cottage for Junius, to whom he repeated his strongly held position, "I will not abide in a house set apart for myself and family alone."[23] Abby knew Hillside to be only barely big enough for her own family of six, but she had no objection to Junius living elsewhere on the property. She respected her brother-in-law's manual skills and his "spiritual exaltation" and wrote him herself, expressing the hope that he would consent to join them in "a domestic community founded on the principle of self support, love, and labor."[24]

Abby knew that she would soon be separated from her own brother by several hundred miles, for Sam May had been called to the pastorate of the Unitarian church in Syracuse, New York. She wrote Hannah Robie that she felt much "commotion" in having to part with "that best of brothers;"[25] but in her diary, she stoically stated her determination to turn this latest loss into personal growth. "It is well ordered that we should be gently and gradually loosened from those ties to the past which may impede the onward movement. I have lost much in early dear friends, but I have gained more independence on myself."[26] Sam moved just as Abby was confronting the task of furnishing Hillside, so she was able to borrow some chairs, a settee, a pine bureau, an oval table, and a bedstead. For Bronson's use in modifying and repairing Hillside, she requested Sam's spare tools, while she begged the boon of a few books for herself, volumes out of fashion at the moment but loved by her "as old friends"[27] - Johnson, Pope, and Bunyan. Both the Mays and the Alcotts were in their new homes by April, and Abby urged Sam to visit, reminding him that he would find neither flesh nor fowl at their table, but he would be welcomed by "free, happy spirits and grateful souls, ready to do you homage for all you have been to them and all you are in yourself."[28]

The move to Hillside coincided with Abby's customary springtime euphoria, a seasonal optimism which, for once, did not wilt in the heat of summer. In fact, the first two years of their two and a half year occupancy were relatively free of anxiety. Bronson's desire for a consociate family came to naught for want of recruits. The girls - fourteen, twelve, ten, and five years of age during the summer of 1845 - were old enough to appreciate their relative security, young enough to relish the simple pleasures afforded by country life and their own high spirits. It was an idyllic time for them, abundant in companionship with one another and with their parents, an era immortalized twenty-five years later by Louisa, in *Little Women*. Though never the rather too perfect, placid Marmee depicted by Louisa, Abby, while at Hillside, did find a modicum of tranquility. With most of her worries at bay for a time, she could, at last, nurture her children in a stable environment, encourage their talents, and participate fully in their recreations.

Neither Abby nor Bronson had changed in essence, but harmony prevailed in the relative absence of debt, failure, and ultraism. Bronson resigned himself to the conviction that a heaven such as he envisioned was possible only in his mind. Perfection on earth was not to be, so he would lead a solitary life in the belief that his personal existence was immaterial. As Abby expressed it to Sam, "The Unseen and Eternal is [sic] his care and hope."[29] He could converse comfortably on philosophical topics with Emerson and Thoreau, but, having been scoffed at by the world and betrayed by friends, he patiently awaited the hour when intolerance and prejudice would crucify him. In order to avoid the sight of the "petty traffic" of the townspeople who passed by on their "mundane... brutish"[30] errands, he planned to screen his dwelling from the road with a row of trees.

Abby, always more of the world than Bronson, determined to acknowledge its existence but at the same time stand apart from and morally above it. She complained to Hannah Robie about Concordians who felt it their right to satisfy curiosity by means of social calls. Nonetheless, no matter how selfish the villagers' motives in claiming rites of hospitality, she would be hospitable. Though she admitted to imperfections in her own nature, consciousness of personal virtue was at the heart of her comments on eliminating them. "It will be no slight task to ravel out threads of these [foibles] which have become woven into my own web of life. If I cannot do this I will destroy the whole fabric and begin again on a different scheme."[31] Whatever the fabric, the pattern remained the same and, in reality, she was not dissatisfied with it. Her human frailties, she was certain, were as nothing in the light of her moral superiority. "Nothing makes one so indifferent to the sins and mosquito-thrusts of life," she said, "as the consciousness of being morally invulnerable."[32] Today, her words leave an unfavorable impression of smug arrogance; but taken in the context of an era in which both church and society explicitly exhorted women to be moral models for their children, her statement simply reflects the truth that she did live every day in generous simplicity and unselfishness.

It was with this sense of being in the right that Abby continued to justify her requests for money. When Sam approved the purchase of Hillside, he also arranged with family members to give her an annual stipend of two hundred and fifty dollars, enabling her to "commence this year free from debt or any embarrassment of a pecuniary nature."[33] As early as February, however, she had to ask her nephew, Hamilton Willis, for one hundred dollars, not to mention smaller sums from other relatives, amounts which she said were trifles to them but everything to her. In June, Miss Robie sent her ten dollars for flour, apples, and potatoes, and Abby adopted a new attitude towards dependency. Asking for assistance had become her employment, she said, the means by which she earned a living for her family.  She was becoming skilled at it, less embarrassed to do it, and didn't hesitate when it became necessary to ask cousin Sam for help with the costs of repairs and renovations at Hillside.  Since there was no need to remodel the old wheelwright shop into a cottage for Junius, they planned to convert part of it to a bath-house in which a system of weights and pulleys was so designed that "even Elizabeth can give herself a bath without help."[34]

Lizzie's journal for 1846 supplements those of her parents in depicting Alcott family life at Hillside.  Out of door activities were of primary importance, and her entries need no dates to indicate the time of year in which they were written.  The gathering of violets, dande-lions, lilacs, daisies, and bright colored leaves sufficiently indicated the progression of seasons.  Lizzie went to the woods in a horse and cart with her father, to search out spruce and larch trees suitable for trans-planting; and, "smiling on everything as if love was as cheap as dirt,"[35] she joined him in the planting of his beans and corn.  Bronson helped Abby plant flowers in new beds by the dooryard; and when he and she set out six apple trees by the garden walk, "the little ones came down to see us," wrote Bronson.  He felt such humble acts served mankind as much as did public activity, and he saw in the setting of trees the equiv-alent of teaching his children, "these human shoots."[36]

Their girls' education remained of the utmost importance to the Alcotts and became as much a part of family living as it was a matter of formal teaching.  They valued well stocked and inquisitive minds, and Bronson conducted conversations after breakfast and supper, provoking ideas and stimulating thought.  The parlor at Hillside bore an unmistak-able air of refinement with its leather bound books, carefully chosen engravings, and parian marble busts.  Bronson was as patrician as ever in appearance and attitude, and Abby wore her heritage with a confi-dence which no amount of hardship could disguise.  She now had a keyboard instrument, a seraphine, which allowed her to give lessons to the three older girls and to accompany the family's daily singing.  "Mu-sic," she said, "is too powerful an agent in domestic life to be neglected."[37]  She, Anna, and Louisa, while sewing of an evening, continued their practice of reading novels aloud to one another, analyz-ing intricacies of plot and character, discussing new ideas for the family theatricals which gave their neighbors and themselves so much pleasure.  Lizzie entertained Abba with *The Arabian Nights, Oliver*

*Twist,* and *Swiss Family Robinson* when the two weren't playing "going to Boston" or dressing up as fine ladies and "having a ball." Anna was old enough to teach these two younger sisters in Bronson's stead when he was kept outside by the demands and pleasures of working in his garden. Though Louisa helped Anna in the classroom, she was as much interested in propelling her charges down the hallway in a wheelbarrow as she was in giving lessons.

There was formal instruction for all of the girls, of course, and it began even before the family was thoroughly settled into Hillside. Heedless of previous experience, Abby invited into her home a teacher from the Northampton community, Miss Sophia Ford, hoping that Miss Ford and Bronson could attract enough paying scholars to keep the family in fuel and clothing. Unfortunately, students were not forthcoming. Miss Ford lived at Hillside only a few months, teaching the Alcott and Emerson children mathematics, geography, drawing, poetry. Anna showed a flair for French, and the younger children read from William Russell's *Primary Reader.* The unruly Louisa loved solitude as heartily as activity and spent quiet, profitable hours composing poetry and reading. Miss Ford was a demanding teacher, and Louisa found it easiest to keep herself in hand when instruction was given out of doors. After a botany lesson in the woods, she observed in her diary that *there* she was able to be good. Following her mother's advice, she was attempting to understand herself better by means of introspective entries. When Abby left her a note, "Hope, and keep busy, dear daughter, and in all perplexity or trouble come freely to your Mother," Louisa replied that she would do so, "for you are the best woman in the world."[38]

Louisa's escape into books led her, in her thirteenth year, to devour Charles Dickens and Sir Walter Scott and to find her way to Plato through *Philothea,* a work by her mother's good friend, Lydia Maria Child. She reflected the influence of both her parents when she chose to copy into her journal, from *Philothea,* a passage by Plato, which posited "everlasting harmony between the soul of man and the invisible forms of creation.... flowers are the angel's alphabet whereby they write on hills and fields mysterious and beautiful lessons for us to feel and learn."[39] There was high thinking going on at Hillside during the summer of 1845, and increasing tension as well, for in August Charles Lane left the Shakers and took up temporary residence with the Alcotts. Abby wrote Sam that Lane was quiet and gentle and seemed saddened by something. His reunion with Bronson was "quite affecting,"[40] but she was made anxious by his presence. Now there were two alien forces in the house, two outsiders seeking to influence and instruct her children. Lane reintroduced the Socratic method of teaching by question and answer, and Louisa recorded some samples of their lessons, Lane as Socrates, she as the disciple, Alcibiades. "How gain love? By gentleness. What is gentleness? Kindness, patience, and care for other people's feelings. Who has it? Father and Anna. Who means to have it? Louisa, if she can."[41]

Abby's natural inclinations still led her to be more indulgent than otherwise with her girls, with the result that Concordians considered them "dreadfull [sic] wild people."[42] She allowed them to climb trees and run freely across fields, believing there was healthy release in physical activity and knowing that Louisa, especially, needed such release. Needless to say, she did not condone irresponsible or selfish behavior in her girls and made it a practice to look into their diaries in a desire to help them over rough spots in their lives and to give them guidance. She recognized that Louisa's creative writing was a "safety valve to her smothered sorrow which might otherwise consume her young and tender heart."[43] Louisa's sorrow was her inability to curb her temper. Abby knew that she was making a great effort "to obtain self possession and repose,"[44] and she did Sophia Ford the justice of acknowledging the woman's favorable influence upon Louisa. Not only did Miss Ford teach botany in the woods, she joined the girls in sloshing across Flint's Pond, from which expedition they all came home wet and muddy, and in Louisa's words, "bawling and singing like crazy folks." Despite the fun, Louisa felt Miss Ford was "particular"[45] in the classroom. Abby, also, felt an increasing unrest under her constant, competing presence, a malaise reminiscent of life shared with Elizabeth Peabody in Boston and with Ann Page at Fruitlands. When Miss Ford announced that she would leave by winter if no more pupils were found, Abby had mixed feelings. She reiterated her own unsuitability for "associative life," but she also expressed disappointment that her children would no longer be under the "influence, and habits, and the lofty integrity of her [Miss Ford's] character." Only her sincere respect for Sophia Ford's rectitude avoided acrimony between the two during a frank discussion of Abby's tendencies towards permissive child rearing. Abby acknowledged some truth in Miss Ford's observation that she would be ill advised to take other children into her home when her own were "such faulty specimens of parental impotence;" but when Miss Ford charged that Abby was desultory and her girls indolent, she responded that Miss Ford was not a mother herself and could know little of the intangibles of a mother's love. If she was not doing right by her girls, why did they give her their unfaltering trust? If she had betrayed this trust, how could it have been so "unerringly sustained?"[46]

Abby was not without an effective means of improving her children's behavior, but it was subtle, anticipating later theories of behavior modification and positive reinforcement. When Louisa was obedient to her parents, kind to Anna, patient to baby, Abby wrote little complimentary notes in her diary. Bronson, too, gave credit where it was due but was equally ready to mete out punishment for misdemeanors, making little Abba read from her slate before joining the family at dinner because she had absented herself from the schoolroom, insisting that Louisa eat altogether apart from the others when she did not put forth enough effort in her journal writing. In disciplinary practices, he and Abby were almost as far apart now has they had been when the children were toddlers, but she supported him when she deemed his punishments appropriate and deserved. "My Louy," she wrote, "I was grieved at your selfish behavior this morning, but also greatly pleased to find you bore so meekly Father's reproof for it.... It is not to be expected that children should always do right; but oh, how lovely to see a child penitent and patient when the passion is over."[47] She accompanied the fine sentiment with some very practical advice. When anger is ascendant, walk or read, but do not talk. Bronson, in his infant diaries, had noted the differences in the personalities of his children and was serenely confident that he could bring Louisa's headstrong tendencies under his control through education. As she grew into adolescence, however, he was forced to revise his theories, writing in his journal, "I once thought all minds in childhood much the same, and that in education lay the power of calling these forth into something of a common accomplishment. But now I see that character is more of a nature than of acquirement."[48] Character was one thing, talent another. Louisa's talent was unmistakable, and both parents recognized and encouraged it.

Birthdays were occasions on which to resanctify family, to give one another gifts regardless of whose birthday it was. When Louisa turned fourteen, her father gave her a book into which he had neatly copied her original poetry. Abby gave Bronson half a ream of paper, and he gave her a rocking chair and also a gold pen in tacit acknowledgment that she possessed a talent which exceeded the mere need to record events and exchange information. Abby was not reticent in admitting her facility with words, commenting that she was no angel, "never aspired to any kind of pinion but a goose quill," but was "very apt to flap that about while there is anybody who cares to see my flight."[49] Her prose was superior to her verse, but the girls were always delighted with her rhymed birthday offerings. Accompanying the gift of a pen for Louisa was a poem which Abby began with the lines, "Oh! may this pen your muse inspire/When wrapt in pure poetic fire."[50] Her birthday note admonished Louisa to use the pen worthily and to aspire towards the formation of character, the *re*formation of habits. Industry, patience, and love would enable her to satisfy her yearning nature and give her peace. Louisa's temperament, Abby told her, was "a peculiar one, and there are few or none who can intelligently help you."[51] Her mother was one of those few.

Abby and her daughter were indeed allies, too much alike in Bronson's eyes, more apt to provoke than accommodate him. "Count thyself divinely tasked," he wrote, "if in thy self or thy family thou hast a devil or two to plague and try thy prowess... Two Devils, as yet, I am not quite divine enough to vanquish - the mother fiend and her daughter." A startling statement but not as extreme as it appears if Odell Shepard, in *The Journals of Bronson Alcott*, is correct in stating that the words "devil" and "fiend" were not used maliciously by Alcott, but rather referred "to persons who seemed to exist primarily for the discipline of the virtuous."[52] If Shepard's premise is valid, Abby would have been justified in using an equivalent epithet about Bronson; for each plagued the other, and by their own lights both were virtuous. But it was she, not he, who did the bending; she, not he who bore the responsibility for their future. She admired his perpetual repose of mind but was frustrated by it. She saw him absorbed in his garden, absorbed in his philosophy, able to keep the two separate and be content, whereas she could not detach her idealistic yearnings from her need for security. Unable to reconcile the two, one intruded upon the other and burdened her with constant malaise. Louisa sensed this in her

mother and was aware of Abby's growing disappointment in her "arrangements for life."[53] In a touching turnabout, daughter wrote mother
a poem of consolation in the early autumn of 1845. Friends and family
had felt free to visit ever since their move to Hillside, and Abby was
contending with both Sophia Ford and Charles Lane in actual residence. Like her mother, Louisa was "dismal" and wished "we [the
Alcotts] could be together, and no one else."[54]

> God comfort thee dear mother
>     For sorrow sad and deep
> Is lying heavy on thy heart
>     And this hath made thee weep.
>
> There is a Father o'er us, mother,
>     Who orders for the best
> And peace shall come ere long, mother,
>     And dwell within thy breast.
>
> Then let us journey onward, mother,
>     And trustfully abide
> The coming forth of good or ill
>     Whatever may betide.[55]

More good than ill soon befell when Sophia Ford and Charles Lane
departed, he to Graham House, a vegetarian establishment in New York
City, she only as far as the Emersons', where she continued to teach
Lizzie and Abba along with little Ellen and Edith Emerson. Miss Ford
often walked the Alcott girls back home to Hillside and continued to be
intimate with the family, the differences with Abby not being so acri-
monious as to have caused an irrevocable rift. Charles Lane was neither missed nor encouraged to return, though return he did for a few
days the following summer. He was not unaware that Abby's feelings
towards him remained the same as they had been at Dove Cottage and
at Fruitlands. She made it very clear that he was not welcome. His
feelings towards her were also unchanged. "Alcott," he said, "kept his
garden clear of weeds and Mrs. Alcott kept the house clear of all
intruders."[56] Unfortunately, intruders who paid had to be looked upon
in a different light. When Miss Robie proposed that Abby take in as a

boarder a fifteen year old retarded girl, Eliza Stearns, she felt compelled to accept as the sum offered, four dollars a week, was badly
needed to supplement the little Bronson earned by chopping firewood.

Abby knew Bronson's "gentle, persevering discipline" would serve
the child well; and she instinctively included Eliza in the warmth of the
family circle despite the fact that she was "in a state of sad mental
imbecility," an irresponsible being who, "like a young child, must be
gradually developed into love, usefulness, and happiness." Asking
innumerable questions and requiring patient answers, Eliza took from
Abby precious time which she would have preferred to spend in pursuits with her own children. She resigned herself and took some comfort in believing her ministrations were helpful, writing Sam, "if by
faithful care of this bewildered child we can make her path more sunny
and straight, I shall be well repaid for the sacrifice of personal comfort."[57] Eliza remained with them for almost two years, at the beginning of which time Abby took a brief but active part in the anti-slavery
movement and at the end of which she took a job as matron of a water
cure spa. The former, significantly, was within the confines of her own
home and a success; the latter was apart from her family and a failure.
In December of 1846 and for much of January and February, 1847,
Hillside was a station on the underground railroad. A runaway slave,
whom they referred to as John, lived with them during that time. He
rose at dawn to chop wood, undiscovered, in the safety of early wintery
mornings. Abby also rose betimes to give him his breakfast and was
rewarded, on the last day of December, "by meeting God. The interview," she wrote in her diary, "was short but real."[58]

Abby was not in danger of becoming apathetic on social issues, but
except for the few months' refuge she furnished John, she did not know
what she could do other than keep as informed as possible. Expanded
anti-slavery activity on her part was not feasible, given her commitment
to family. In an introspective frame of mind, she began to consider the
distinction between being and doing. She could not *do* for abolition,
but neither was she *doing* for her family; she was merely *being*.
Henceforward, she would actively attempt to support them. "I must
think action here is a duty. Contemplation is necessary to recruit and
adjust, but doing is coextensive with being."[59] Accordingly, she
announced to Sam, "I have taken the ship into my own command."
Bronson was becoming restless but believed that venturing out of his
seclusion would inevitably involve him in discomfort or conflict, an

apprehension borne out when Horace Mann refused to let him speak at a teachers' conference held in Concord, because "his political opinions were esteemed hostile to the existence of the state."[60] Abby was earning a few dollars by boarding two of the teachers attending the meeting, and she was looking for children to board in the summer, in addition to Eliza Stearns. In keeping with her resolution to *do*, she said she would "gladly take a subordinate place in some institution if I could thereby see my children provided for justly and happily sustained without any anxiety or distrust."[61] Bronson felt he would be safe only in a hut on Walden Pond, with beans, and books, and peace, but Abby, continuing her nautical metaphor, "had rather sail on the vast ocean of life in a well trimmed ship than anchor myself on the shores of a lake."[62]

Inasmuch as she kept meticulous accounts, she knew the state of her pocketbook down to the last penny. She saw the way to no further economies since she was already having to manage "without many things which we really need as common comforts."[63] They were in debt two hundred dollars, had neither money nor credit and, worst of all, the girls were aware of the situation and "wretched at our predicament."[64] Anna, scholarly and somewhat experienced in teaching, having instructed her siblings and the Emerson girls, volunteered to accept the invitation of her cousin, Elizabeth Willis Wells, to live with her in Walpole, New Hampshire, and take a school there. Abby was uneasy but knew that Anna had "a great deal of resolution and exemplary patience,"[65] that there was, in any case, no choice. Though the Alcotts needed the money, and though Abby had always said she wanted her girls to have trades, this move would separate family members from one another. An alternative might be to "combine our various gifts,"[66] her own for literature, Anna's for languages, and Elizabeth's for music, in order to open a school of their own. The notion was unrealistic but she was desperate to "do as other people do,"[67] to support themselves without constant appeal to friends for help. She was concerned about Louisa whom she felt required "retirement, agreeable occupation, and protective provident care about her. She has most decided views of life and duty. And nothing can exceed the strength of her attachments, particularly for her mother. She reads a great deal. Her memory is quite peculiar and remarkably tenacious."[68] Unable to fit Louisa's talent for writing into the family school proposal, she actually took steps to arrange painting lessons, for which Hannah Robie agreed to pay, so that Louisa could decorate and sell boxes and articles of papier mache. In this farfetched scheme, Abby was less than her usual, practical self, and it came to nought. Abba May was the gifted artist of the family, still too young to contribute to the Alcott sinking fund.

In the midst of Abby's earnest efforts to engage her girls in keeping the family afloat, Bronson offered an unwelcome view. "Make no arrangements for them. The place or work will come when they are prepared. Anna no sooner was ready than the niche she could best fit was provided without any effort of ours - a little domestic school."[69] His insistence that Providence would provide put Abby out of patience but did not deter her from seeking solutions, knowing as she did that he would "yield to any plan of mine. He is so helpless as things now are."[70] Astonishingly, she hit upon a communal scheme involving her brother Charles, his wife, and baby. She proposed that he sell his house, come to live with them, and invest one hundred and fifty dollars in "livestock" - cow, pig, chickens, doves - which would make them more self sufficient. Charles had more sense than to accept, and when he declined, there seemed no choice but to sell Hillside. If they could not remodel their life there, they must abandon it. Autumn crops had to be brought in before Abby could turn her attention to reclaiming the interior of the house, which was in such a shabby state that no sensible buyer would make an offer until repairs were made. As the squash and pumpkins began to ripen, Bronson chose to immerse himself in building a rustic bower, a sylvan temple of willow and other supple woods, for his friend Emerson. This left it to his wife to bring in the harvest while at the same time discharging her duties as homemaker and securing the services of carpenter, painter, and walldraper. As a consequence, her comments carried more bite than usual and, though written to Sam, did not escape her husband's knowledge. After God made the animals and declared them good, she said, He created woman merely to satisfy Adam's fancy for a companion, pronouncing no benediction upon her but, rather, a tacit curse. She has, therefore, always been an indefinable medley of good and evil, angel and devil. "I think God is a little ashamed of this piece of his handiwork and therefore takes little account of us. We owe man a grudge for desiring us and then caring so little for providing for us."[71]

When Bronson collected Abby's journals and letters after her death, he laboriously copied page after page, often interspersing her writings with letters and documents of his own. In retrospect, pondering whether he had been sufficiently attentive to his obligations, he inserted at the end of the material for 1847 a rough draft of his thoughts on the matter. "Was it from some defect of character I have not aimed to acquire a livelihood for the sake of [living] either for myself or my family?" He had become aware, too late, that he could earn a modest competency through lecturing. By 1847, he had met with no such success. Had he but known that he possessed gifts which would allow him to pursue the aims of his life without compromising his ideals, he would have "delighted in the fruit." Acknowledging that his wife had become "worn and aged with cares,"[72] he failed, even after her death, to acknowledge the true extent of his own responsibility.

Abby, having resolved to *do*, did. She put herself in touch with Dr. Samuel Gridley Howe, who proposed opening "an asylum for idiots,"[73] and she applied to Mr. Calvin Farrar for the position of matron at his new water cure spa in Waterford, Maine. She preferred the latter, having learned through Eliza Stearn's constant presence just how demanding it was to be in close proximity to the retarded. The thought of living apart from husband and children dismayed her and put her in the paradoxical position of having to consider leaving her family in order to save it. Anna was, of necessity, away in Walpole; and what with all the confusion attendant upon renovating Hillside, Abby had reluctantly sent Elizabeth to Miss Robie's for an indefinite stay. Abby accepted the need for Anna's absence but could no more tolerate Lizzie's than the quiet child could thrive away from her natural family. Fetching her homesick daughter home betimes, Abby was spared making a decision because Mr. Farrar was unable to recruit sufficient patients for the winter of 1848. There were strong arguments in favor of accepting when the time came, however. Abby had earlier expressed a willingness to take even a subordinate job in an institution if it paid well enough, but this was no menial position. She would be next in command to the director, and the proposed salary of five hundred dollars a year would free the family from debt. Hydropathy was familiar to her and acceptable, merely an extension of her own belief in cold water bathing. The spa offered a modified Graham diet and would be run in accordance with the homeopathic principles in which she believed.

While the offer pended, Abby practiced her own brand of medicine right in Concord, which "has been one great hospital for the past month. Sickness and death all about us." As she dispensed herbal teas, she railed against incompetent doctors practicing interventionist, allopathic medicine. In nursing a neighbors' family, she witnessed the confident, conflicting blustering of two doctors regarding the case of a small child.  One diagnosed disease of the brain, the other inflammation of the bowels, while "Death stood ready to quiet doubt and relieve the sufferer."[74]  She avowed that simple nursing at the early onset of symptoms, common sense, and mother wit could have saved the child's life and the mother's grief.  Nature was better than drugs, the effect of which were not thoroughly understood.  She was all too right in this judgment.  When Louisa contracted typhoid as a nurse in Washington during the Civil War, calomel was administered with the result that she suffered unnecessarily from the debilitating, long term effects of mercury poisoning.

Those who sought relief from water cures had no such dire diseases, certainly nothing contagious.  Hydropathy was a facet of the reform movement of the mid-nineteenth century, with a goal, according to the *Water-Cure Journal*, of universal health, virtue, and happiness.  To this end, water was consumed internally in great quantities and liberally applied to the skin in the form of soaks, showers, plunges, rubdowns, and even body wraps of linen strips which were kept wet for the purpose of drawing out impurities.  Abby decided to accept the matronage of the Waterford Water Spa on a three month's trial basis, beginning in May, 1848, rationalizing the separation from her family by convincing herself that she would doubtless be able to discover "its [Waterford's] capability to support me and my family if by uniting our purposes we could live by laboring here."[75]  Bronson had been offered a teaching position in conjunction with his wife's work and had already declined outright, but she hoped his objections could be overcome.  He was supportive of her, however, and wrote Anna that all were being stoic in the face of this disruption of family life.  "I honor the good Mother for this brave deed of hers, purchased at the cost of so many enjoyments, taking her from those whom she loves and has served so well, and whom she still loves and serves in the pains of absence....  Would that some Power as propitious might task my Gifts, and fill my hands too with work and my table with bread.  But 'tis not thus with me and I submit to the decrees of fate, till times and men discover and use me, as I would be used."[76]  He urged all to correspond regularly with "the dear woman"[77] and to write plainly so as to spare the poor eyesight with which she was perpetually afflicted.

Waterford, though isolated, wore a quiet village charm and sophistication not unlike that of both Concord and Walpole. The spa was on a lake, with magnificent views of New Hampshire's White Mountains and plenty of paths and trails for the walking which was very much a part of the hydropathic regimen. Emerson's aunt, Mary Emerson, passed her summers there, and Elizabeth Peabody proposed to go for the cure. Intellectual stimulation was a given, and Mr. Farrar, director, teetotaler, and abolitionist, espoused the causes important to Abby. She did not go to Waterford entirely alone, reluctant to leave little Abba at home and obligated to keep the care of Eliza Stearns under her direct supervision. She planned to have Eliza undergo the water cure although she had little confidence in its efficacy for the retarded. The three, weary upon arrival, were given a supper of applesauce, breads, and a simple cake, and then shown to their sleeping quarters, one large room with three beds. Mr. Farrar was kind to her and respectful, but after a few days' observation, she did not return the compliment. She felt him desultory and "without any fixed law of moral or physical discipline."[78] His establishment, she found, was sadly deficient in organization but, fortunately, he deferred everything to her. She prided herself on bringing order out of chaos, feeling her way quietly into the hearts and confidence of staff and patients alike, putting love and exalted thought into her labors. She awoke each morning to find herself "the bone, sinew, and great aorta of the water cure body."[79]

Soon established in a routine, she habitually did a day's work before breaking her fast. As always, early morning was a time of inspiration. Here in this scenic Alpine setting, God found her even as she sought Him and gave her "a cheerful heart for every duty, a quick wit for every emergency, a brave hand for every labor."[80] She rose at four a.m. to wrap Eliza in her wet sheet, then flew through the passageways to the baths for her own plunge, douche, or spray. Back again in her room, she dressed, then either looked out upon the lake, read, or wrote until five o'clock when she went to see that all was in order in the kitchen. From there she went to the breakfast room to see that the glasses were nicely cleaned and then on to the drawing room to arrange the books, sweep, and dust. At six o'clock, she unpacked Eliza from her sodden wrappings, awakened Abba, and set the two to walking the grounds or exercising on the piazza until breakfast, after which she gave out bed linen and supervised the removal of slops from the bedrooms. At eleven, she gave Eliza a dripping sheet and a washdown, then organized her to sew or clean, whichever was most pressing. Dinner was at half past noon. She found the scene at every meal to be a theater piece, so diverse were the guests' displays of character, notions, and opinions. In the early afternoon, Abby consulted with Mr. Farrar on dietary matters and saw to it that the patient's rooms were in order.[81] As the day waned, she could at last take Abba and Eliza on their favorite walk, a time to savor the sublimity of lake and mountains and to breathe the scent of fragrant fruit trees in glorious springtime blossom.

Pleased to be well accepted by people previously unknown to her and not a little buoyed in self-confidence as a consequence, she was nonetheless having second thoughts. She wrote Bronson within two weeks of her arrival, "I begin to wonder more at myself how I came to this decision to leave you. It is a great experiment on the heart and life of a family to sever it occasionally, make it bleed at every pore, reunite, heal, and live again." Though her action might serve to strengthen individual family members, she realized, also, that "the wholeness, unity, sacredness has been invaded." She began having dreams about those she had left in Concord - Elizabeth, crying for want of Abby's help with her music; Louisa, running down the lane, hair flying, bursting into tears as she screamed, "Mother, is it you?" Awaking from the dream, Abby was drenched in real tears of her own, "almost in a wet sheet but not packed."[82] Louisa was much on her mind, old enough, at almost sixteen, to have a trade but having none. In her mother's absence she left nothing undone for the comfort of her father and sister, but she was restless and unfocused. Elizabeth, Bronson reported, was "the tidiest of house maids"[83] and keeping up a good heart. In Waterford, while Abby agonized over the pros and cons of remaining there, she realized that she must at least return little Abba to Concord, where she would no longer be exposed to "sights and sounds which are disastrous to the innocence and purity of childhood."[84] Anna was the only one of her children about whom she was reasonably comfortable. "Her little school gives her agreeable employment, and she sees society at Cousin Elizabeth's which is favorable to the cultivation of her manners."[85] Manners, she told Anna, in concert with courage, truthful purpose, and reason would see her through the difficulties of life.

Bronson kept a miniature of Abby on his desk, where he could see it while dispatching news of household events and the fruits of his cogitations. To remind her of those remaining in Concord, Abby asked him to draw and send to her a sketch of Hillside, with likenesses of

Elizabeth and Louisa looking out of the window. He and she corresponded regularly, as they had done when he was away in England six years earlier and, now as then, distance served to smooth over differences. "Something better than has ever yet occurred for us must come of this separation," she wrote him. "Your letters are fresh and full, and breathe of early morning air, as well as moist [sic] with the dews of early affection. Despair is no paragraph in our chapter."[86] Taking a dispassionate view now that she was no longer the recipient of charity, she lauded his spirituality as "the best blessing of my life." Rereading the sermons of James Martineau, she found a passage which reconfirmed her defense of Bronson's idealism. God gives to some the honor of renown through work, *doing*, whereas to others, He gives the blessing of truly *being*, of living "simply to express themselves, to stand between heaven and earth, to mediate for our dull hearts, their life [sic] a soliloquy of love and aspiration."[87]

Before long, Bronson's letters to Waterford included messages from Abba, who was safely home again in Concord but who, indulged little lady that she was, missed her mother and cried from both jealousy and pique when her sisters received letters but she did not. Abba said she wished she could have remained at the spa, wrenching her mother's heart more than she knew, adding one more burden to this real life pilgrim's pack while Louisa, Lizzie, and Abba played at *Pilgrim's Progress*, climbing up the stairs from The City of Destruction to The Celestial City, journeying over their hillside "with script and staff and cockle-shells in their hats." Anna returned from Walpole in July and added her theatrical flair to more elaborate productions in the barn. As Louisa wrote in her later *Sketch of Childhood*, "We dramatized the fairy tales in great style. Our giant came tumbling off a loft when Jack cut down the squash-vine running up a ladder to represent the immortal bean."[88] In a more serious vein, Anna, now proficient in German as well as French and reading Krummacher's parables in the original, instructed Elizabeth in those languages and both Lizzie and Abba in arithmetic, geography, writing, and drawing. Having to imagine rather than participate in daily life at Hillside, their mother could no longer bear to live apart. Family remained the warp and the woof of her being, exerting its inexorable pull. She returned home at the conclusion of her three month's commitment to Mr. Farrar, vowing to keep the family together, refusing to let circumstances "sunder them apart."[89] Despair, she knew, was "paralysis of the soul"[90]

Early September brought "beautiful weather without, not so clear and benign within. Short means, long doubts." Bronson made application to teach at the district school but, in Abby's words, "a child is preferred." He was denied the position, ostensibly because he was not a church goer, but she believed it to be because he would have commanded too high a salary. Properly indignant that he should ask for bread and be given a stone, she railed against townspeople once again. "How destitute of sense and sentiment is this world of Concord, looking well to its pockets."[91] Neighbors complained that her husband would hold no job, but when he attempted to secure work for which he was well qualified, they refused him. As for his not going to church, she didn't hesitate to point out the failings of those who had left it to the Alcotts to give supper and lodging to an immigrant family which had recently been turned away by hypocritical Christians. Small wonder she still preferred to live without friends when friendships with such as these would cause her to compromise or abandon her principles. "I love friendship, but I am pledged to the [invincible] virtues of justice, punctuality, fidelity, and pity." Her disdain for the piety of those who were moved by Christ's teachings only on Sunday mornings moved beyond the confines of Concord when she began to look elsewhere for practical solutions to their poverty. "I apply for part of a house in Cambridge, thinking a small school can be obtained for Anna. I am advised that 'Mr. A's religious opinions are repugnant to the Christian world of Cambridge.' I suggest my willingness to become the matron of an idiot institution. I am warned of the prejudices the public entertains against my husband's theories. Indeed! Believing and practicing the folly of loving our neighbour as ourself; doing justice and loving mercy; truly we deserve to suffer."[92] Though Abby was a woman given to sarcasm as a defense, her words on this occasion were exceptionally bitter.

Her resilient spirit carried her through this personal Slough of Despond, enabling her to express hopeful resolve on her forty-eighth birthday. Determined not to allow the peace and joy of life to be destroyed by brooding and discontent any more than by poverty and slander, she wrote a prayer in her diary. "Let me dwell then as far as possible on the beautiful and true; try to live in less anxiety for means; trust more to unseen Providence; and do cheerfully with a hoping heart and willing hand what each day presents to be done."[93] Louisa gave her mother the gift of two collars and a poem.

Home! Home! hath a blessed sound
 Wherever I may be;
And the sunny hours of a happy youth
 Gaze gaily up to me.

Oh few there are in the great cold world
 Full as it is of woe,
Who have no place where love can dwell
 A home, however low.

To the most forlorn and friendless one
 Will some sweet image come,
Of gentle words and happy hearts
 A mother's love and - home.

There's not a flower in the fields
 No green leaves on the tree
I have nothing but my heart's best love
 Mother, to offer Thee.[94]

Poor though the Alcotts were, Abby was reassured by Louisa's verses that the love she had bestowed upon her family had taken deep root and would see them, together, through whatever might be in store.

# Chapter Six

---

## Sister of Charity

*They saw and felt that a genuine woman
stood down there among them like a sister, ready with head, heart, and hand to
help them help themselves; not offering
pity as an alms, but justice as a right.*

Christie Devon from *Work*
by Louisa May Alcott

As Abby approached her fiftieth year, she finally found an acceptable
way to earn the competency she sought for the support of her family.
The work was a logical extension of her charitable acts towards those
even more destitute than she, and it came about through the efforts of
Hannnah Robie. Abby wrote her from Hillside that, regardless of her
own poverty, she wanted to bestow charity as best she could, "for in
every influence where mercy goes out, grace is abundantly poured in....
If I cannot give new clothes to the destitute neighbor, I can patch the
old ones. If I cannot feed the children, I can wash them, which is
almost as essential to health."[1] As a result of her own benevolent
undertakings, Miss Robie was well aware of Boston's need for a
woman with Abby's skills and empathy and was able to find enough
sponsors to offer her a job as missionary to the poor at a salary of thirty
dollars a month. Abby accepted unhesitatingly and moved her family

to Dedham Street, Boston, in November, 1848, thus becoming a full-time, paid social worker, one of the first, if not the first, in the city. Now, having "long toiled for the oppressed,"[2] she was saddened only by the need to accept compensation for work she would so willingly have done for love.

Abby had always been a relentless critic of the ills of society and still blamed them upon the selfishness of individuals and institutions. Ironically, Bronson's utopian experiment failed because of the insistence of its members upon singular means and motives. After witnessing at first hand the divisiveness of self-interest, Abby looked more than ever to the natural family to foster cooperative behavior and to instill values. Her own family certainly confirmed the theory. Anna, serious and capable, put the family's well-being before a strong desire to become proficient in languages, going to work as a governess as soon as the Alcotts moved to Boston. Louisa did the household chores at Dedham Street until Lizzie took over, and then she and Anna taught students together, at home. Louisa remained restless, for all her willingness to help, and even at age sixteen dreamed of adding to the family income through writing. Hers was an active personality, said Abby. "I believe there are some natures too noble to curb, too lofty to bend. Of such is my Lu."[3] Now ages thirteen and eight, Lizzie and Abba had lessons with Elizabeth Peabody, who had a bookshop on West Street. Bronson let space next door for the purpose of giving conversations, which, to Abby's relief, paid his rent. On Monday evenings, she sometimes joined him there with his transcendentalist friends for a sort of soiree, but doing so gave her little pleasure. "I find myself less congenial in these higher harmonies and look on this banquet of beauty and exquisite elegance with incredulity."[4] Only when excluded from philosophical conversation, as at Fruitlands, did she feel any desire to participate. Discussion of society's ills was another matter, especially now that she was personally involved in trying to understand and remediate the problems of Boston's poor. Bronson had had his chance to translate his ideals into action. Now it was her turn as she attempted to convert social theory into practice.

The English socialist, Robert Owen, whom Bronson had met while abroad, paid the Alcotts an impromptu visit at Hillside shortly before Abby was asked to become missionary to the poor, or, as she preferred to be called, sister of charity. Owen engaged her interest immediately as his view of society's evils was much like her own. His elaborate terminology included disappointment of the affections, intemperance, pecuniary difficulties, disorganization, and religious perplexities.[5] Though personal prejudice against Irish immigrants and their Catholicism shadowed her tenure as missionary, she overcame it when dealing with the Irish on a personal basis and continued to preach, with a clear conscience, that love was the cornerstone of a society free from corruption. She urged that workers shun spirituous liquors and that employers pay fair wages. She proselytized for labor unions and advocated a district system for the distribution of aid. Truly a compassionate sister of charity, she told her employers, "My heart has always been pledged to the cause of the destitute and oppressed. Now my time shall be sacredly devoted to their relief."[6]

Rather than plunging into her work indiscriminately, Abby set herself the tasks of surveying the pattern of alms-giving in Boston and determining the overall situation of each family or individual who applied to her for aid. She soon realized that charity, being temporary and often degrading, was not the best means of relief. Lack of employment and inadequate wages were so obviously the root causes of poverty and crime that she determined, early on, to give high priority to finding jobs for the unemployed, remarking, "We do a good work when we clothe the poor, but a better one when we make the way easy for them to clothe themselves, the best when we so arrange society as to have no poor."[7] To accomplish this lofty goal she offered several solutions, not the least of which was her advocacy of "labor associations... to protect the masses from the cupidity of the speculator and capitalist."[8] She frequently used the word justice in this regard. Workers were free to demonstrate their solidarity and bring power to bear against unjust positions taken by employers. One of her clients, Mrs. Hummel, was unable to collect payment for sewing twelve coats because the customer disputed the bill, claiming the work was not well done. Abby knew for a certainty that the garments were perfectly well made and penned a diatribe in her diary, ending with a passionate, "When will the rights of the labourer be recognized."[9] Mrs. Hummel, on her own, had no recourse.

"Because some want so much," wrote Abby, "many cannot have [enough.]"[10] If workers could but share some small fraction of ownership in the factories which employed them, she believed that poverty would be reduced and that pride of ownership would be an incentive for workers to better themselves. She spoke on behalf of such a plan;

but knowing that factory owners were unwilling to see their profits diminished, she was aware that managerial self-interest would not be easily eradicated. In time, unions might succeed; a few benevolent capitalists might see the light. New movements, Abby knew, took root slowly, "breathed from individual to individual, from family to family.... At last a word is spoken, the right word in the right time and place, a word which appeals to the hearts of all.... A compact body is collected under one stand and a watchword is given, and every man knows his friend."[11]

One of the means by which ideas spread was through literature - newspapers, journals, books. She read the works of social theorists avidly and came upon a scheme by a Frenchman, Joseph DeGerando, who proposed that young women contribute thirty cents a month to a common fund in order to place girls of poor families into apprenticeship. Each contributor should take an interest in a specific girl and, as her sponsor, furnish her with such necessities as soap. Abby concurred. "I think we need in this city some such provisional arrangement to protect a large mass of young females unprovided for by any employment societies or charitable institutions, who become reckless or abandoned for want of that love and care which should provide for and protect them at this tender period of their lives."[12] Not to mince words, and she did not, prostitution was one of the evils with which she had to contend and with which she dealt compassionately. In answer to criticism that she was exposing her girls too directly to life's unsavory aspects, she replied, according to Louisa, "I can trust my daughters, and this is the best way to teach them how to shun these sins and comfort these sorrows. They cannot escape the knowledge of them; better gain this under their father's roof and their mother's care."[13] A girl of sixteen, just Louisa's age, was one of the outcasts Abby took into her home for a few days, asking, "Who will love and protect her from the sharks of lust that await to devour her last remnant of innocence, whose cloak of charity so ample or so warm that it will screen and save her. Let me try!" When told such an attempt was quixotic, Abby asserted that Christ himself was "the Don of Quixots" for ministering to sinners and prostitutes. He defied the multitude, and she would do no less. At the end of a week, she took the girl, Mary Ann Moore, to a home for "helpless, unprotected children"[14] on Albany Street, run by a woman with whom she agreed that sin which resulted from poverty was to be pitied and shown a tender mercy.

Abby's overview of Boston's charitable organizations led her to conclude that the word organization was ill used. City-wide refuges such as the one for wayward children on Albany Street were practical, she agreed, but for dispensing food, clothing, fuel, and medicines, she urged adoption of a neighborhood system, which would allow the missionary in each to know her clients intimately and offer dignity and compassion along with employment and aid. In presenting her case to officialdom, she pointed out that under a ward system fraud would be at a minimum and efficiency at a maximum. Although she had discovered as many as forty benevolent societies in Boston, it was clear that they were at cross purposes, subject to abuse, and inconvenient to charity workers and clients alike. In arguing her point, she offered a short but graphic narrative. "I see no propriety in the poor of Northampton Street seeking Deacon Grant of Cambridge Street for a note to Dr. Bowditch in Summer Street, or for a woman in Broad Street to get a recommendation from Groton Street to the President of the South Friends in Bedford Street for an order on Small, the grocer, who keeps above Dover Street.... Our Sisters of Charity get dog-weary with this nonsense. If they are not always as amiable as angels, it is because angels have wings and are not subject to old legs and new shoes."[15]

When Abby was hired by Hannah Robie and her friends, she was given little assurance that she would always have at hand the means with which to aid the poor once she found them. Although the ladies donated used clothing and petty cash, their offerings were insufficient. Abby found she had to knock on the doors of old acquaintances soliciting aid, not for herself now, but for others. A few of her relatives refused her because she did not attend church. "Alas!" she said, harping on the hypocrisy of the pious. "Every day finds me busy, yes, *spent* in doing my Father's will. His business alone occupies me."[16] She wore herself out searching for donations and clients alike. Word of mouth brought many of the destitute to her home with their requests for alms, but when they knocked at the door of 29 Dedham Street, one of the Alcott girls was likely to say her mother was out, traversing the city on this or that errand of mercy. Abby refused to tolerate such haphazard arrangements for long. She gathered her sponsors together and gave them an ultimatum. They must keep the purse adequately supplied and the charity basket overflowing. They must form committees to solicit orders for fuel, groceries, and medicines. Furthermore, they must meet with her monthly for a report on destitute visited and alms dispensed. Some of these reports were published in the *Christian Register*, but Abby complained, "Much of their pungency is lost by the retouches of the conservative editor."[17]  Small wonder her words were edited. She pulled no punches, especially later when she berated subsequent sponsors who failed to fulfill their responsibilities but who, nonetheless, had the gall to question her effectiveness.

So efficient was Abby, in fact, that she soon came to the notice of an established entity, the South Church Benevolent Society and Relief Fund, under the general direction of the Reverend Mr. Huntington. The women of its sewing circle asked her to superintend their charitable efforts at a salary of fifty dollars a month, the sum Abby told them was the very least she could accept and have any hope of supporting her family.  As it was, she knew herself well enough to realize that she would be all too apt "to encroach upon this private purse for public needs and uses.  I cannot always stop to count consequences when starvation and destitution is at my door wailing its want and pleading its necessities.  I must stop the wail with a slice from my own loaf."[18]  She expected the women to do no less, making so bold as to suggest that a few among them might "adopt" a poor family, teaching the mother household thriftiness, securing adequate employment for the father, inculcating in the children a habit of personal cleanliness. That was too much to ask, but at the end of March, 1849, they did secure for her a room on Washington Street, for the purpose of centralizing aid.  She still visited the poor in their homes, the destitute in their hovels; but her Relief Room was open at stated hours during which "the poor and rich could be put into communication... a kind of neutral ground, a receptacle for your surplus substance and a source from which your organized charities might flow."[19]  Benefactors could bring clothing or orders on grocers; clients could come to receive aid, give notice of need, and seek help in finding employment. There had been no action at City Hall with regard to a ward system, but that did not stop Abby from establishing a distribution center of her own.

Neighborhood cooperation remained one of her dominant themes. She worked with the poor as well as for them and looked for ways in which they could work for each other.  True to her conviction that cooperation was one means to a better society, she tried to reduce what she saw as destructive isolation of poor families by encouraging them to share.  To the woman with two wash tubs and one flat iron she said, in effect, go to your neighbor who has two flat irons but only one tub.

Put your resources together and you will both be the better for it. Every once in a while she found herself heartened by evidence that there were some Christians who obeyed Divine Law, which was love. A Methodist minister referred her to the Conant family, unnecessarily as it turned out. The husband, who had injured his hand, was not rehired because his employer had found a substitute for less pay. Parishioners rallied round, found temporary work for him, replenished the cupboard, clothed the child, and procured comforts for his wife, who was ill. Abby lauded these Methodists but recounted their beneficence as a prelude to chastising the ladies of the sewing circle. The Conants, she pointed out, were good; their neighbors were good. When the destitute were not good, when they had fallen into slovenly or evil ways, the ladies gave aid reluctantly, if at all. Abby objected strenuously to this unjust selectivity. "If we find destitution without sin as its cause or consequence, we should sympathise and relieve it. If we find poverty with sin as its cause and sorrow its result, we should pity and reform it, in all cases showing a tender but wise mercy."[20]

No matter the cause or result of their destitution, Abby emphasized the need to restore and maintain the dignity of the poor. In one of her early reports, she left no room for doubt as to exactly where she stood. "We may legislate in wisdom, we may multiply our charity schemes, but never until society looks upon poverty as an incident of Man's condition, not as a crime of his nature, shall we see any permanent or beautiful results from our laws or our alms-giving."[21] Finding jobs for the poor, supplying tools instead of alms, she insisted, would give them belief in their own power and dignity in the eyes of all. Rather than patch up and perpetuate inadequate conditions, help them find employment; before branding them as beggars, test them as laborers. The ladies of the South Church Sewing Circle continued to receive the full benefit of their missionary's passion and eloquence in her monthly reports. From her secular pulpit she went on to preach that despair paralyzed the heart just as surely as hunger starved the body. Give the poor hope; penetrate the secrets of their anxious hearts; replace their brooding with jobs. Knowing well the healing power of work and recalling the restorative powers of nature, she offered the ladies a unique analogy to make her point. "The sweat of the brow is to the Soul what dew is to green herbage."[22]

Abby empathized more with the poor than with the well-to-do but believed women of all classes were a potent moral force. Increasingly, she dealt with the females of families in her care, mothers whose responsibilities were in the home, daughters she hoped to influence for the good. The needle, she said, was the only tool by which she could obtain a subsistence. Who should know better than she! Believing that there was most contentment and least vice in poor families where the mother was a needle-woman, she began holding sewing classes in her home one afternoon a week; but when she circulated a petition for the introduction of sewing instruction into the public schools, the women she approached for signatures were less than enthusiastic. In a reprise of her old tune that the finery of the wealthy encouraged pettiness and often clothed selfishness, Abby branded these women as "equivocally polite" and "guilty of displaying more jewelry than brains."[23] Addressing the sewing circle in a monthly report, she was hardly less blunt when she complained that poor, underpaid young women were distorting their spines and ruining their eyes over delicate stitches for needless frills and furbelows. If the cost be their health, their wages were earned at too dear a price. A related matter was also much on Abby's mind. "Young, destitute girls," she said, "claim much of my time, all my sympathy." Would the ladies please refrain from giving inappropriate cast-off garments to the young women in their employ. In their ignorance, these girls flaunted themselves in imitation of their benefactors' inordinate attention to "Paris riggins," inviting trouble. In donning her mistress' hat, feathered with an ostrich plume, a young servant girl unwittingly wore a "flag of availability."[24]

While she was at it, Abby served up a diatribe against the literal and figurative cost of fashion in food. The rich ate red meat and white bread; the poor purchased them in imitation and at unnecessary expense, starving as much from lack of knowledge of what to eat as from lack of food itself. Teaching economy and nutrition became an integral part of Abby's service to her poor. The Graham diet with which she was so familiar became the basis of her instruction. Coarse bread cost little and was rich in nutrients; beans were inexpensive and a tasty substitute for meat. When she came across an article in the New York *Tribune* which expanded on this theme, she wrote the author and urged him to publish it as a tract, "so persuaded am I of its truth and utility." One section of the article gave her pause, however. She had entered into her work as a sister of charity without much baggage, but she carried a prejudice against oat meal, which well-to-do Bostonians felt was fit only for pigs and horses. She had to accept the logic of the article's author, however, as it echoed her own so exactly. He claimed that oat meal supplied the greatest nutriment for the least money and was a cheap food which needed only to be fashionable "to be extremely popular among all laborers, all of whom, to say nothing of other classes, eat too much fine flour bread."[25]

Abby took seriously her opportunity to promote healthy and moral living, not hesitating to speak her mind though it offend benefactors. She once refused to accept an order on a grocery store because the owner sold liquor. "The order for thirty dollars which Mr. Mayo so generously gave me, I could not conscientiously occupy, as it is one way I enter my protest against the use of spirituous liquors, not to patronize the seller." Traffic in ardent spirits, she said, was degrading to the vendor and destructive to the buyer. Having seen so much despair, poverty, and crime resulting from drink, she would never knowingly send anyone where it could be had. She added that health could be ravaged as much by the habit of filth as by that of drink, but cleanliness was easier to achieve than temperance. "I as often carry *soap* as *soup* to [the poor], so convinced I am that food goes to the hungry mouth with four-fold efficacy when carried by clean hands, and the floor that is frequently washed becomes hallowed ground, though trodden by unshod feet."[26]

In her own home, needless to say, Abby practiced what she preached with regard to temperance, cleanliness, and diet, but the family was cramped for space at Dedham Street, and she was only too glad to accept when Mrs. Savage offered them, rent free for the summer, her spacious Temple Place residence. Here Bronson isolated himself, feverishly writing his metaphysical work, *Tablets*, and here he suffered a debilitating apotheosis, succumbing to the intensity of the experience just as he had at Brick Ends in 1844. That Abby continued with her social work is evident from her reports, but neither diary entries nor letters to Sam remain to shed light on her state of mind. Bronson spent most of late summer and early fall recovering in Concord under the care of Mrs. Hosmer and her daughter, Sarah. He benefited from Emerson's attentiveness and, as his cough improved and his strength returned, he was further restored by long walks with Thoreau. Abby, immersed in her work, left the renewal of his health and sanity to these understanding friends, though she and the girls kept in touch by post and sent him clean shirts and sundries for his comfort. When at last he was able to sleep without seeing "goblins," he invited her to come to Concord. With touching perception which indicated awareness of her needs as well as his, he wrote, "Come, and leave that Poor Self, and the Poor creatures you enrich, for one clear day, before the winter's campaign opens to us both."[27]

Winter was on both their minds. Abby mused, "Shall our relief ship ride the winter ocean swift and joyous or shall we take in all sail, moor our hulk in some haven of selfish safety?"[28] Though the work of missionary was exacting a personal toll, her answer was to sail on. Taking stock on her birthday, she noted that the forty-nine years which had closed over her life left her "in a position of great responsibility and labour,"[29] in a job which was poorly understood. At the beginning of October she had moved her family to 12 Groton Street. More than ever, since there was space enough to accommodate a relief room, work was inseparable from life. In reply to a note from Louisa which "breathed in my office so softly, so sweetly," she assured her daughter that her words had not fallen on deaf ears or a cold heart. Her time was much occupied, she told Louisa, but doing for her children was the equivalent of doing for herself, so closely bound were they all. Their lives had changed, would change. "The [forward] tide of our existence takes us a little farther each day."[30] They must, all of them, sail on.

The Groton Street Relief Room was forward progress in Abby's eyes, a neighborhood model which might make "some of our sleeping partners [at City Hall] rouse themselves. I have been distressed and oppressed by their sluggishness."[31] Reiterating the advantages of centralized aid, she praised her room as an example of a place "where the Rich may freely send and the Poor confidingly go."[32] The poor did go, to the extent that she almost feared the relief room would become a retreat for the indolent. The rich did not send, not enough at any rate. Devoted to charitable work herself, she assumed the ladies of the sewing circle would assist her willingly, but their increasing apathy obliged her to resume soliciting aid herself. Worse, they were guilty of a haughtiness which demeaned and humiliated those poor coming legitimately for help. "The pauper at our gates," she told them, "asks for bread, and we pause to examine her credentials.... Let us approach them confidingly, not as dictators or givers of [alms] alone, not as spies on their household arrangements, nor let us carry any sense of superiority with us."[33] Treating the poor with too much severity and too little love reduced them to deception and denied them dignity. Finding them work, she reminded the ladies, would restore that dignity and eliminate the need for alms.

The broadside for the Groton Street Relief Room read "Best German, American, and well-recommended Irish help procured at shortest notice." Sharing the prejudice of her class against the Irish, Abby wanted to make it clear that she would be particularly selective in offering their services as maids, cooks, and seamstresses. She believed they could make something of themselves if only they would be industrious and careful of their wages, but their habits of improvidence and self-indulgence appeared irrevocably fixed. Equally dismaying in her view, Protestant charity was promoting Catholicism, which was not "a life-giving, soul-gaining religion of truth and love." She signed no petitions to admit additional immigrants, insisting that those who were already here must first be maintained. "Freighting a ship for starving Ireland," she warned, "warms our enthusiasm... but I fear we too often freight a basket for Cove Alley." As illustration she did not hesitate to include in her monthly report a comment that was as demeaning as any the ladies of the sewing circle could have uttered. After the potato rot in Ireland, she said, "We sent what we could spare from our cupboards and meal tubs over to them, but like mice they have followed on its trail and have come over to take cupboard, tub, and all. We are or soon shall be infested with the least desirable part of European population." Only when she turned from the general to the specific did she display the Christian charity she professed to have in such abundance. "I am accosted in the streets every day by those [Irish] who, having been driven by fear of famine or oppression, have gathered up their last fragment of earthly possession and find their way here for protection or employment. I cannot pass by. I must whisper a word of encouragement or hope to them.... Their life boat is drifting, a small rope may save it."[34]

Abby knew the Irish suffered; she knew their wants were "human and incident to our common nature;" but she expressed her uncharitable, not to say un-Christian, view in more than one report. Telling the ladies that she preferred blacks, she gratuitously added, "To me they are far more interesting than the God-invoking Irish, who choke with benedictions or crush you with curses." The colored, by contrast, "their very skin a cross," quietly bore the oppression heaped upon them by prejudice. The children of Sarah Hill, a destitute black client, were

excluded from public school because of their complexion. Uninte-
grated and uneducated, what was to become of such children? She
reminded the South Church ladies that Bronson had been forced to
leave Boston "despised and rejected of teachers, because he admitted a
girl of tawny skin into his school at Beach Street."[35] Each ward, she
insisted, should have a good school "for our colored brethren," but "disagreeable interviews at City Hall with principalities and powers"[36] were
no more effective in bringing about educational equality than they were
in promoting a district system of alms, distribution. She had achieved
the latter in her own ward, number eleven. All she could do regarding
education was, three evenings a week with Anna and Louisa, teach
adult negro women to read, write, and make out their bills for washing.

Poor Abby was beset from all sides. Officialdom was uncoopera-
tive; almoners were angry when she had no alms to give; the ladies of
South Church blamed her when it was they who failed to honor their
commitment to keep the purse and the sewing basket full. In her January report she pulled no punches, telling them, "I have had an abundance of censure from the rich, misrepresentation by the poor. Mine is
no enviable position." The following month she was angry to the point
of sarcasm. "I will interrupt your social enjoyment this evening as little
as possible, although I have allowed myself to feel a sort of right to
your attention on these occasions, as none other has been offered me to
communicate with most of you. Our relief room offers few attractions
and your Missionary's character I have lately heard was very good but
her manners not agreeable.... Shall I close the door for the next and last
month of our connexion, or may I hope to have the pleasure of occasionally welcoming you on its threshold?"[37] Neither chiding nor sarcasm brought results. Worse, Abby's faith in her ability to control
circumstances was badly undermined, and each defeat brought with it
further distress. In addition to the difficulties of procuring and distributing aid, she was wearing herself out by sitting long hours with the
sick and dying. Though grateful that she still had a "willing heart and
ready hand,"[38] she had to acknowledge that she was no longer able to
work effectively.

On a stormy night in early April, 1850, with but few present, Abby
read her final report. Frustration and fatigue were the immediate reasons for her resignation, but underlying all else was the unwillingness
of others to share her concern about the causes of poverty and crime.
She admitted it was hard for her, too, not to yield "to a morbid sympa-

thy with the symptoms of destitution and despair;" but even in the act of dispensing alms in answer to the question "What shall we do?" her thoughts were never far from "Why is it so?"[39] Her response to the latter remained lack of work and low wages. When feasible, she sought jobs for her clients, making a nuisance of herself if she thought the pay inadequate. For her, work was no longer possible. She was exhausted. When she told the ladies, "The winter is over but not gone. The spring has come but is not here,"[40] she was speaking as much of the bleakness within herself as that of nature without. "My embarrassments are insurmountable," she wrote in her diary, "and I feel I must push the family claim to its remotest argument." Though the peer in poverty of those she had so recently served, birth and education placed her in a position she could not put aside. Relatives must come to her aid.

Sam was in Boston the month she resigned. Were there not, she asked him, "superfluous means somewhere that can keep us where we belong?"[41] She knew he loved her too well to allow despair to overtake her, but what was she to do? Neither she nor Bronson would compromise their ideals. Both had found suitable work; both had failed because of "the false requisitions of society.... I make this appeal to you, my brother... what, where, how to do. We ask no man what or how we should be."[42] Kindred, including Sam, saw only that Bronson would not do as everybody else and support his family. Bronson countered with the statement, "No explanation can take the place of deeds in [others'] eyes, and I must stand for the time as a thriftless if not a heartless and incapable fellow. So let it seem; but let it not be so."[43] His wife and children, he assured Sam, knew he was not indifferent to their welfare. Whether through Sam's efforts or Abby's, temporary relief was forthcoming from such as felt compassion if not understanding. Cousin Sam Sewall and nephew Samuel Greele contributed cash. Brother Sam placed an order on Furbush, the grocer, for thirty dollars. Uncle Samuel May, her father's brother, offered them his mansion at Atkinson Street, rent free, while he and his family were away for the summer.

Just as Abby was beginning to regain health and hope, she exposed her family to smallpox by feeding some immigrants in the garden at Atkinson Street, leading to the subsequent illness of all the Alcotts. It almost seemed as though compassion were her fatal flaw and she the heroine of a Greek tragedy in which hubris played no small part. This proud woman had said, when Emerson's little son died of scarlatina in

1842, "I cannot offer sympathy to these dear suffering mothers, for I see so much culpable neglect of the means of living."[44]    Now, by choosing human compassion over maternal discretion, she put in jeopardy all she cared for most.    Bronson was severely stricken and she badly so, enough to write that she would "never forget the discomforts of such a sickness."[45]   The girls all succumbed, but with lighter cases. Abby's homeopathic medicine saw them through the various crises though, in Louisa's words, "We had a curious time of exile, danger, and trouble."[46]  Even Hannah Robie, dissuaded from visiting lest she carry contagion to others, would have been unable to cheer Abby, who, Bronson recorded, was "disconsolate and cannot be comforted."[47] Louisa often found her mother weeping, a circumstance which strengthened her determination to provide for her.  "She is a very brave, good woman, and my dream is to have a lovely, quiet home for her, with no debts or troubles to burden her."[48]  For the moment, Louisa had to be satisfied with earning what she could through teaching and sewing.

After "the small-pox summer," the Alcotts went to a rented house in High Street, bordering on a slum.  There Abby ran an employment agency "which grew out of her city missionary work and a desire to find places for good girls."[49]   She had opened her Ladies Help Exchange while still at Atkinson Street and simply moved it to High Street, offering herself as proof that work prevented destitution, if not poverty.   Several of her relatives took her to task for employment beneath her dignity; but she countered, "I have outlived the flummery of that.  If I did not think that I was eminently qualified to extend to the one the protection they need in this exacting and cruel world, and to the other the agency they require to place the best adapted to each family..., I should turn in disgust from an occupation which absorbs time, quiet, and domestic privacy."[50]  Operating the Ladies Help Exchange, she insisted, gave her dignity of the highest order.   Her agency was respected because she was honest and because she followed up placements to make certain that both employee and employer were well served.   While she found jobs for foreign and American women as cooks, maids, and seamstresses, she and the girls kept house without servants.  Lizzie was general housekeeper while Abba continued her schooling, and the two oldest girls took students in the parlor; but the combined earnings of Abby, Anna, and Louisa barely brought in enough to live on.  In Louisa's words, they were "poor as rats."[51]

Sam wrote his sister, "When I think of your trials, I am almost distracted for you. It seems very cold counsel to say hold on bravely and be of good cheer, but what else can I say. If you do not keep up your courage, all will be lost."[52] Doing for others always helped buoy Abba's spirits, and she was able to tell Sam that she had sent "twenty colored women to service in the country, where for the present they will be safe." She told him she might yet have to suffer the penalties of the law, but she was ready and willing. "There are higher laws, the infringements of which I fear more."[53] Her concern with earthly legality centered around the recently passed Fugitive Slave Law, under which the federal government approved the return to their owners of runaway slaves. Skin color put even freed slaves at risk, and the women Abby sent to the country were the safer for her doing so. In February, 1851 a slave by the name of Shadrach was caught under the act but was rescued, taken secretly to Concord, and sent to Canada on the underground railroad. During the trial of his rescuers, Abby noted that a turning point had been reached. Abolitionist ideas which had previously been controversial were now "strong conviction."[54]

Anti-slavery sentiments were in the ascendency as was advocacy of the rights of women. In a rare public act on behalf of female enfranchisement, Abby initiated a petition calling for equal participation in the framing of laws, demanding that the women of Massachusetts be allowed to vote on amendments to and alterations of the state constitution. There were seventy-three signatories to the document which read, in part,

> The People's authentic act of 1852 delegated power to this Convention to submit amendments and alterations of the Constitution to the people, in such a manner as they, the said Constitutional Convention, might see fit to direct. We note, in that act, first, that the alterations and amendments are to be submitted to the People, of which we claim to be a component part, and secondly, that your Honorable Body have full control over the manner in which the popular will is to be ascertained. We, therefore, women of Massachusetts as aforesaid, do respectfully request the Constitutional Convention now in session to ordain that, when the said amendments and alterations are submitted to the People for their ratification and adoption, all women, residents of the Commonwealth, who have attained the full age of twenty-one years, shall be entitled to vote on the same, and that their votes shall be counted as of equal value and potency with those of men. And we submit this request, in order that in case our power to govern ourselves shall be deemed to be transferred out

of our own hands, where it naturally belongs, it may be so transferred by
our consent and in order also that the government of the Commonwealth
may really be constituted by the consent of the governed.[55]

The petition was rejected, but Abby continued to harangue on the
subject of women as a component part of the People, telling all who
would listen that females had the right to think, to feel, and to live. She
wrote Sam, "I say to all the dear girls keep up, be something in yourself. Let the world feel at some stage of its diurnal revolution that you
are on its surface alive, not in its bowels a dead, decaying thing."[56] Her
own girls received the message from infancy. As adolescents and
adults they proved the worth of their mother's child rearing methods,
showing a skeptical world that they were not "dreadfull wild people."
Each found fulfillment in her own way, taught by Abby that the freedom to be an individual was a right limited only by moral constraints
and the law of love. For all her emphasis on family, she did not seek
her own fulfillment through her children, nor did she thwart their independence any more than she allowed her own to be thwarted. Though
fiery of temper and sharp of tongue, she set for them an example of
sacrifice and service which was not limited to her few years in the public eye as missionary to the poor and agent for their employment.

# Chapter Seven

## Marmee

*I'm not ambitious for a splendid fortune, a fashionable position, or a great name for my girls. If rank and money come with love and virtue, also, I should accept them gratefully, and enjoy your good fortune; but I know, by experience, how much genuine happiness can be had in a plain little house, where the daily bread is earned, and some privations give sweetness to the few pleasures.*

Marmee to Meg and Jo
from *Little Women*

Years of uncertainty and toil had aged Abby perceptibly. She wrote Sam that she was becoming corpulent and lethargic, that her days of service were numbered, but "when summoned I shall at least not be found rusty for lack of use."[1] Only her thick chestnut hair remained of her youth. Giving each of her girls a long strand for remembrance, she observed, "the gray hairs are insidiously stealing among them, these heralds of age, these autumn leaves of time."[2] She was ready to withdraw from the responsibility of supporting the family, and the family was but a few years short of being able to relieve her of her cares. In 1852, she sold the house in Concord, Hillside, to Nathaniel

Hawthorne and his wife, Sophia Peabody, thus enabling her to lease a large place on Boston's Pinckney Street. There she worked at keeping a boarding house for almost three years, claiming never to have laboured so much to so little purpose. "We are gaining nothing by this large family, but shall scarce pay for extra salt in the various porridges for daily use."[3] Bronson was having more success than she. Honored by Harvard College with an invitation to give a series of lectures on modern life, he was also about to go on the first of several trips, mostly remunerative, to give conversations in the "West" - Cincinnati, Cleveland, Buffalo, Rochester, Syracuse. In November, 1853, he wrote to tell Abby, whom he called his "scarce believing comforter," that a draft for one hundred dollars was on the way. "I wish it were millions and as opulent as her generosities have been for these long years past to me and mine."[4]

Syracuse was an important stop on Bronson's itinerary, for Anna was teaching there under the patronage of Sam May. Thoughts of the resulting family reunion comforted Abby, who wrote them a letter from Bronson's study, where "manuscripts stand like sentries to guard the consecrated spot."[5]   She missed Bronson and feared for Anna, who was unwell and whose "affectionate nature leads her to dwell too much on absent people."[6]   Separation was a way of life for the Alcotts from mid-century on, the girls grown up and often away from home, Bronson traveling for months at a time. Once Abby wrote him, "Where are you? So quiet, so hush about your doings and movings. Pray make a dot somewhere on your journey that we may know you are really measuring geographical miles, and not clean gone out of time and space."[7] His lapse was an exception. Correspondence amongst family members was prolific, informative, and loving, and letters were either copied or sent round from one to another. Abby was both a real and a symbolic unifying presence, interacting all the more with events in the lives of her husband and children as they relieved her of the need to support them. Mother became Marmee and, with the publication of *Little Women*, Marmee became the idealization of nineteenth century motherhood. Abby knew that separations were inevitable, that future brought chance, that time brought change, but she told the girls she was ready to share their trials and progress. Letters and love would "chain the bond closer as we are distanced, and chance will find us invulnerable to her worst decrees."[8]

Inasmuch as her four girls had survived childhood, death was a separation Abby no longer dwelt upon. Lizzie, sometimes called Beth, was always Abby's "home child."[9] Never robust, her contribution to the family was light housekeeping, when able. During the summer of 1853, her health was so poor that she had to pass the month of August in the country with Willis relatives in Walpole, New Hampshire. From there, she wrote her mother a very private letter, not to be shared. Walpole, she said, was a dream come true, a beautiful place in which she had time to enjoy herself and do as she liked. She was feeling so much better that she had begun to sew again, trying to be of use. "You can't think, dearest Mother, how wicked I feel when I think of the time I have been wasting here.... Oh, if my blessed worn out mother and the dear toiling sisters at home could only rejoice with me in the quiet and beauty of this lovely spot, how happy I should be. I hope there is a good time coming, when all my dear 'pathetic family' may be at rest and enjoy the happiness which will be all the sweeter for being so long strived for. I wonder if poor people don't love each other better than rich ones, who have no sorrows and troubles to bind them to one another. I am sure I love my home and family better for every struggle and trial I share with them, and my joys are always sweeter when I have them to rejoice with me."[10]

Lizzie did not contract her fatal illness until three years later, and Anna was not yet engaged although five years older than the age at which Meg March, her fictional counterpart in *Little Women*, became betrothed. Abby feared that both Anna and Lizzie were oppressed by the uncertainty in their lives, while she believed that Louisa, like Jo March, was capable of meeting whatever destiny had in store. Abba, now called May at her request, did not make personal sacrifices to the extent that Anna and Louisa did, being the youngest and much petted. She was not quite as preoccupied with fun and fine gowns as the fictional Amy March, however. She studied at the Bowdoin School to become a teacher until it became evident that she was a gifted artist, a "little Raphael," as the family called her. May eventually added to the family income by taking art students of her own and by painting decorative objects, pot-boilers, she called them, the equivalent of the melodramatic tales Louisa wrote for ready money. *Flower Fables* was Louisa's first book, published when she was twenty-two and presented to her mother on December 25, 1854. Abby copied the accompanying note into her journal. "Into your Christmas stocking I have placed the

first fruits of my little talent, knowing that you will accept it with all its
faults and look upon it merely as an earnest of what I may yet do, for
with so much to cheer me on I hope to pass in time from fairies and
folks to men and realities."[11]    All the birthday pens and encouraging
notes from mother to daughter were bearing fruit very sweet to both.

Family theatricals, encouraged by their mother from the time the
girls were little, gave Louisa another outlet for her creativity, one not
limited to home, for she took an intense interest in Boston theater.
Home, in any case, was more a matter of the heart than the dwelling
from the mid-fifties onward.  Sacred in its essence, a cathedral for family loves and hopes, Abby remained at its center and created a haven
for the others to return to.  Orchard House, in Concord, was the home
Marmee presided over in real life, but two years in Walpole preceded
the Alcotts' return to Concord and saw the beginning of Lizzie's final
decline.  Fact furnished Louisa with material for that saddest of chap-
ters, the death of Beth.  In the summer of 1855, Abby, exhausted and
eager to escape Boston, gratefully accepted Benjamin Willis' offer of a
house in Walpole.  There she and Lizzie remained while Anna, Louisa,
May, and Bronson came and went as required by their teaching, writing, studying, or lecturing.  The second summer, Lizzie came down
with scarlet fever, caught from some poor children to whom Abby was
ministering.  Already in poor health, Lizzie was unable to regain her
strength and was still convalescing a year later.  Abby found some
solace, even occasional joy, as spring's divine "Artist Cultivator" made
beauty and order out of Walpole's winter chaos, giving to hills and
fields "a radiant touch like a fine enamel."[12]  But as Lizzie continued to
decline, Abby's concern intensified, and she began to devote herself
almost exclusively to her home child.

In August she took her to the shore at Lynn, Massachusetts, hoping
the sea air would revitalize her.  At first, this experiment with salt water
bathing restored some color and animation to Lizzie's emaciated form;
but the weather turned raw and rainy, and after the first week she lan-
guished without improvement.  Doctors called in for consultations did
nothing but confirm Abby's long-held belief that there was no such
thing as a science of medicine.  It was but one "prolonged guess."  The
physicians could not agree as to whether Lizzie's affliction were of the
lungs or of the brain.  The only consensus was that she should return to
"the comforts of home and the society of her family."  Abby, at least,
had gained needed physical and spiritual strength from the stay at the

seashore. Nature, as always, revived her and enabled her to carry on. She wrote Sam that her anxiety subsided "before the immensity of ocean, the grandeur of the rocks, the serenity and sublimity of the starlit heavens."[13]  Supreme law manifested itself through its beauty and order, its love and power, and she would submit to its decrees.

A return to Concord seemed best, although Abby would have welcomed any practical alternative. She had previously found there neither happiness nor prosperity. "Concord again receives us," she wrote, "I hope under better auspices than before. They cannot well be worse. Hope on!"[14]  The Alcotts decided to purchase the house next door to their former home, Hillside, and rented half a house near the center of town while renovating their new place, Orchard House. Abby made the comment, "Our life has been a migratory one for the past twenty years, but repose must come even if we take it in "Sleepy Hollow."[15]  This cemetery, wooded and peaceful, was not to be her final resting place for another twenty years, but it became her daughter's before winter was truly over. Lizzie vacillated between forced cheerfulness and "unutterable distress;"[16] but for a while, Abby deluded herself that she was gaining on her illness and even spoke of housing some of the participants expected in Concord for an anti-slavery meeting, "depending on my baby."[17]  The most recent medical opinion pronounced Lizzie's disorder to be "atrophy or consumption of the nervous system, with great development of hysteria."[18]  She was, in fact, much agitated by the doctor's presence and wept all the time he was there. Abby, Anna, Louisa, and May took care of Lizzie in turns, and occasionally Louisa carried her downstairs; but by mid-January Dr. Geist told them that Lizzy's case was hopeless, and her bedroom became the center of the family circle. Abby sent for Bronson, who was in Cleveland, and wrote Sam, "I can lay no purer offering on the alter of the Lord than this gentle spirit."[19]

On Sunday, March 14, 1858, Abby wrote in her diary, "Elizabeth passed quietly into Shadow Land." Her account of Lizzie's passing is every bit as poignant as Louisa's of Beth in *Little Women*. The death watch began on Friday evening when she asked her father to take her into his lap and wanted to know whether all were gathered about her. Upon being reassured that they were, she asked to have the window open, breathed hard, and said, "Oh heavenly air." On Saturday she was uneasy, begging for morphine and ether, rousing towards midnight to say, "Well now, Mother, I go, I go.  How beautiful everything is tonight." Lizzie lingered until three in the morning, and Abby described her passing immediately, while the peacefulness of the scene obscured the earthly import of the loss. "She kept up a little inaudible monologue till 1 o'clock, when a shade passed over her face and a light vapour seemed to pass over her head and dissolve into the air. I said, 'This is the spirit passing off.' The shadow was the angel of death veiling the mortal while it puts on the spiritual. What a moment. I said in my heart, 'Fold her, Oh God! in thine arms and let her henceforth be a messenger of love between our human hearts and thee.'"[20] Together, Abby and Bronson sat with her departed form, trying to find solace in the lesson that they all were "wiser for her life, holier for her death."[21]

Abby was no longer a churchgoer, but she believed in God and in a life hereafter. Lizzie died during Lent, and in an image both secular and religious Abby wrote Sam, "It has been an intense Lent, a long Passion week. May the stone be rolled from this grave of my affections that I may live."[22] Louisa wrote that her mother often sat, thereafter, in Lizzie's empty chamber, "trying to believe that she shall never hear Lizzie's voice again or see her dear face on the pillow."[23] Monday, the day after her death, the Reverend Mr. Huntington came to Concord to read the funeral service. The loving hands of Waldo Emerson, Henry Thoreau, Frank Sanborn, and John Pratt carried the coffin across the threshold and placed it in the carriage which bore her remains to Sleepy Hollow. Abby always observed the anniversary of her death and termed it "the inexplicable trial of my life."[24] After moving the family into Orchard House that summer, she went to the cemetery with votive offerings of violets and roses and wept "that her gentle presence is not among us to grace and enjoy this beautiful home."[25]

Orchard House became the happy place depicted by Louisa in *Little Women*. Many of the sisters' experiences while at Hillside were incorporated into the novel, though family theatricals were a common thread which bound their interrupted Concord life into the book's seamless whole. Anna, Louisa, and May began to call their mother Marmee just as did Meg, Jo, and Amy March. In depicting her as placid as well as practical and charitable, Louisa had for her model the woman Abby became once insecurity no longer threatened. There was a sense of fun at Orchard House. Of an evening, if Louisa had no family play in rehearsal, there might be literary games or charades, often with the Hawthorne family from next door. The composition of nonsense rhymes led to general jollity, sometimes at the expense of the subject. Nathaniel Hawthorne wrote this of Bronson.

> There dwelt a Sage at Apple-Slump,
>     Whose dinner never made him plump;
> Give him carrots, potatoes, squash, parsnips and peas,
> Some boiled macaroni without any cheese,
> And a plate of raw apples to hold on his knees,
> And a glass of sweet cider, to wash down all these,
> And he'd prate of the Spirit as long as you'd please,
>     This airy Sage of Apple-Slump.[26]

Reminiscing about a visit to Orchard House, Lydia Maria Child concurred with those who found Bronson's philosophical meanderings unintelligible, specifically his *Orphic Sayings*, but she praised his architectural taste, writing:

> When they bought the place, the house was so very old, that it was thrown into the bargain, with the supposition that it was fit for nothing but fire-wood. But Mr. Alcott... let every old rafter and beam stay in its place; changed old ovens and ash-holes into Saxon-arched alcoves; and added a wash-woman's shanty to the rear. The result is a house full of queer nooks and corners, and all manner of juttings in and out... The capable Alcott-daughters painted and papered the interior themselves. And gradually the artist-daughter filed up all the nooks and corners with pannels [sic] on which she had painted birds, or flowers; and over the open fire-places she painted mottoes in ancient English characters. Owls blink at you and faces peep from the most unexpected places.[27]

Activity, joy, and love filled Orchard House, helping Abby accept, though not forget, the loss of Lizzie.

Less than a month after her sister's death, Anna announced her engagement to John Pratt, son of Minot Pratt, once a resident of the Brook Farm community. Here was yet another loss of sorts because, as Abby admitted, Anna had seemed theirs exclusively; but she was prepared to let all her daughters follow their natural bents, and Anna, she knew, had "a large love nature."[28] Her affections were free from selfishness, and therein lay the key to contented conjugal relations. The Alcotts had long known the Pratts, and Abby knew John to be kind and of unimpeachable character. When Anna accepted his hand, he was working for his uncle, a flour merchant on Central Wharf in Boston, so there was also the promise that she would be well provided for. Abby indulged "the pleasant little conceit of Anna's"[29] that she be married on the anniversary of her mother's wedding, so on May 23, 1860, Sam May performed the ceremony, just as he had for his sister thirty years before. May relatives gave the bride a gift of money "so that Anna takes forty dollars in gold for her dower as well as a legion of virtues with which to bless her husband."[30] Anna wore silver-gray silk with John's favorite flower, lily of the valley, tucked into her bosom and hair. Abby pressed a fragrant stem into her diary and wrote that she hoped her daughter would "find herself fully possessed of the strength, endurance, all abiding love, to meet the exigencies and aspirations of wedded life."[31] None of Abby's journal fragments about the wedding offer commentary on her thirty years of marriage to Bronson, but later entries attest to her continuing love for him, and earlier entries well document her endurance to meet the unique exigencies of their relationship.

Anna wrote her mother a letter on "the last day when in the eye of the world I am Annie Alcott," assuring Abby that she would always consider herself "your Annie as long as I keep myself good enough to deserve the name of daughter to so excellent a mother."[32] The couple went to live in Chelsea, Massachusetts, and Abby made haste to visit in order to satisfy herself that all was cosy and in good order. Reassured that John's business prospects were good, with a salary of six hundred dollars a year from Taylor and Co., and that Anna's habits of economy and prudence would keep spending within their means, Abby returned to Orchard House satisfied but lonely. Lizzie was gone forever. Anna was in a home of her own. May planned to go to Syracuse to teach as Anna had done before her, for she felt she could earn more for the family there than in Concord. Louisa was often in Boston; but Bronson, to Abby's pride and pleasure, had been appointed Superintendent of Schools in Concord and had ceased traveling for a time. His return to everyday aspects of education pleased her as much as the town's recognition, for she still loved the man more than the philosopher. An earlier portrait of him, recently retouched by the artist, Carolyn Hildreth, emphasized his asceticism whereas the original had depicted him as he was and as she wished him to be, dressed simply and in keeping with "the severe simplicity and rectitude of his life." Mrs. Hildreth did the unacceptable when she made him appear "rapt seer and prophet" more than husband and father by draping a mantle about his shoulders and softening the background "as if moonlight had cast a shadow," touching him with divinity. The artist appeared to have "worked with the down from an angel's wing rather than with a crayon."[33] Abby preferred the crayon.

Bronson was not the only Alcott to have "risen a peg or two"[34] in the eyes of Concord. Abby wrote Sam that both Louisa and May were acknowledged as artists, the one with words, the other with pencil and paint. A story by Louisa, "Love and Self Love," was published by the prestigious *Atlantic Monthly* in 1860, prompting Abby to comment that Louisa's previous successes with short fiction for newspapers had "matured her powers for this last [latest], best effort." She felt that Louisa had a remarkable ability to depict everyday scenes and ordinary people, though perhaps her shades were "a little too dark," her lights "too rosy." Later, in annotating her mother's diary, Louisa wrote the words "good criticism."[35] As proud of May as of Louisa, Abby was, nonetheless, objective in her comments about both daughters, observing that May had talent, if not genius. "The former perceives what is already revealed. Genius reveals."[36] Both Abby and Louisa wanted May to have every opportunity to nurture her talent; and eventually, once Louisa had provided for Marmee's comfort, she was able to assure her sister of professional training abroad. In 1860, it was Hannah Robie who offered to pay for drawing lessons. "How generous this woman has ever been to me and mine," wrote Abby. "Helping most cheerfully at the right time and right place."[37]

Abby remained the hub of her family as private and public events circled about her. Abolition and women's rights were two issues in which she retained a keen interest, though she rarely took an active part. The abolitionist, John Brown, was convicted of treason and hung in December, 1859, following his raid on the arsenal at Harper's Ferry. In her diary for December 31, Abby wrote, "The last day of the year. It seems to close with the obsequies so usual to the interment of the dead; the white shroud which nature has prepared for the remains of the old year.... John Brown's martyrdom has perhaps been the event of 1859. The Confederacy is shaken to its foundation.... The hour and the man both came at last to reveal to the South their sin and to the slaves their saviour."[38] Brown had spent time with Concord's abolitionists. Abby and Bronson had been impressed with his courage and "readiness to strike a blow for freedom,"[39] so it was natural that they should welcome his family after his trial and hanging and that Abby, who scoffed at ordinary social functions, should hold a reception for his widow. The following year, John Brown's daughters, Anne and Sarah, ages seventeen and fourteen, boarded for a time with the Alcotts. The Civil War was raging by then and Abby celebrated her sixty-first birthday with unaccustomed solemnity. The usual exchange of tokens and poems took place amidst sewing and knitting for Union soldiers. At the conclusion of the war, after General Lee surrendered to General Grant at Appomattox, she annotated her journal with a comment which indicated she knew the job was not yet finished. "Now if the laws can protect civil rights then peace will indeed prevail throughout this troubled nation."[40]

Louisa had been in Washington as an army nurse, leaving Concord in December, 1862. Abby, though aware of the dangers, bore her departure bravely. Had she not, Louisa might well have changed her mind. The two were tearful at their final embrace, and Louisa almost lost her courage, calling out, "Shall I stay?" "No, go!" answered Abby, "and the Lord be with you."[41] After four weeks of unsanitary conditions and overwork, Louisa fell critically ill with typhoid-pneumonia and had to be brought back home by her father. He, Abby, and May nursed her through three weeks of delirium and a lengthy convalescence. It was not until the end of March that she was able to leave her sick room. Abby was enormously relieved, not only by Louisa's improving health, but also by good news from Anna. On the evening of March 28, 1863, Bronson arrived home from Boston in a snowstorm and burst open the door of Orchard House to announce the birth of Frederick Alcott Pratt. Louisa and May poured out questions. Marmee wept and smiled and kept saying, "I must go right down and see that baby."[42] Anna's second child, John Sewall Pratt, was born just over two years later. These two grandsons were all the more precious to Abby since she still quietly mourned the loss, at his birth, of her own baby boy.

Louisa was seldom completely well after the typhoid contracted while an army nurse. Years later Abby feared that illness might be "the bitter drop in this cup overflowing with success."[43] Louisa's health was permanently undermined by the effects of mercury poisoning, the result of being dosed with calomel while sick in Washington. She turned her experiences with the wounded and dying soldiers to good advantage, however, by writing the poignant volume, *Hospital Sketches*. When negotiating the contract with her publisher, she told him she devoted her earnings to the care of her parents, "for one possesses no gift for money making and the other is now too old to work any longer for those who are happy and able to work for her."[44] Abby's gratitude for the comforts Louisa provided mingled with pride in her maturing talent, and she predicted that Louisa would become a respected author. It might take many years, "but she will have no mean rank assigned her now. She is in the vestibule of the temple, but the high altar is not far off."[45]

As her means made her more independent, Louisa often chose to live in Boston, where her work would not be interrupted; but whenever Abby took one of her "sick-turns,"[46] Louisa left her desk to care for Marmee. Two of the novels, *Work* and *Moods*, required reworking over long periods of time, and the writing of both was occasionally disrupted by Abby's illnesses. Each woman was concerned about the other, and Abby worried that the intensity with which Louisa was working might further damage her health. When Louisa was living at Orchard House and Abby able, she brought her daughter "cordial cups of tea,"[47] fretted because she wouldn't eat, and sewed her a silk cap with a red bow like the one Jo March wore while "scribbling." Louisa dedicated *Moods*, her "first romance," to her mother and in the letter accompanying the gift copy, Louisa wrote that she would be satisfied if the novel made a little money, "and you in some measure repaid for all the sympathy help and love that have done so much for me in these hard years. I hope Success will sweeten me and make me what I long to become more than a great writer - a good daughter.[48] While Abby appreciated the tone and intent of the note, she felt that Louisa's powers were greater than she knew and hoped that public acclaim would help her realize the full extent of her capabilities.

Part one of *Little Women* was published in October, 1868, fulfilling the expectations of the mother and allaying the doubts of the daughter, though Louisa denied that an exceptional talent had created the March family. "The characters," she said, "were drawn from life, which gives them whatever merit they possess; for I find it impossible to invent anything half so true or touching as the simple facts with which every day life supplies me."[49] After the birthday breakfast Bronson escorted his wife to her big red chair in the study, Freddy and Johnny Pratt blowing little trumpets and prancing before them. Anna, Louisa, and May marched behind, "glad to see the dear old mother better and able to enjoy our little fete." Louisa knew that time was altering "the ener-getic, enthusiastic home-mother into a gentle, feeble old woman, to be cherished and helped tenderly down the long hill she has climbed so bravely with her many burdens."[50] Part two of *Little Women* was pub-lished the following April, and Abby prophetically declared that Louisa had developed the four girls' various fates so truly that the book would see "permanent value and increasing demand."[51] The first part, she said, left off as the four sisters were endeavoring to do something use-ful with their lives. In the second part, the March girls' futures were not precisely those of the Alcott models, but the Marmee of both the fictional and the real families took pride in daughters who had grown up as she wished, contributing to the improvement of society, each in her own way.

Because poor health now prohibited exertion, Abby had unaccus-tomed leisure time. She passed many hours rereading her journals, and her new entries expressed a slowly evolving contentment. Still fond of analogies, she compared the family's journey through time to a voyage, all of them in the same boat. Her "log book," her diary, took on value for them all, she wrote, "tho not very accurately kept by the pilot."[52] Their boat had been much buffeted about by adverse winds and rough tides, but as she neared port the skies were more serene, the gales gen-tler. Louisa, whose steady hand was now on the helm, commented, "I never expect to see the strong, energetic 'marmee' of old times, but, thank the Lord, she is still here though pale and weak, quiet and sad. All her fine hair gone and face full of wrinkles, bowed back and every sign of age. Life has been so hard for her and she so brave, so glad to spend herself for others."[53] During her final years, Abby had the rare ability to accept necessary care with good grace. She wrote that "im-paired health and defective sight"[54] compelled her to consider herself, but she did so with a concern for others which lessened the burden for all. The love she had bestowed on her family came back a hundred fold, and her girls embodied all the virtues of womanhood she had sought to instill. Anna was competent and content as wife and mother and, from time to time, took her parents into her home when it was deemed best to close Orchard House. May was sensible despite her love of pretty things, an accomplished artist and loving daughter. Louisa fulfilled her dream for Marmee, who now could sit in a pleasant room with neither work, nor care, nor poverty to worry her, though social issues still captured her attention.

Women's suffrage roused her to express something of her old fire and indignation. On April 19, 1875, Concord celebrated the centennial of the battle which began the American Revolution. All Abby's former feistiness returned as she drew a parallel between the colonists' protest against taxation without representation and women's current disenfranchisement. Into her diary she entered a vigorous protest. Women must claim and secure their rights, she said, even unto defying the government that withheld them. Louisa went to the speakers' tent that day, only to discover that no arrangements had been made for ladies. She was able to report justice of sorts to her mother, however, for the speakers' platform collapsed. Abby retorted that the men should not have left out the women's suffrage plank. The Woman Suffrage Association was planning a convention for Concord the following month, and in anticipation of it Abby compiled a list of the one hundred Concord women who paid taxes, not one of whom was allowed to vote. A recently published pamphlet showed that one tenth of all revenue from property taxes in the Commonwealth of Massachusetts was paid by women. Taxing them without giving them the privilege of voting was not only alarming, it was "a gross injustice of the system" and "contrary to the spirit and letter of the Constitution." Abby wanted wives, mothers, and daughters to protest, to petition, "to clamour for the right of suffrage."[55]

In *Little Women*, Marmee declared, "Don't shut yourself up in a bandbox because you are a woman, but understand what is going on, and educate yourself to take your part in the world's work, for it all affects you and yours." Abby could well have spoken those words herself and would have added that taking part in the world's work imposed responsibility and reason. Her values never wavered, but she no longer supported the nineteenth century ethos which ordained that men and women orbit in separate but equal spheres. Those spheres, she now saw, were not equal; society had condemned women to a subordinate role. Moving forward with the times, she rejected the beliefs that women should understand but not act upon issues, that they should send sons but not daughters into the affairs of the world. She urged females to forward their own emancipation and insisted, "They must help make the laws, be educated as jurists, doctors, divines, artists, bankers. It will occupy and give dignity to their minds and lives."[56] Anna chose the life which suited her, that of homemaker in the nineteenth century tradition, and Abby rejoiced in this choice for this daughter. Louisa and May disliked "conventional fetters."[57] Their careers spoke to Abby's vision.

May did some fine original work, but she was best known for her reproductions of J.M.W. Turner, called by the British art critic, John Ruskin, the best that had ever been done. Whenever she was in Europe to study and paint, she wrote Marmee faithfully and was sure to include delightful sketches of the sights. Reluctantly, fearing her mother might die during her absence, she set sail for the Continent in the autumn of 1876. The following spring a jubilant May wrote, "Sing for joy, dear Marmee."[58] She had been honored by the hanging of a still life at the prestigious Paris Salon. A little sisterly rivalry prompted further comment from May. "Who would have imagined such good fortune, and so strong a proof that Lu does not monopolize all the Alcott talent. Ha! ha! sister, this is the first feather plucked from your cap."[59] She sent home a portrait of herself by a friend, Rose Peckham, which Abby proclaimed an exact likeness, though she did have one reservation. May was wearing a hat which Abby found much too fashionable, too suggestive of the artificial trappings of Paris society. She would have much preferred May's pretty blue velvet snood.

In her letters, May described people and places, cities and countryside, knowing that her mother would enjoy pouring over the details. A ride in a shady glade "full of ferns, Solomon's seal, and field flowers"[60] reminded May of the woods at home, walks with Marmee, cups of tea taken together on a rustic bench of Father's design. May had been happy in Concord, and Abby now found it more to her liking as villagers recognized the worth of her husband and daughters. The town was sanctified for her by the fact that Lizzie's remains were buried in Sleepy Hollow, and she wished her own to be placed beside her. Abby believed it of little consequence where the body was finally laid, for all is dust. "Yet," she said, "I must own a preference to the final resting-place; to rest among our kindred is a desirable thing to look forward to, even if we are insensible to the fact. After that the birds of the air, the dews from heaven, the Stars above us, even the snows of winter, are beautiful to contemplate as our companions in their seasons. The daisies will not forget to smile above me, and the sweet clouds of heaven moisten their throats with tender rain."[61]

Ill with heart disease and soon to join Lizzie, Abby declared herself prepared to be patient as the infirmities of age impaired her faculties. Her life, she said, had been filled with trials she found hard to accept and was not prepared for. Condemnation of Bronson had been even harder to bear than poverty. She perceived herself as having been impulsive but not vindictive as she "writhed under the injustice of society;"[62] but she rejoiced, at last, to see her "grand, strong women established in life on their own merits and capabilities,"[63] and Bronson, her "dear old man,"[64] achieving success with his writings and conversations. "The world," she wrote, "must acknowledge and honor him, for his efforts to improve it and advance the best interests of education and morality, temperance and free religion."[65] For her part, she had done her best. God was just and would punish or forgive as He saw fit.

In September, 1877, Louisa wrote in her journal, "Marmee had a very ill turn, and the doctor told me it was the beginning of the end." Fluid in her lungs, a result of heart disease, was causing Abby much suffering and she "longed to go."[66] She asked Louy to stay by her and wrote May a good-bye to which she responded from Paris, "My Dear Marmee, Your little note nearly broke my heart, not to be there with my arms round your neck when you are so ill."[67] Bronson, called to Concord from his childhood home in Wolcott, wrote May that she could not hope to see her mother alive even if she sailed immediately. Trying to soothe her mind he added, "The dear patient is patience itself, every virtue that shone during her active life, now burns the more brightly during her weakness. Not many daughters have been blessed with a mother so unselfish and so noble."[68] At Abby's urgent insistence, Louisa moved her into Anna's new home, the old Thoreau house, where she died at twilight on November 25. It was a peaceful end. She waved good-bye to a little picture of May and said to Bronson, "You are laying a very soft pillow for me to go to sleep on." Thinking herself a girl again, she called Louisa "Mother" and smiled, saying "A smile is as good as a prayer."[69]

After a simple funeral service, Abby was laid to rest next to Lizzie. William Lloyd Garrison was among those who spoke, and he remarked that when he first went to Boston in 1830, to lecture against slavery, the only three people to stay afterwards and express interest were Bronson Alcott, Sam Sewall, and Sam May. Now, after forty seven years, all but Sam May, who died in 1871, were gathered to mourn Abby, who had so staunchly supported their cause. No less was she an advocate for all suffering fellow creatures. Lydia Maria Child commented that Abby, though absorbed in her family's welfare, "was always prompt to help in righting wrongs and alleviating sufferings. These dispositions were, indeed, an inheritance. No one is surprised to find any member of the May family habitually right-minded and kindly, because everybody knows they cannot help it."[70]

In *Little Women*, Louisa immortalized her mother's goodness for all the world to read; but in a journal entry following an autumn visit to Sleepy Hollow, she recalled that goodness privately and succinctly with imagery from nature not unlike that of her mother. Asters rather than daisies smiled above the grave, pines sang overhead, and red-leaved blackberry vines trailed over the mound and about the little white stone at its head. "Among the tall grass over her breast a little bird had made a nest. Empty now, but a pretty symbol of the refuge that tender bosom always was for feeble and sweet things."[71]

# Notes

## Chapter 1: Marriage

1. "I was the youngest of..." Autobiography, AMA Fragments.

2. " 'To be good is to be happy'..." Joseph May to Abigail May, Sept. 6, 1811, Memoir AMA. (Until her marriage, the notes will refer to Abigail May as AM rather than Abigail May Alcott, AMA.)

3. "strangers" AM to Joseph May, May 4, 1818, Memoir AMA.

4. "My mother's most striking trait... She loved the doing..." Memoir AMA.

5. "Firm in the Christian faith..." AMA Fragments.

6. "He led a useful..." Memoir AMA.

7. "spared no expense..." Thomas J. Mumford, *Memoir of Samuel Joseph May* (Boston: Roberts Brothers, 1873), 22.

8. "Nothing is of unimportance..." SJM to AM, August 14, 1815, Memoir AMA.

9. "With a little practice... You must forgive..." Louisa May to AM, July 5, 1816, Memoir AMA.

10. "in trifling occupation... made me a new being..." AM to her parents, Oct.10, 1819, Memoir AMA.

11. "I may yet..." AM to Eliza May Willis, July, 1819, Memoir AMA.

12. "a good shake of the hand" AM to Joseph May, Jan. 13, 1819, Memoir AMA.

13. "My mind, character, and feelings..." AM to her parents, March 25, 1819, Memoir AMA.

14. "Should [I] not succeed..." Memoir AMA.

15. "[Haste] is a great waste..." SJM to AM, June 13, 1819, Memoir AMA.

16. "Cheerfulness is..." SJM to AM, May 29, 1819, Memoir AMA.

17. "demons" SJM to AM, June 13, 1819, Memoir AMA.

18. "allowed to refuse visiting" through "Philosophy activates..." AM to her parents, Oct. 10, 1819, Memoir AMA.

19. "a full statement..." AM to Joseph May, June 13, 1825, Memoir AMA.

20.. "unbecoming the father... in a whisper... My father..." AM to Thomas May, October 9, 1826, Memoir AMA.

21. "Children, until within..." Diary, April, 1829, Memoir AMA.

22. "the defects of our Common Schools..." SJM, "An Address to the Normal Association," Bridgewater, Mass., August 8, 1855. Madelon Bedell, *The Alcotts* (New York: Clarkson N. Potter, Inc., 1980), 344.

23. "The child is the book." Odell Shepard, ed., *The Journals of Bronson Alcott* (Boston: Little, Brown and Company, 1938), 12.

24. "It is not the string of names..." ABA MS Journal, March 17, 1828.

25. "at once felt... I have never..." Mumford, *Memoir SJM*, 122-123.

26. "moral health..." through "divine agents..." AM to ABA, Sept. 16, 1827, Memoir AMA.

27. "It would add much..." through "I shall pass..." AM to ABA, July 16, 1827, Memoir AMA.

28. "a friend... I went into... might have been more familiar..." Aug. 5, 1828, Memoir AMA.

29. "There was nothing..." Shepard, *Journals*, 12.

30. "I cared for nobody..." April 20, 1829, Memoir AMA.

31. "I have been conquered..." AMA Fragments, 1828-1829.

32. "strange infatuation..." through "tender, holy interest and affection." Aug. 5, 1828, Memoir AMA. Her summary of this tumultuous period is all to be found in this single, long diary entry.

33. "I am engaged..." through "I have something to love..." AM to SJM, August, 1828, Family Letters, 1828-1861.

34. "moral mentor..." through "is the most interesting..." AMA Fragments, 1828-1829.

35. "expect no more... to be decided... He must approve..." Aug. 5, 1828, Memoir AMA.

36. "pride of opinion..." through "It shall become tame..." April 20, 1829, Memoir AMA.

37. "He has delicately sketched..." AMA Fragments, 1828-1829.

38. "I burst into tears... I seemed not to have..." AM to ABA, June 10, 1829, Memoir AMA.

39. "the greatest affliction... Human wisdom..." AMA Fragments.

40. "It shall be discharged..." April 20, 1829, Memoir AMA.

41. "nearer and dearer..." AM to Lucretia May, Jan. 30, 1829, Memoir AMA.

42. "an intelligent friendship..." AM to Lucretia May, Feb. 4, 1829, Memoir AMA.

43. "Circumstances may separate..." AM to ABA, June 10, 1829, Memoir AMA.

44. "His plan..." AM to Joseph May, July 15, 1829, Memoir AMA.

45. "Mr. Alcott's visits..." through "Let us love..." Joseph May to AM, July 6, 1829, Memoir AMA.

46. "It is Mr. Alcott's wish... I am fallible..." AM to Joseph May, July 15, 1829, Memoir AMA.

47. "good brother" July 18, 1829, Memoir AMA.

48. "dear Louisa's orphans... It was a responsibility..." July 26, 1829, Memoir AMA.

49. "To the children... I am persuaded..." Joseph May to AM, Aug. 26, 1829, Memoir AMA.

50. "assurance of kind feelings... pecuniary embarrassments" AM to Joseph May, Sept. 22, 1829, Memoir AMA.

51. "doubt and apprehension... with the confidence... Reason urges..." AM to Joseph May, Feb. 18, 1830, Memoir AMA.

52. attended by Elizabeth Peabody... Louise Hall Tharp, *The Peabody Sisters of Salem* (Boston: Little, Brown and Co., 1950), 5.

53. "and that is saying... beams of the honey-moon" AMA to Lucretia May, June 15, 1830, Family Letters, 1828-1861.

## Chapter 2: Motherhood

1. "love is..." through "His school has diminished..." AMA to SJM, June 15, 1831, Family Letters, 1828 -1861.

2. "is worth a 100 dollars... strongly marked by practical wisdom... blush into obscurity..." AMA to SJM, July 25, 1830, Family Letters, 1828-1861.

3. "not lived an hour..." through "My happiness..." AMA to SJM, March 27, 1831, Family Letters, 1828-1861.

4. "I have no rules... I never go out..." AMA to SJM, Aug. 11, 1831, Family Letters, 1828-1861.

5. "little paradise" through "I believe a little patience..." AMA to SJM, May 22, 1831, Family Letters, 1828-1861.

6. "prostrated... with his body... pestilence..." AMA to SJM, Aug. 24, 1831, Family Letters, 1828-1861.

7. "held in horror..." AMA to SJM, August 11, 1831, Family Letters, 1828-1861.

8. "suffering for intellectual society" AMA to SJM, Aug. 24, 1831, Family Letters, 1828-1861.

9. "It is a thankless..." AMA to SJM, Feb. 20, 1833, Family Letters, 1828-1861.

10. "We hardly earn... return the compliment... may be the last..." AMA to SJM, Aug. 24, 1831, Family Letters, 1828-1861.

11. "We continued..." Autobiography, AMA Fragments.

12. "one of those periods... peculiarities and... firmness of purpose... the greatest volatility..." July 24, 1842, AMA Diary, 1841-1844.

13. "The primal soul..." copied July 24, 1842, by AMA into Diary, 1841-1844. Written by ABA October, 1832.

14. "unknown evils" AMA to Jane Haines, April 9, 183[3], Memoir AMA.

15. "a sprightly... an active pantomimic... I find in my contact... " AMA to SJM, Feb. 20, 1833, Family Letters, 1828-1861.

16. "discriminating" through "the measure..." AMA to Jane Haines, April 9, 183[3], Memoir AMA.

17. "When I stick..." AMA to SJM, June 22, 1833, Family Letters, 1828-1861.

18. "yet so intelligent..." through "Am I doing..." AMA to SJM, June 22, 1833, Family Letters, 1828-1861.

19. "cessation from labor... by change... We do not make..." AMA to SJM, Oct. 20, 1833, Family Letters, 1828-1861.

20. "bold thinkers... soar high..." AMA to SJM, October 20, 1833, Family Letters, 1828-1861.

21. "of the mushroom order... I am more familiar..." AMA to SJM, June 22, 1833, Family Letters, 1828-1861.

22. Dorothy Quincy. She was the subject of Oliver Wendell Holmes' poem, "Dorothy Q."

23. "a good subject... even in her foibles" Shepard, *Journals*, 13-14.

24. "folly and flummery" AMA to SJM, June 22, 1833, Family Letters, 1828-1861.

25. "They always seemed..." Milton Meltzer and Patricia G. Holland, eds., *Lydia Maria Child, Selected Letters, 1817-1880* (Amherst: The University of Massachusetts Press, 1982), xii.

26. "be sold into Georgia" AMA to SJM, March 3, 1834, Family Letters, 1828-1861.

27. "go aground" "This would be an excellent thing... " AMA to SJM, Jan. 19, 1834, Family Letters, 1828-1861.

28. "good enough for heaven..." AMA to SJM, Dec. 11, 1833, Family Letters, 1828-1861.

29. "for with all sorts..." AMA to Mrs. Haines, n.d., Memoir AMA.

30. "knows where to say..." AMA to SJM, Jan. 19, 1834, Family Letters, 1828-1861.

31. "determined we shall not leave..." AMA to SJM, March 3, 1834, Family Letters, 1828-1861.

32. "You must say..." AMA to SJM, Jan. 19, 1834, Family Letters, 1828-1861.

33. "I am now alone.... " ABA MS Journal, Ap. 22, 1834.

34. "Mr. Alcott would consider..." Meltzer and Holland, *Lydia Maria Child*, 142.

35. "misunderstanding and unkind thoughts" AMA to SJM, Aug. 24, 1831, Family Letters, 1828-1861.

36. "I try to suppress..." AMA to SJM, Sept. 1, 1834, Family Letters, 1828-1861.   Bedell, in a note for page 135 of *The Alcotts*, cites the Shattuck Papers at the Massachusetts Historical Society as the source for suggesting that Abby was at this time "deranged." She was certainly physically unwell, and her normal excesses of temperament were no doubt exacerbated by circumstances. It cannot be taken from this comment that she was necessarily psychologically unfit.

## Chapter 3: Marital Discord

1. "would never put his mind..." Tharp, *The Peabody Sisters,* 92-93.
2. "I never knew..." Elizabeth Peabody, *Record of a School*, 3rd ed. (Boston: Roberts Brothers, 1888), 89.
3. "You have taken the knowledge..." Ibid., 145.
4. "more like a sepulchre..." AMA to SJM, Sept. 1, 1834, Family Letters, 1828-1861.
5. "elevated moral sentiment" through ""I believe that my husband..." AMA to SJM, Sept. 7, 1834, Family Letters, 1828-1861.
6. "fidelity to the pursuit..." July 21, 1842, AMA Diary 1841-1844.
7. "thoughtless expenditure... yield to expenses... You have made several important mistakes..." JM to AMA, Oct. 1, 1834, Memoir 1878.
8. "If my husband were a spendthrift..." through "Ever since this excellent man..." AMA to SJM, Oct. 6, 1834, Memoir 1878.
9. "in the ghostly folds..." AMA to SJM, Feb. 22  1835, Family Letters, 1828-1861.
10. "connected with the sin... the slave mother..." AMA Diary, Jan. 2, 1836, Memoir 1878.
11. "unique and transcendent... to aid in..." AMA to SJM, Jan. 20, 1835, Family Letters, 1828-1861.
12. "The word atom..." Elizabeth Peabody, *Record of a School*, 1st ed. (Boston: James Munroe and Company, 1835), 202.
13. "From neglecting this mode..." Ibid., 9.
14. "most successfully with others" AMA to Lucretia May, April 12, 1834, Family Letters, 1828-1861.
15. "the delicate and yet necessary work" Shepard, *Journals*, 47.
16. "from the radiance..." Ibid., 55.
17. "He who kindles..." Ibid., 51.
18. "the sentiment of humanity" Ibid., 55.
19. "less to him..." April 1, 1842, AMA Diary 1841-1844.
20. "truly good... benumbed" AMA to Lucretia May, April 12, 1835, Family Letters, 1828-1861.
21. In May... Both Abby and Bronson give May 14 as the date, she in her Autobiography, he in a note for the year 1835 in his Memoir 1878.
22. "I shall endeavor..." Shepard, *Journals*, 57.

23. "a oneness with the Divinity" Ibid., 67.

24. "an angel of love and peace" Sophia Peabody to Mrs. William Russell, July 25, 1836, Memoir 1878.

25. "I am growing selfish..." AMA to Elizabeth Peabody, August, 1835, Memoir 1878.

26. "He did nothing." AMA to Joseph May, Sept. 3, 1835, Memoir 1878.

27. "a few thoughts... but the one thing needful... in the forms..." AMA to Joseph May, May 6, 1835, Memoir 1878.

28. "began to sojourn..." JM to AMA, Oct. 8, 1835, Memoir 1878.

29. "As I was the queen..." Ednah D. Cheney, *Louisa May Alcott, Her Life, Letters, and Journals* (Boston: Roberts Brothers, 1890), 27.

30. "noisy and boisterous" "little time for thought" "tired of living in..." AMA to Mrs. Anna Alcott, November, 1835, Memoir 1878.

31. "I *will not* be overcome" Jan. 1, 1836, Memoir 1878.

32. "by making them reflect..." ABA Journal, Oct. 8, 1835, ms copy, Fruitlands Museums.

33. "incapable of appreciating... If this is the state..." Elizabeth Peabody to Mary Peabody, Nov., 1835, Bedell, 108.

34. "undoubting faith..." Anna Thaxter to AMA, Jan. 7, 1836, Memoir 1878.

35. "an old-fashioned wooden house..." AMA to Mrs. Anna Alcott, June 5, 1836, Memoir 1878.

36. "We shall then..." ABA Journal, March 26, 1836, ms copy, Fruitlands.

37. "What does love make?" through "The spirit makes the body..." Alice O. Howell, ed., *How Like an Angel Came I Down* (Hudson, New York: Lindisfarne Press, 1991), 61, 73-74.

38. "in the spirit of friendship" Elizabeth Peabody to ABA, Aug. 7, 1836, Memoir 1878.

39. "melodious repose" through "makes me retreat..." Sophia Peabody to Mrs. William Russell, June 25, 1836, Memoir 1878.

40. "build up his school... tottering... AMA to Chatfield Alcott, Nov. 20, 1836, Memoir 1878.

41. "savior" "weary and heavy laden" AMA to Mrs. Anna Alcott, Nov. 20, 1836, Memoir 1878.

42. "far exceeded" Autobiography, AMA Fragments.

43. "sweetly and quietly" ... through "a combination of nutritive..." AMA to SJM, April 23, 1837, Family Letters, 1828-1861.

44. "committed no offense..." Shepard, *Journals*, 88.

45. "I rail..." AMA to SJM, April 23, 1837, Family Letters, 1828-1861.

46. "virtue and wisdom" ABA Journal, April, week XIV, 1837, ms copy, Fruitlands.

47. "subjects connected..." Shepard, *Journals*, 63.

48. "without satisfaction... a learner late..." ABA Journal, week XXII, June, 1837, ms copy, Fruitlands.

49. "vulgar aims... an Idea without..." Nov., 1837, Shepard, *Journals*, 94, 96.

50. "My good wife... Again you have been called... as good an Abolitionist..." ABA to AMA, June 8, 1837, Memoir 1878.

51. "I would not say... " AMA to SJM, June 21, 1837, Family Letters, 1828-1861.

52. "continual illness..." Emerson to ABA, Aug., 1837, Memoir 1878.

53. "Many think your aunt... She is unsparing..." AMA to Miss E. Willis, July 2, 1837, Memoir 1878.

54. "We are as poor... by her brilliant... A great revolution..." AMA to SJM, Oct. 3, 1837, Family Letters, 1828-1861.

55. "remnants of the dishes..." ABA Journal, week XLIV, Nov., 1837, ms copy, Fruitlands.

56. "Why? Because it is thought..." AMA to Mrs. Anna Alcott, Feb. 25, 1838, Memoir 1878.

57. Dr. Windship, either her brother-in-law or her nephew, both of whom were doctors.

58. "I am getting hardened... leaving my excellent... the strife of mortal things..." AMA to SJM, April 22, 1838, Family Letters, 1828-1861.

59. "Even in my own home..." ABA Journal, April, 1838, week XLII, ms copy, Fruitlands.

60. "scantily supplied..." ABA Journal, week I, Jan., 1838, ms copy, Fruitlands.

61. "give tacit assent to... mutual forbearance" AMA to Mrs. May, June 3, 1838, Memoir 1878.

62. "delicate health, precarious state... though I could speak... the progress of our reunion..." AMA to JM, June 3, 1838, Memoir 1878.

63. "one of the facts..." Shepard, *Journals*, 115.

64. "wise example... the wishes of his heart... sweet satisfaction" AMA to JM, Feb. 3, 1839, Memoir 1878.

65. "full grown..." Autobiography, AMA Fragments.

66. "deposit the body..." AMA annotation on letter JM to ABA, April 6, 1839, Memoir 1878.

67. "But my thrill..." ABA annotation on a letter to Mrs. Anna Alcott, March 17, 1839, Shepard, *Journals*, 119.

68. "in fine order" Anna's diary, July 25, 1839, Family Letters and Diaries, 1837-1850.

69. "O stupid..." ABA Journal, Dec. 9, 1839, ms copy, Fruitlands.

70. "It never was so dark..." AMA to Mrs. Anna Alcott, May 9, 1838, Memoir 1878.

71. "God shall provide..." ABA Journal, Sept. 24, 1839, ms copy, Fruitlands.

72. "To My Wife" Two versions, one at Fruitlands Museums, one copied into AMA Diary, 1841-1844.

73. "for another experiment..." AMA to SJM, March 13, 1840, Memoir 1878.

## Chapter 4: Con-sociate Family

1. "enfeebled" "a more vigorous..." AMA to SJM, March 13, 1840, Memoir 1878.

2. "A spirit must..." AMA to JM, April 5, 1840, Memoir 1878.

3. "his love of neatness..." AMA to SJM, April 26, 1840, Family Letters, 1828-1861.

4. "liberality of sentiment..." AMA to SJM, March 13, 1840, Family Letters, 1828-1861.

5. "talk mystical... Mr. Ripley and Miss Fuller... only by bread..." AMA to HR, April 26, 1840, Memoir 1878.

6. "No one will employ..." AMA to SJM, Nov., 1840, Jessie Bonstelle and Marian deForest, *Little Women Letters from the House of Alcott* (Boston: Little, Brown and Company, 1914), 176.

7. "slight compensation..." Ibid., 176-177.

8. "I should like..." Ibid., 177.

9. "never sell his..." letter, recipient unknown, Nov., 1840, Memoir 1878.

10. "Life is within us..." AMA to JM, April 5, 1840, Memoir 1878.

11. "I should not often want..." AMA to HR, Oct. 22, 1840, Memoir 1878.

12. "transcendental farming" "in carrying little offerings..." AMA to Hannah Robie, August 4, 1840, Memoir AMA.

13. "than the usual way..." Hannah Robie to her sister, Dec. 6, 1841, Memoir 1878.

14. "an exquisite sense... I cannot get rest... the world of want... furnished a good many... re-established" AMA to SJM, August 30, 1840, Family Letters, 1828-1861.

15. "don't care-ism" "that life shall bring..." AMA to SJM, Nov. 15, 1840, Family Letters, 1828-1861.

16. "the threads wrought..." Sept. 16, 1842, AMA Diary, 1841-1844.

17. "own little sphere" "in the orbit..." AMA to JM, Jan. 27, 1841, Memoir 1878.

18. "annihilate... I cannot gee..." AMA to SJM, Jan. 24, 1841, Family Letters, 1828-1861.

19. "in kind words..." AMA to LMA, Dove Cottage, n.d., Memoir AMA.

20. "Love your duty..." AMA to ASA, Dec. 24, 1840, Family Letters and Diaries, 1837-1850.

21. "queer stories" Anna's Journal, Sept. 20, 1839, Family Letters and Diaries, 1837-1850.

22. "loved by many... something like confidence... if weighed..." AMA Diary, Feb., n.d., 1841, Memoir 1878.

23. "We have in no wise..." AMA to SJM, April 15, 1841, Family Letters, 1828-1861.

24. "Wisdom must be fed..." AMA to SJM, Oct. 20, 1833, Family Letters, 1828-1861.

25. "the worm gnawing..." AMA to SJM, April 4, 1841, Family Letters, 1828-1861.

26. "anything that is temporary..." May 17, 1842, AMA Diary, 1841-1844.

27. "with those who are free..." August, 1841, AMA Diary, Memoir 1878.

28. "Why are men icebergs..." Aug., n.d., 1841, AMA Diary, Memoir 1878.

29. "Accept it... losing the view..." ABA to AMA, Oct. 8, 1841, AMA Diary, 1841-1844.

30. "it was the only way..." HR to her sister, Dec. 6, 1841, Memoir 1878.

31. "the color of... [If] his body don't... their senior" AMA to SJM, Jan. 17, 1842, Family Letters, 1828-1861.

32. "the fostering care..." March 6, 1842, AMA Diary, 1841-1844.

33. "one of mercy..." March 6, 1842, AMA Diary, 1841-1844.

34. "Wife, children... the belief that..." April 1, 1842, AMA Diary, 1841-1844.

35. "lenient to his..." May 9, 1842, AMA Diary, 1841-1844.

36. "reality in her life..." June 17, 1842, AMA Diary, 1841-1844.

37. "How elastic... Some flowers..." May 11, 1842, AMA Diary, 1841-1844.

38. "a death knell... a shroud" May 9, 1842, AMA Diary, 1841-1844.

39. "I am enjoying... full melody..." July 8, 1842, AMA Diary, 1841-1844.

40. "circulating so much..." May 19, 1842, AMA Diary, 1841-1844.

41. "Father dear..." June 24, 1842, AMA Diary, 1841-1844.

42. "the joy I feel..." July 24, 1842, AMA Diary, 1841-1844.

43. "frolick joys... whose unsleeping love..." Richard L. Herrnstadt, ed., *The Letters of A. Bronson Alcott* (Ames: Iowa State University Press, 1969), 83.

44. "indissoluble chains" AMA to SJM, June 26, 1842, Family Letters, 1828-1861.

45. "Mr. A. lives..." Aug. 22, 1842, AMA Diary, 1841-1844.

46. "My hour shall..." Aug. 22, 1842, AMA Diary, 1841-1844.

47. "united scheme of life" Sept. 8, 1842, AMA Diary, 1841-1844.

48. "content with anything" Sept. 16, 1842, AMA Diary, 1841-1844.

49. "My mind to me..." Sept. 8, 1842, AMA Diary, 1841-1844.

50. "If he sees... All is received..." April 1, 1843, AMA Diary, 1841-1844.

51. "stupid inattention... Graham is not..." March, n.d., 1842, AMA Diary, 1841-1844.

52. "Happy days..." Oct. 21, 1842, AMA Diary, 1841-1844.

53. "frowned down... stupidly obtuse... give me one day..." Nov. 29, 1842, AMA Diary, 1841-1844.

54. "that devil come..." Lane to Oldham, Nov. 26, 29, 1843, *Harland Typescript*, Fruitlands.

55. "Mrs. A. has passed..." Lane to Oldham, Nov. 30, 1842, Ibid.

56. "glad to resume..." Jan. 1, 1843, AMA Diary, 1841-1844.

57. "unusual quietude..." Jan. 4, 1843, AMA Diary, 1841-1844.

58. "a pleasant way..." Jan. 15, 1843, AMA Diary, 1841-1844.

59. "excellencies" Lane to AMA, Feb. 1, 1843.

60. "with benignity toward... desirous of access... beneficial effects in..." Herrnstadt, *Letters*, 99-100.

61. "to be employed..." March 6, 1843, AMA Diary, 1841-1844.

62. "I enclose a picture..." March 12, 1843, microfilm, Concord Free Public Library.

63. "Then humbly take..." March 16, 1843, AMA Diary, 1841-1844.

64. "scarcely tenantable" June 14, 1843, AMA to SJM, Family Letters, 1828-1861.

65. "tasteful buildings..." June 10, 1843, newspaper clipping in AMA Diary, 1841-1844.

66. "It is a beautiful..." Clara Endicott Sears, *Bronson Alcott's Fruitlands* (Boston: Houghton Mifflin Company, 1915), 100.

67. "true men and women... putting away the... there is much to..." June 1, 1843, AMA Diary, 1841-1844.

68. "a public tavern..." AMA to Hannah Robie, Jan. 21, 1844, Memoir 1878.

69. Christy Greene. There is some question whether Greene was at Fruitlands, but in Anna's diary for Fruitlands she wrote caringly about Christy, her teacher. Also, the adult Anna Alcott Pratt wrote a letter to Frank Sanborn in which she recalled the presence of Greene clearly and with fondness. Alcott Family Papers, Fruitlands Collection.

70. "higher intelligences who..." AMA to Prudence Ward, newspaper clipping, Concord Free Public Library.

71. "I am sure..." Sears, *Fruitlands*, 91.

72. "somewhat relieved by..." August, n.d., 1843, AMA Diary, 1841-1844.

73. "has good sense... too morbidly... I do not allow..." AMA to SJM, Sunday morn [Aug. 6, 1843], Family Letters, 1828-1861.

74. "There is a fat... A woman may live..." Aug. 26, 1843, AMA Diary, 1841-1844.

75. "People have been..." AMA to SJM, Nov. 11, 1843, Family Letters, 1828-1861.

76. "little short of..." Lane to Oldham, Nov. 26, 29, 1843, *Harland Typescript*.

77. "Perhaps Lane is..." LMC to Augusta King, Sept. 19, 1843, Meltzer and Holland, *Lydia Maria Child*, 202.

78. "for I will know..." AMA to SJM, Nov. 11, 1843, Family Letters, 1828-1861.

79. "Mrs. Alcott has..." Oct. 30, 1843, *Harland Typescript*.

80. "The right people..." AMA to Charles May, Nov. 6, 1843, Memoir 1878.

81. "to cheer the scene..." Dec. 25, 1843, AMA Diary, 1841-1844.

82. "All Mr. Lane's..." AMA to SJM, Jan. 11, 1844, Memoir 1878.

83. "tedious... My satisfaction is... to some employment..." AMA to Hannah Robie, Jan. 21, 1844, Memoir 1878.

84. "Several calls for..." Jan. 16, 1844, AMA Diary, 1841-1844.

## Chapter 5: Natural Family

1. "disagreeable dependencies" "Should like to see..." Jan. 28, 1844, AMA Diary, 1841-1844.

2. "soul-sick" March 22, AMA Diary, 1841-1844.

3. "allied to a shadow" AMA to Charles May, April 28, 1844, Memoir 1878.

4. "have advantages over... move an inch" AMA to SJM, Jan. 11, 1844, Family Letters, 1828-1861.

5. "no sphere in which... more neatness... no advance... association in labor" Feb. 17, 1844, AMA Diary, 1841-1844.

6. "perish under dependence" March 4, 1844, AMA Diary, 1841-1844.

7. "Quite satisfied..." AMA to Hannah Robie, March 12, 1844, Memoir 1878.

8. "I enjoyed this..." Shepard, *Journals*, 240-241.

9. Lovejoys. AMA to SJM, April 9, 1844. "I have made a proposition which Mr. and Mrs. Lovejoy have acceded to - and the Mother agrees too - I have taken for six months or a year half the house at Still River which the Mother was to occupy."

10. "a little bathing room" AMA to SJM, April 9, 1844, Family Letters, 1828-1861.

11. "What a holy..." April 24, 1844, AMA Diary, 1841-1844.

12. "bring forth abundantly..." AMA to SJM, April 24, 1844, Family Letters, 1828-1861.

13. "a hero *worth*... See this great, noble..." Aug., 1844, AMA Diary, 1841-1844.

14. The fact that James Martineau was the hated Harriet's brother was of no consequence, especially as James and Harriet had their own differences.

15. "in the spirit's deepest..." Aug. 4, 1844, from Martineau's "Kingdom of God Within Us," AMA Diary, 1841-1844.

16. "Geehale - An Indian Lament" Annie M. L. Clark, *The Alcotts in Harvard* (Lancaster, MA: by the author, 1902), 33.

17. "a field of action..." July 14, 1844, AMA Diary, 1841-1844.

18. "a plain house" Herrnstadt, *Letters*, 114.

19. "help to mature... keep a rational... time, life... The great idea..." AMA to SJM, Oct. 6, 1884, Family Letters, 1828-1861.

20. "If we perform..." Herrnstadt, *Letters*, 114.

21. "a sad illustration..." Nov. 12, 1844, AMA Diary, 1841-1844.

22. purchase of Hillside. Bronson's journal for Jan. 2, 1845, states that the purchase price of $1,350 was met through Abby's legacy plus money from Emerson.

23. "I will not abide..." Herrnstadt, *Letters*, 117.

24. "spiritual exaltation" "a domestic community..." Jan. 1, 1845, AMA Diary Fragments.

25. "commotion" "that best of brothers" AMA to Hannah Robie, April 17, 1845, Memoir 1878.

26. "It is well ordered..." March 17, 1845, AMA Fragments.

27. "as old friends" MA to SJM, Feb. 21, 1845, Family Letters, 1828-1861.

28. "free, happy spirits..." AMA to SJM, April 17, 1845, Family Letters, 1828-1861.

29. "The Unseen and..." AMA to SJM, April 17, 1845, Family Letters, 1828-1861.

30. "petty traffic... mundane... brutish" Shepard, *Journals*, 177.

31. "It will be no slight task..." April 1, 1845, AMA Diary Fragments.

32. "Nothing makes one..." AMA to SJM, April 17, 1845, Family Letters, 1828-1861.

33. "commence this year..." Jan. 1, 1845, AMA Fragments.

34. "even Elizabeth can..." AMA to SJM, June 8, 1845, Family Letters, 1834. 28-1861.

35. "smiling on everything..." AMA to SJM, June 8, 1845, Family Letters, 1828-1861.

36. "the little ones... these human shoots" Shepard, *Journals*, 176.

37. "Music is too..." March 4, 1844, AMA Diary, 1841-1844.

38. "Hope, and keep... for you are..." Cheney, 42.

39. "everlasting harmony between..." Joel Myerson and Daniel Shealy, eds., *The Journals of Louisa May Alcott* (Little, Brown and Company: Boston, 1989), 55.

40. "quite affecting" AMA to SJM, Aug. 9, 1845.

41. "How gain love?..." Myerson and Shealy, *Journals*, 56.

42. "dreadfull wild people" Joel Myerson and Daniel Shealy, eds., *The Selected Letters of Louisa May Alcott* (Boston: Little, Brown and Company, 1987), 4.

43. "safety valve to..." AMA to SJM, April 17, 1845, Family Letters, 1828-1861.

44. "to obtain self..." March 16, 1845, AMA Fragments.

45. "bawling and singing... particular" Myerson and Shealy, *Letters*, 4.

46. "associative life... influence and habits... such faulty specimens... unerringly sustained" Sept. 5, 1845, AMA Fragments.

47 "My Louy, I was..." Cheney, 46.

48. "I once thought..." Shepard, *Journals*, 173.

49. "never aspired to... very apt to..." AMA to SJM, April 23, 1837, Family Letters, 1828-1861.

50. "Oh! may this pen..." Nov. 29, 1846, AMA Diary Fragments. The final two lines in this source, "Love guide your pen, inspire your theme/And from each note a gush of gladness stream," differ from those recorded by Cheney, page 54, "Truth guide your pen, inspire your theme/And from each note joy's music stream."

51. "a peculiar one..." Nov. 29, 1846, AMA Fragments.

52. "Count thyself divinely... to persons who..." Shepard, *Journals*, 173.

53. "arrangements for life" [Aug.], 1845, AMA Fragments.

54. "dismal" "we could be..." Cheney, 43.

55. "God comfort thee..." LMA to AMA, 1845, copied by Anna into her diary, Bonstelle, 134.

56. "Alcott kept his... " Frank B. Sanborn, *Bronson Alcott at Alcott House, England, and Fruitlands, New England* (Cedar Rapids, Iowa: The Torch Press, 1908), 98.

57. "gentle, persevering... in a state of... like a young child... if by faithful care..." AMA to SJM, Nov. 2, 1846, Family Letters, 1828-1861.

58. "by meeting God...." Dec. 31, 1846, AMA Fragments.

59. "I must think..." AMA to SJM, Feb. 8, 1847, Family Letters, 1828-1861.

60. "his political opinions..." Shepard, *Journals*, 195.

61. "gladly take a subordinate..." AMA to SJM, Aug. 2, 1846, Family Letters, 1828-1861.

62. "had rather sail on..." AMA to SJM, Feb. 8, 1847, Family Letters, 1828-1861.

63. "without many things..." Jan., 1847, AMA Fragments.

64. "wretched at our..." AMA to SJM, Sept. 12, 1847, Family Letters, 1828-1861.

65. "a great deal of..." AMA to Anna, Nov. 9, 1847, Memoir AMA.

66. "combine our various gifts" AMA to SJM, Feb. 29, 1848, Family Letters, 1828-1861.

67. "do as other people do" AMA to SJM, Feb. 13, 1848, Family Letters, 1828-1861.

68. "retirement, agreeable occupation..." AMA to SJM, Feb. 29, 1848, Family Letters, 1828-1861.

69. "Make no arrangements for..." AMA to SJM, Feb. 13, 1848, Family Letters, 1828-1861.

70. "yield to any..." AMA to SJM, Feb. 13, 1848, Family Letters, 1828-1861.

71. "I think God is..." AMA to SJM, Nov. 3, 1847, Family Letters, 1828-1861.

72. "Was it from some... delighted in the fruit... worn and aged..." ABA, rough draft inserted after a letter to Anna dated Dec., 1847, Memoir AMA.

73. "an asylum for idiots" AMA to SJM, April 16, 1848, Family Letters, 1828-1861.

74. "has been one great... Death stood ready..." AMA to SJM, Sept. 12, 1847, Family Letters, 1828-1861.

75. "its capability to..." May, n.d., 1848, AMA Fragments.

76. "I honor the good..." Herrnstadt, *Letters*, 139.

77. "the dear woman" Ibid., 140.

78. "without any fixed law..." May, n.d., 1848, AMA Fragments.

79. "the bone, sinew, and..." May 20, 1848, AMA to ABA, Memoir 1878.

80. "a cheerful heart for..." AMA to ABA, June, n.d., 1848.

81. Schedule at Waterford, AMA to ABA, May 20, 1848, Memoir 1878.

82. "I began to wonder... the wholeness, unity... Mother, is it you? almost in a wet..." AMA to her family in Concord, May 27, 1848, Memoir 1878.

83. "the tidiest of house maids" Herrnstadt, *Letters*, 143.

84. "sights and sounds which..." May, n.d., 1848, AMA Fragments.

85. "Her little school..." May, n.d., 1848, AMA Fragments.

86. "Something better than... Your letters are fresh..." AMA to ABA, May 25, 1848, Memoir 1878.

87. "the best blessing... simply to express..." AMA to SJM, June 14, 1848, Family Letters, 1828-1861.

88. "with script and staff... We dramatized the..." Cheney, 31.

89. "sunder them apart" AMA to SJM, Sept. 17, 1848, Memoir 1878.

90. "paralysis of the soul" AMA to SJM, Sept. 17, 1848, Memoir 1878.

91. "beautiful weather without... a child is... How destitute of..." Sept. 1,2,&3, 1848, AMA Fragments.

92. "I love friendship... I apply for part..." Sept. 17, 1848, AMA Fragments.

93. "Let me dwell..." Oct. 8, 1848, AMA Fragments.

94. "Home! Home!..." Oct. 8, 1848, birthday poem, LMA to AMA, copied by AMA into AMA Fragments. In Memoir 1878, ABA copied a poem more generally known to Alcott scholars, beginning "I hope that soon, dear mother."

## Chapter 6: Sister of Charity

1. "for in every influence..." AMA to Hannah Robie, Dec. 13, 1846, Memoir 1878.

2. "long toiled for..." Fragments of Reports while Visitor to the Poor, henceforward referred to as Reports. These monthly reports to those employing her are fragmentary and not always in Mrs. Alcott's hand. Some are duplicates, with slight variations in wording.

3. "I believe there are..." AMA Help Book, Jan., 1850, Memoir AMA.

4. "I find myself less..." AMA to SJM, Jan. 29, 1849, Family Letters, 1828-1861.

5. disappointment of the affections... AMA to SJM, Dec. 10, 1845, Family Letters, 1828-1861.

6. "My heart has always..." Reports.

7. "We do a good work..." Reports

8. "labor associations..." Reports.

9. "When will the rights..." Oct. 10, 1849, AMA Fragments.

10. "Because some want..." Reports.

11. "breathed from individual..." AMA Fragments.

12. "I think we need..." Reports.

13. "I can trust my..." Sandford Salyer, *Marmee* (Norman: University of Oklahoma Press, 1949), 144.

14. "Who will love and... the Don of Quixots... helpless, unprotected children." Jan. 24, 1849, AMA Fragments.

15. "I see no propriety..." Reports.

16. "Alas! Every day..." March 6, 1849 AMA Fragments.

17. "Much of their pungency..."  AMA Diary Fragments, 1849, Memoir 1878.

18. "to encroach upon this..." Jan. 1, 1849, AMA Fragments.

19. "the poor and rich..." Reports.

20. "If we find destitution..." Reports.

21. "We may legislate in..." Reports.

22. "The sweat of the brow..." Reports.

23. "Equivocally polite... guilty of displaying..." n.d. AMA Fragments.

24. "Young, destitute girls... Paris riggins... flag of availability." Reports.

25. "so persuaded am I... to be extremely..." AMA Fragments.

26. "The order for thirty... I as often carry..." Reports.

27. "goblins... Come, and leave that..." Herrnstadt, *Letters*, 152.

28. "Shall our relief ship..." AMA to Mrs. Hyde, Aug. 25, 1849, filed with Reports.

29. "in a position of..." Oct. 8, 1849, AMA Fragments.

30. "breathed in my office... The forward tide..." AMA to LMA, Sept. 29, 1849, Memoir AMA.

31. "some of our sleeping..." AMA Fragments.

32. "where the Rich may..." Salyer, 139.

33. "The pauper at our..." Reports.

34. "Best German... a life-giving... Freighting a ship... We sent what we... I am accosted..." Reports.

35. "human and incident to... to me they are... their very skin... despised and rejected..." Reports.

36. "for our colored... disagreeable interviews..." AMA Fragments.

37. "I have had an... I will interrupt..." Reports.

38. "willing heart and..." March, 1850, AMA Fragments.

39. "to a morbid... What shall we... Why is it..." April 4, 1850, AMA Fragments.

40. "The winter is over..." Reports.

41. "superfluous means..." AMA to SJM, April 14, 1850, Family Letters, 1850-1855.

42. "the false requisitions..." AMA to SJM, April 14, 1850. Family Letters, 1850-1855.

43. "No explanation can..." Shepard, *Journals*, 232.

44. "I cannot offer sympathy..." March, 1842, AMA Diary, 1841-1844.

45. "never forget the..." May 29, 1850, AMA Diary Fragments, Memoir 1878.

46. "We had a curious..." Myerson and Shealy, *Journals*, 62.

47. "disconsolate and cannot..." Shepard, *Journals*, 231.

48. "She is a very..." Myerson and Shealy, *Journals*, 63.

49. "the small-pox... which grew out of..." Myerson and Shealy, *Journals*, 67.

50. "I have outlived..." AMA to Miss Mary May, Aug. 8, 1851, Memoir 1878.

51. "poor as rats" Myerson and Shealy, *Journals*, 65.

52. "When I think of..." SJM to AMA, Oct. 15, 1850, Family Letters, 1850-1855.

53. "twenty colored women... There are higher laws..." AMA to SJM, Feb. 28, 1851, Family Letters, 1828-1861.

54. "strong conviction" AMA to SJM, Nov. 10, 1851, Family Letters, 1828-1861.

55. "The People's authentic act..." Family Letters, 1850-1855.

56. "I say to all..." AMA to SJM, April 12, 1853, Family Letters, 1828-1861.

## Chapter 7: Marmee

1. "when summoned I..." AMA to SJM, Dec. 14, 1851, Family Letters, 1828-1861.

2. "the gray hairs are..." Oct. 8, 1856, AMA Fragments.

3. "We are gaining nothing..." AMA to ABA, Nov. 17, 1853, Family Letters, 1850-1855.

4. "scarce believing... I wish it were..." Herrnstadt, *Letters*, 173.

5. "manuscripts stand like..." AMA to ABA, Oct. 30, 1853, Family Letters, 1850-1855.

6. "affectionate nature leads..." AMA to ABA, Nov. 19, 1853, Family Letters, 1850-1855.

7. "Where are you?..." AMA to ABA, June 27, 1852, Family Letters, 1850-1855.

8. "chain the bond closer..." AMA to her daughters, Oct. 8, 1851, Family Letters, 1850-1855.

9. "home child" AMA to ABA, Aug. 5, 1853, Family Letters, 1850-1855.

10. "You can't think..." Lizzie to AMA, Aug. 10, 1853, Family Letters, 1850-1855.

11. "Into your Christmas stocking..." Dec. 25, 1854, AMA Diary Fragments. This version differs slightly from Myerson and Shealy, *Letters*, 11.

12. "Artist Cultivator" "a radiant touch..." May 23, 1857, AMA Fragments.

13. "prolonged guess... the comforts of home... before the immensity..." AMA to SJM, Aug. 25, 1857.

14. "Concord again receives us..." Sept. 20, 1857, AMA Fragments.

15. "Our life has been..." June 1, 1857, AMA Fragments.

16. "unutterable distress" AMA to SJM, Dec. 8, 1857, Family Letters, 1828-1861.

17. "depending on my baby" AMA to SJM, Dec. 8, 1857, Family Letters, 1828-1861.

18. "atrophy or consumption..." Jan., 1858, AMA Diary Fragments.

19. "I can lay no..." AMA to SJM, Jan. 21, 1858.

20. "Elizabeth passed quietly... Oh heavenly air... Well now, Mother... She kept up..." March 14, 1858, AMA Fragments.

21. "wiser for her life..." AMA to SJM, March 19, 1858, Family Letters, 1828-1861.

22. "It has been an..." AMA to SJM, March 19, 1858, Family Letters, 1828-1861.

23. "trying to believe..." Myerson and Shealy, *Letters*, 33.

24. "the inexplicable trial..." Autobiography, AMA Fragments.

25. "that her gentle presence..." June 30, 1858, AMA Fragments.

26. "There dwelt a Sage..." Caroline Ticknor, *May Alcott - A Memoir* (Boston: Little, Brown and Company, 1927), 53.

27. "When they bought the place..." Meltzer and Holland, *Lydia Maria Child*, 535.

28. "a large love..." n.d., 1858, AMA Fragments.

29. "the pleasant little..." April 9, 1860, AMA Fragments.

30. "so that Anna takes..." May 22, 1860, AMA Fragments.

31. "find herself fully..." May 23, 1860, AMA Fragments.

32. "the last day when... your Annie..." May 23, 1860, AMA Fragments.

33. "the severe simplicity... rapt seer... as if moonlight had... worked with..." Jan. 25, 1857, AMA Fragments.

34. "risen a peg..." AMA to SJM, March, 1860, Family Letters, 1828-1861.

35. "matured her powers... a little too dark... too rosy... good criticism" Jan., 1860, AMA Fragments.

36. "The former perceives..." Feb. 15, 1860, AMA Fragments.

37. "How generous this woman..." 1860, AMA Fragments.

38. "The last day of..." Dec. 31, 1859, AMA Fragments.

39. "readiness to strike..." Shepard, *Journals*, 316.

40. "Now if the laws..." Dec. 31, 1861, annotation, AMA Fragments.

41. "Shall I stay?..." Ticknor, *May Alcott*, 55.

42. "I must go right..." Myerson and Shealy, *Letters*, 83.

43. "the bitter drop in..." April 20, 1872, AMA Fragments.

44. "for one possesses..." Myerson and Shealy, *Letters*, 87.

45. "but she will have..." June 14, 1863, AMA Fragments.

46. "sick-turns" n.d., 1861, AMA Fragments.

47. "cordial cups of tea" Myerson and Shealy, *Journals*, 103.

48. "and you in some measure..." Myerson and Shealy, *Letters*, 106.

49. "The characters were drawn..." Ibid., 118.

50. "glad to see the... "the energetic, enthusiastic..." Myerson and Shealy, *Journals*, 166-167.

51. "permanent value and..." April 15, 1869, AMA Fragments.

52. "log book... tho not very..." June 14, 1865, AMA Fragments.

53. "I never expect to..." Myerson and Shealy, *Journals*, 153.

54. "impaired health and..." Nov. 16, 1868, AMA Fragments.

55. "a gross injustice of... contrary to the spirit... to clamour for" May 1, 1875, AMA Fragments.

56. "They must help make..." April 19, 1875, AMA Fragments.

57. "conventional fetters" Meltzer and Holland, *Lydia Maria Child*, 534.

58. "Sing for joy..." Ticknor, *May Alcott*, 193.

59. "Who would have imagined..." Ibid., 192.

60. "full of ferns..." Ibid., 143.

61. "Yet, I must own..." Ibid., 176-177.

62. "writhed under the..." Dec., 1872, AMA Fragments.

63. "grand, strong women..." Nov. 29, 1875, AMA Fragments.

64. "dear old man" Jan. 25, 1875, AMA Fragments.

65. "The world must acknowledge..." Dec. 31, 1872, AMA Fragments.

66. "Marmee had a very... longed to go" Myerson and Shealy, *Journals*, 205.

67. "My Dear Marmee..." Ticknor, *May Alcott*, 245.

68. "The dear patient is..." Ibid., 246.

69. "You are laying a... a smile is..." Myerson and Shealy, *Journals*, 206.

70. "was always prompt to..." Martha Saxton, *A Modern Biography of Louisa May Alcott* (Boston: Houghton Mifflin, 1977), 346.

71. "Among the tall grass..." Myerson and Shealy, *Journals*, 217.

# Selected Bibliography

**Manuscript Sources**
  **(by permission of the Houghton Library, Harvard University)**

Abigail May Alcott Diary, 1841-1844. (AMA Diary, 1841-1844)
      Shelf mark: 59 M-311 (1)
Abigail May Alcott Fragments. (AMA Fragments) Mostly diary entries.
      Shelf mark: 59 M-311 (2)-(19)
Amos Bronson Alcott, Memoir 1878. (Memoir 1878) ABA copies of AMA's
      diaries and letters, hand written after her death in preparation for a biogra-
      phy, never written.
      Shelf mark: 59 M-306 (23)
Family Letters, 1828-1861. Mostly AMA to Samuel J. May (SJM)
      Shelf mark: 59 M-305 (25)
Family Letters and Diaries, 1837-1850.
      Shelf mark: 59 M-305 (24)
Family Letters and Diaries, 1850-1855.
      Shelf mark: 59 M-305 (26)
Fragments of Reports while Visitor to the Poor  (Reports)
      Shelf mark: bMS Am 800.23 (247)
Memoir Abigail May Alcott. (Memoir AMA) Small collection of her papers.
      Shelf mark: 59 M-306 (28)

[In order to facilitate the reading of manuscript sources, minor changes
have been made in punctuation and capitalization, and most spelling has
been corrected.]

## Books

Bedell, Madelon. *The Alcotts*. New York: Clarkson N. Potter, Inc. 1980.

Bonstelle, Jessie and Marian deForest. *Little Women Letters from the House of Alcott*. Boston: Little, Brown and Company, 1914.

Cheney, Ednah D. *Louisa May Alcott, Her Life, Letters, and Journals*. Boston: Roberts Brothers, 1890.

Clark, Annie M.L. *The Alcotts in Harvard*. Lancaster, Massachusetts: by the author, 1902.

Herrnstadt, Richard L., ed. *The Letters of A. Bronson Alcott*. Ames: Iowa State University Press, 1969.

Howell, Alice O., ed. *How Like an Angel Came I Down*. Hudson, New York: Lindisfarne Press, 1991.

Meltzer, Milton and Patricia G. Holland, eds. *Lydia Maria Child, Selected Letters*. Amherst: The University of Massachusetts Press, 1982.

Myerson, Joel and Daniel Shealy, eds. *The Journals of Louisa May Alcott*. Boston: Little, Brown and Company, 1987.

Myerson, Joel and Daniel Shealy, eds. *The Selected Letters of Louisa May Alcott*. Boston: Little, Brown and Company, 1987.

Mumford, Thomas J. *Memoir of Samuel Joseph May*. Boston: Roberts Brothers, 1873.

Peabody, Elizabeth. *Record of a School*. Boston: James Munroe and Company, 1835.

Salyer, Sanford. *Marmee*. Norman: University of Oklahoma Press, 1949.

Sanborn, Frank B. *Bronson Alcott at Alcott House, England, and Fruitlands, New England*. Cedar Rapids, Iowa: The Torch Press, 1908.

Sears, Clara Endicott. *Bronson Alcott's Fruitlands*. Boston: Houghton Mifflin Company, 1915.

Shepard, Odell, ed. *The Journals of Bronson Alcott*. Boston: Little, Brown and Company, 1938.

Tharp, Louise Hall. *The Peabody Sisters of Salem*. Boston: Little, Brown and Company, 1950.

Ticknor, Caroline. *May Alcott, a Memoir*. Boston: Little, Brown and Company, 1927.

# Index

# About the Author

Cynthia H. Barton is an educator and author, who has been engaged in Alcott research for many years. For the issue of *Cobblestone Magazine* devoted to Louisa May Alcott, she wrote an article about their experiment in communal living at Fruitlands, in Harvard, Massachusetts. Ms. Barton is the biographer of the founder of the Fruitlands Museums, Clara Endicott Sears, and was a speaker at a symposium on transcendentalism held at the Museums. She is a lecturer at the Bronson Alcott School of Philosophy in Concord, Massachusetts, and a contributor to the Orchard House publication, *Portfolio*.